MODERN SCHOOL PSYCHOLOGY

MODERN SCHOOL PSYCHOLOGY

By

M.U. Qureshi

ANMOL PUBLICATIONS PVT. LTD.

NEW DELHI - 110 002 (INDIA)

ANMOL PUBLICATIONS PVT. LTD.
H.O.: 4374/4B, Ansari Road, Daryaganj,
New Delhi-110 002 (India)
Ph.: 23278000, 23261597
B.O.: No. 1015, Ist Main Road, BSK IIIrd Stage
IIIrd Phase, IIIrd Block,
Bangalore - 560 085 (India)
Visit us at: www.anmolpublications.com

Modern School Psychology

First Published, 2004
Reprint, 2006, 2008

PRINTED IN INDIA

Printed at Mehra Offset Press, Delhi.

Contents

Preface

Education is a vast discipline and Teachers' Training is a vital part of it. The responsibilities of the educationists and educators are focused on the task of providing better training to the future teachers for their better learning and proper development. Needless to say that this responsibility can only be exercised, if the trainers are equipped with the required knowledge of the subject concerned. That's why it becomes essential for making adequate provisions for each course to the student-teachers or teacher trainees. The present series is designed for providing a solid workable base for all course-papers. It has been prepared strictly according to the syllabus of the B.Ed class, prescribed by the UGC for different universities.

No doubt, there are so many other books on the subject, available in the market, written by worthy authors. However, every writer has his or her own style and way of presentation. The present work also has its own features and characteristics.

In preparation of this series of texts, the editor had to refer to the works of other authors and information sources. The editor feels a deep sense of gratitude for incorporating their ideas in the text. Hopefully, this series would serve as a 'ready to refer' tool for all teachers, teacher-students and others.

— Editor

1

Role of School

Ethos of Schooling

School ethos implies moral nature or environment of the school, its guiding principles, its distinguishing character and its sentiment.

The concept of an ideal ethos of a school has been very beautifully summed up by S. Bala Krishna Joshi, an eminent headmaster of a well managed school as, "A school is not a mere brick and mortar structure housing a miscellany of pupils and teachers; a school is not a market place where a heterogeneous crowd gathers with diverse objects; a school is not a rigorous reformatory where juvenile suspects are kept under vigilant watch, a school is a spiritual organism with distinctive personality of its own; a school is a vibrant community centre, radiating life and energy all round; a school is a wonderful edifice, resting on the foundation of goodwill-goodwill of the public goodwill of the parents; goodwill of the pupils. In a word, a well conducted school is a happy home, a sacred shrine, a social centre, a state in miniature and bewitching Brindavan, all beautifully blended into a synthetic structure."

Significant Elements

It is not without reason that the Education Commission 1964-66 observed "The destiny of India is now being shaped in her class-rooms. On the quality and number of persons coming out of schools and colleges will depend our success in the great adventure of national reconstruction."

Following factors in the school ethos greatly influence children's' learning and then overall growth and development.

Training in the Art of Living Together: "We do not visualize the school as merely a place of formal learning, whose main concern is to communicate a certain prescribed quantum of knowledge but rather as a living and organic community which is primarily interested in training its pupils in what we have called the gracious "art of living", observed the Secondary Education Commission.

Development of Child's Entire Personality: We would like the school to see if it can provide a richly varied pattern of activities to cater to the development of its children's entire personality. It has to formulate a scheme of hobbies, occupations and projects that will appeal to draw out the powers of children of varying temperaments and aptitudes.

Provision of a Stimulating Environment: The primary concern of the school should be to provide for its pupils a rich, pleasant and stimulating environment which will evoke their manifold interests and make life a matter of joyful experience.

Transformation into Activity School: The school must be transformed into an "activity school" because activity has an irresistible appeal for every normal child and in his natural path to the goal of knowledge and culture.

We do not visualize that these schools will have dull, routine ridden formal lessons in the class plus a number of independent unrelated extra-curricular activities which have no intrinsic relationship with them either in contents or methods. The entire programme of the school will be visualised as a unity and inspired by a psychologically congenial and stimulating approach, the so-called 'work' being characterised by the feeling of joy and self expression usually associated with play and hobbies, and these having something of the meaningful and purpose which are normally considered a special feature of academic work. Thus by planning a coherent programme of these different activities, rich in stimuli, the school will not be frittering away either the time or the energy of the pupils but will be heightening their intellectual powers also side by side while training them in other fine qualities.

***Opportunities for Self-Discipline*:** Discipline in the school will not be a matter of arbitrary rules and regulations enforced through the authority of the teachers helped by the lure of rewards or the fear of punishment. The students will be given full freedom to organise functions, to conduct many of the school activities through their own committees and even to deal with certain types of disciplinary cases. In this way, discipline will be maintained through the influence of the social group and it will gradually lead to the development of self-discipline.

No school can develop into an educative community, capable of releasing the students' creative capacities, if the teachers maintain a stiff forbidding attitude towards their pupils and try to maintain their authority through various kinds of punishments whilst the pupils, on their part, stand in awe of them and are not prepared to share their problems and difficulties with them.

The School as a Centre of Community Service: Another thing which will distinguish this school from most of the traditional schools is that it will be organised as a community.

***Providing Work Experience and Socially Useful Work*:** We expect the school to devote special attention to craft and other productive work and thus redress the balance between theoretical and practical studies which have been upset for many years.

Democratic Classroom Climate	*Autocratic Classroom Climate*
1. Students are teacher-guided.	1. Students are teacher dominated.
2. The students are guided by the teacher in the choice of many activities.	2. The teacher plans activities without conferring with the pupils.
3. The groups suggests and proposes supplementary work-all of which is reviewed and appraised by the group.	3. All the supplementary work is chosen and assigned by the teacher.
4. The student aid in planning the academic work, make suggestions and proposals.	4. The students answer questions asked by the teacher.
5. The pupils share with teacher in establishing standards of achievement.	5. The teacher sets up standards of achievement without conferring with the pupils.
6. The students share with the teacher the responsibility of appraising their work.	6. The students are not conferred with in appraising their growth.
7. Students are encouraged by the teacher to make suggestions concerning their work.	7. The teacher ignores suggestions of the pupils.
8. The students can move about the room with comparative case and without disturbing the work.	8. The students can move only with the permission of the teacher.
9. Students are encouraged to correct their mistakes.	9. The teacher directs pupil activities.
10. The daily programme is elastic and can be changed as the group decides.	10. The teacher decides when pupils are to stop working on one subject and when to start on the next. Daily programme is rigid.
11. The teacher adopts an exploratory attitude.	11. The teacher gives directions in a firm manner.
12. The teacher tries to understand the child.	12. The teacher works according to set procedures.
13. The teacher is sympathetic.	13. The teacher springs awe and fear.

Contd.

Democratic Classroom Climate	*Autocratic Classroom Climate*
14. The teacher tries to find reasons for misbehaviour.	14. The teacher arbitrarily punishes pupils for misbehaviour.
15. The teacher takes into consideration the individual differences of the students.	15. The teacher treats all children alike.
16. Children are naturally affectionate and are encouraged to show affection.	16. Teacher is cold to child's affection and does not reciprocate.
17. Every child is provided with an opportunity to contribute and to lead a group.	17. Only the aggressive and brighter children contribute and lead.
18. Materials and books are provided for all mental levels in a grade.	18. One level of supplies is furnished for single grade no matter what the ability range.
19. Students are grouped properly.	19. Students are grouped on administrative reasons.
20. The students express themselves freely.	20. There is no such freedom of expression.
21. Curriculum is flexible to meet with the needs of each child.	21. Curriculum is definite and same goals are set for all the children.
22. Teachers co-operate with other teachers to study problem students.	22. Teacher normally does not participate in group study of pupils.
23. Teachers encourage parents to visit school for a closer relationship between home and school.	23. Teachers discourage parents from visiting school because according to them it disrupts the schedule.
24. School atmosphere is reflected by student's remark, "I like School."	24. School atmosphere is reflected by student's remark "I don't like school."
25. Students committees assume responsibility for selecting equipment and supplies needed.	25. Teacher or the principal assumes responsibility for selecting and purchasing supplies and equipment.

Comprehensive Curriculum: Curriculum should fulfil psychological and social needs of the students.

Guidance and Counselling Services: These should be adequate.

Human Relations: Students should be made acquainted with the principles of developing good harmonious relations.

Atmosphere in Class

Meaning of Classroom Climate: Class-room climate implies classroom environment in which the change of behaviour or learning takes place through interaction in the group which consists of students of various shades and the teacher who is the leader of the group. In the process of learning, the mental health of the group is an important factor. As a leader, the teacher is expected to create democratic environment. His democratic behaviour in the classroom can steer constructive and inspirational individual as well as group activities in the right direction.

General Suggestions: Apart from the above mentioned factors for creating a democratic classroom climate, following suggestions should prove very useful:

1. It would be desirable for a teacher to throw some light on the qualities of leadership so that students choose their leaders wisely and the teacher is able to influence the class through its leaders. However it must be stressed that teacher must remain neutral in the selection of leaders.

2. The behaviour of the leader of the group is imitated by the members of the group.

3. Suggestion plays a big role in influencing the group behaviour. The suggestions put forward by the leader of the group are readily accepted.

4. The recent studies have made it clear that for bringing about changes to the individual, we must bring about changes in the characteristics of the group. The teachers, therefore, should adopt appropriate group methods in the class and through these influence the attitudes of the members of the group. Group training is better than individual training.

Role Model

Teacher's Personality: It has been rightly observed, "While books can teach, only personality can educate." A good personality includes: (a) Impressive Appearance (b) Modulated Voice (c) High Character (d) Effective Power of Communication.

Mahatma Gandhi observed, Woe to the teacher who teaches one thing with the lips and carries another in the heart."

Personality of the child in the desired dimension cannot be developed if the teacher who is the model to be followed lacks personality. Example is better than precept is an old saying, and it is absolutely true for the teaching profession. No amount of sermons from the teacher can make appreciable head way. A teacher teaches not only by 'What he says' but very largely by 'what he is'. Children are imitative and suggestive by nature. They imitate the dress, voice, habits and manners of their teachers. On several occasions, the likes and dislikes of teachers become the likes and dislikes of their students. Children who are in the plastic period of their lives are easily influenced by their teachers. 'Man know thyself' is the advice given by sage Yajnavalkya in India and the philosopher Socrates of Greece. The teachers must undergo a spiritual inner training. They should try to find out their own shortcomings and remove them. Ryburn has observed, "Self-analysis on the part of a teacher is a necessary equipment" Montessori stresses that every teacher worth his salt must destroy these sins: pride, anger, sloth, sensuality and envy. He should be partly a doctor, partly a scientist and completely religious. He must acquire a moral alertness, patience, love and humility. Writing about the role of the teachers, Lauri has observed, "If a teacher has not an ideal aim, he had better to take to shop keeping at once, he will there doubles find an ideal within his capacity."

Dynamic Methods of Teaching: The Secondary Education Commission (1952-53) has very rightly observed, "Every teacher and educationist of experience knows that even the best curriculum and the most perfect syllabus remains dead unless quickened into life by the right methods of teaching and the right kind of teachers."

A wise teacher can make his class-room teaching-learning easier and effective if he can direct group dynamics into constructive paths.

Through group discussion and activity methods, the teacher would give the individual student a chance to participate actively and to contribute to group work in the class. Some specific group techniques which could be used for the improvement of the group are:

(i) Buzz session, in which a small group of five or six students participate, is organised for purposes of stimulating discussion.

(ii) Role playing, in which problems of handling a situation are dramatised for the benefit of the group.

(iii) Brain storming, in which a group is organised for stimulating discussion.

(iv) Catharsis, in which a planned group expression of problems of concern to the group is provided.

(v) Recreational experiences, in which opportunities are provided for participation in dramatics, picnics, parties, etc. to improve the morale.

Effective Interpersonal Communication: Good teaching is interpersonal communication. Teaching is a two-way communication. As the name indicates, interpersonal communication is the presence of the facility to seek reactions, information etc. One way communication i.e., telling or lecturing by the teacher denies the facility to the learner to seek clarification, confirmation etc. The learners do not get the opportunity to develop interpersonal relationships. Interpersonal communication has a built-in-system of feedback. It ensures that further information and clarification etc. are provided wherever possible. The receiver or the learner gets an opportunity to understand the message or the content of the communication.

Healthy interpersonal communication is the sound basis of sound instruction or teaching.

Ego-involvement: The personality of the child should be given its due recognition. Emerson has observed, "The secret of education lies in respecting the pupil"

Constructive and Creative Discipline: The teacher's attitude towards his children should be sympathetic but firm.

Stimulus Variation and the Teacher: It has been generally observed that children are not able to attend to one thing for a very long period. The effectiveness of the teaching- learning process in such a situation depends to a great extent on the stimulus variations used by the teacher behaviour. Some of the common teacher behaviours in the class-room which fall under variation are:

1. Teacher movement
2. Teacher gestures
3. Changes in speech pattern

4. Changes in sensory focus

5. Changes in postures.

Reinforcement: Praise and Blame "Praise like gold and diamond owes its value to scarcity", writers Robinson Johnson. It implies that this technique should be employed with great care. These may be classified as:

(a) *Positive Verbal Reinforcement:* Following a pupil's answer, the teacher verbally indicates pleasures at the pupil's response by the use of words like 'Good,' 'Fair', 'Excellent,' 'Correct', etc.

(b) *Positive Non-Verbal Reinforcement:* This includes: Nods and smiles.

Teacher's friendly movements towards pupils.

Teacher's friendly look.

Teacher writing student's response on the blackboard.

(c) *Negative Non-Verbal:* This comprises gestures, sneering, frowning, expression of annoyance, impatience, etc.

(d) *Negative Verbal:* This includes comments like 'No,' 'Wrong,' 'No good,' 'Poor', 'Of course not,' etc.

Learning combined with creative Humour and Appropriate Laughter: An experienced teacher once observed, "I consider a day's teaching-learning wasted, if we do not have a hearty laugh."

Teacher as a Guide: Sri Aurobindo writes in the regard, "The first principle of true teaching is that nothing can be taught. The teacher is not an instructor or a task master, he is a helper and a guide. His business is to suggest and not to impose. He does not impart knowledge to the pupil: he shows him how to acquire knowledge for himself."

The Assessment

The teacher should keep an eye on the progress of every child. He should maintain a proper record of the same. He should inform his pupils about the success achieved by them. This will develop a sense of achievement among the pupils. This will also lead to achievement-motivation.

QUESTIONS

1. Explain the meaning of school ethos. What are the educational implications of school ethos? How can appropriate school ethos be built?

2. State the meaning of class-room climate. What type of climate *i.e.,* democratic or autocratic would you prefer? Mention the reasons in support of your answer.

3. Differentiate between democratic class-room climate and autocratic class-room climate. Which of the two would you prefer? State reasons for the same.

4. "While books can teach, only personality can educate." Explain this statement and bring out the role of the teacher in the teaching-learning process.

5. What types of practices should a teacher adopt in making learning effective and inspirational?

6. Write notes on

   (i) Stimulus variation and the teacher.

   (ii) Effective interpersonal relation in the class-room, and

   (iii) Role of praise and blame in learning.

2

Role of the Society

Different Elements

Among the social factors, other than the school, the five major groups that affect learning are: the family or the home, the class or the caste, the community and the rural-urban background. Learning is also affected by the tribal non-tribal background.

Familial Factors

American President Abraham Lincoln used to say, "Whatever I am and whatever I hope to be, I owe to my mother." Shivaji and Gandhiji expressed the same feelings. Educationists, psychologists and sociologists, all agree that the family is the most important single influence on the development and learning of the child. It has been said by Jemni, the author of 'Brahmasutra'. "The child learns the best lesson of citizenship between the kiss of the mother and care of his father." The parents are the transmitters of the cultural and social standards Parents as the first teachers lay the foundations of the preliminary education/learning. Most of the education/ learning at this stage is at the unconscious level. While communicating or interacting with the child, the parents unknowingly impart knowledge, develop skills and inculcate values. The way in which the parents communicate with the child, and their choice of words have a lasting impact on the personality of the child.

Family is the primary school of citizenship. It is the family which teaches the child how to get along with others. The family teaches the lessons of co-operation and give and take. A family can play the role of the 'cradle of all virtues.'

Effective relationship of the child with the parents is a crucial factor in the development of the personality of the child. The parent-child bond is one of love, security and trust.

The parents must understand that no two children are alike and therefore their approach in dealing with different children must differ.

Parents can learn much about their children if they observe them carefully.

A child's natural curiosity forces him to explore new things. He wants independence and freedom. The parents must understand this fact fully.

Parents need not to be too rigid or too liberal to introduce toilet training in early years.

Parents should encourage the child to communicate. They should tell simple stories and sing songs etc. This will help the child to feel secure.

Meeting the child's physical needs is of prime importance. Malnutrition is a very common problem in India and it is to be checked. The diet of the child has to be a balanced one as it affects learning.

Food must be nutritious. Efforts should be made to develop regular eating habits.

Common childhood illness and accidents adversely affect the learning of the child. Timely immunization is one way to prevent diseases. Adequate amount of sleep is necessary for the health of the child. Parents should give due importance to hygienic living.

Parents should provide ample encouragement and opportunity for exercise.

Intellectual development is very rapid during early childhood years. The child asks too many questions which should be answered patiently by the parents. Parents should encourage child's development of language skills.

It is essential for parents to help the child in taking decisions and choosing alternatives to solve problems.

Parents should recognise the emotional needs of the child to make his life better and richer. Child's need for security should be realized by the parents. He should be accepted as an individual. He should be relieved from anxiety. He wants love and it should be made available to him. Non fulfilment of these needs may develop later problems of maladjustment.

Significant Roles of the Parents: Directly as well as indirectly, the following roles of the parents affect learning:-

1. Parents as caretakers of physical needs of the children.
2. Parents as givers of security.
3. Parents as providers of love and affection.
4. Parents as role models for children to emulate
5. Parents as ideal disciplinary environment-constructive creators as well as creative.
6. Parents as developers of attitudes, skills and values.

7. Parents as providers of comfort in times of trouble.
8. Parents as admirers of children's achievements.
9. Parents as motivators and stimulators.
10. Parents as acceptors of limitations and assets of children.
11. Parents as providers of an overall stimulating environment.

Negative Aspects

Great psychological damage is caused to young children from poor family relationships. Three forms of psychological damages are caused to young children. First, the young child who develops an angry attitude towards a strict parents is likely to develop an unfavourable attitude towards all adults outside the home also.

Second, poor relationships in the family, for example, feeling of unloved and unwanted in the family may lay the foundations of an inferiority complex.

Third, unfavourable family relationships make children unhappy and keep them upset. The children remain emotionally disturbed.

Role of Economy

Undoubtedly class and socio-economic factors play a significant role in development and learning of children. The type of environment they provide to their children has a great bearing on learning.

It is very difficult to classify the society into water-tight compartments. Nevertheless Indian society on the socio-economic basis can be classified as: (i) Class of people below the poverty line

(ii) Lower class i.e., just above the poverty line class (iii) Lower middle class (iv) Middle class (v) Upper class (vi) VIP class (very Important Persons' class).

(i) Class of people below the poverty line constitutes nearly one-third of India's population. This class, by and large, has failed to derive benefit from educational facilities and incentives provided by the government. Almost the entire class can be placed under the category 'illiterate.' It is so much engrossed in making both ends meet that it can hardly think of providing education to its children.

(ii) The lower middle class, though conscious of the benefit of educating children, is still not able to make the maximum benefit of educational and learning opportunities and incentives.

(iii) The middle class has been able to make use of the facilities provided by the government to a considerable extent. It recognises the importance of learning and is quite keen that its children occupy respectable positions in the society. However, barring a few sections of this population, majority of its children go to local bodies/ government schools which in general lack suitable buildings, equipments, libraries workshops etc. The standard of teaching-learning is on the lower side. It is true that this class has also produced great scholars, professionals and eminent persons in various fields. But the proportion is not very high.

***Upper class/VIP Class*:** This class makes all possible efforts to send its children to public schools of varying standards but in general higher than state-run schools. Public schools provide better schooling facilities to their students. Quite a good proportion of students educated in these schools occupy prestigious positions in different walks of life.

The community must provide a pure, simple and a well balanced environment. It must eliminate evil influences on the child. It should provide secular examples to children.

The various institutions in the community such as Panchayats, Mahila Mandals. Youth Clubs etc., should be involved in the development and learning of children.

The community and especially 'play groups' of young children exercise a considerable influence on their personality development. The activities of these play groups are highly imaginative and educative. Following are the learning and educative values of play groups in the community.

1. Children learn to cooperate.
2. Children learn to respect other's right and duties.
3. Children get opportunities for both leadership and followership training.
4. Children develop social attitudes.
5. Children get opportunities to play together and thus become conscious of the differences that exist in attitudes, values and behaviour in children of the neighbourhood.
6. Children get valuable information about their neighbourhood.

The community must ensure that the play-groups/peer groups provide suitable environment.

Attempts should be made to educate the parents to develop interest, skills and knowledge in child care.

The community and the especially the rural community must take interest in establishing educational institutions. In rural areas, it is generally expected to provide land for the school buildings.

The inter-relatedness of the community and the school must be adequately understood in our country. The community should not treat school as an institution outside the community. There should be a friendly-oriented partnership between the school and the community.

Apart from cooperating in various instructional programmes of the school, the community can offer assistance to the school in various areas like the following:

1. Electrification of the school building.
2. White washing and minor repairs of the school building.
3. Construction of compound walls.
4. Provision of sheds for cooking meals.
5. Donations of land for various purposes.
6. Painting of biack-boards.
7. Supply of portraits of national leaders.
8. Supply of stationery and books to the poor students.
9. Supply of uniforms to the poor students.
10. Supply of utensils.
11. Supply of play materials.
12. Offering free services by individuals like doctors.

Social Backdrop

There is no doubt that a conducive environment helps to draw out the best in child-body, mind and soul. However, rural schools, in general, lack such a learning environment. Rural schools are usually housed in poor buildings. They also lack equipment and various learning facilities. Qualified and experienced teachers, when posted to rural schools, are always in the look out of transfers to urban schools. Thus students are deprived of their services.

Rural societies are conservative and traditional by and large. This fact also makes a lot of difference in the learning outcomes of students.

In the urban areas, there are several well-maintained school libraries, museums, research institutes etc. which serve as resource centres of learning. Students get a much wider exposure to new technology. Competition among institutions and students is also very keen.

All the above mentioned factors lead to wide differences in learning.

In spite of the recommendations of several education committees and commissions, we are far away from the goal of providing equal opportunities to learners. Much ground in this regard still remains to be covered.

QUESTIONS

1. "Family is the first school of learning". Explain this statement and bring out the role of the family in the learning of the child.

2. Explain the role of the following in the learning of the child.

   (i) Class and socio-economic factors in learning.

(ii) Role of the community in the learning of children.

(iii) Rural-urban background and learning of children.

3. "Too much stress on individualization leads to social maladjustment". Show how far this statement is justified. In what way can good teaching combine the benefits of both individual and group oriented learning experiences?

3

Significance of Psychology

In a simple language, educational psychology implies the application of principles and practices of psychology to the various dimensions of education with a view to modify the behaviour of the learner in an educational environment so that he amicably adjusts himself with the society with maximum of satisfaction and security. Thus educational psychology is the applied branch of psychology in an educational setting.

Following definitions would enable us to understand the true meaning of educational psychology in its various facets.

In the words of Anderson, "While general psychology is a pure science, educational psychology is its application in the field of education with the aim of socialising an individual and modifying his behaviour".

E.A. Peel considers educational psychology as the 'science of education.'

Crow and Crow put it as, "Educational psychology describes and explains the learning experiences of an individual from birth through old age."

According to Skinner, "Educational psychology is that branch of psychology which deals with teaching and learning." He has also observed, "Educational psychology covers the entire range and behaviour of the personality as related to education."

Judd considers educational psychology as "the science which explains the changes that take place in the individuals as they pass through the various stages of development".

Stephen regards educational psychology as "the systematic study of the educational growth and development of a child."

The Encyclopaedia of Educational Research states, "Educational psychology is the study of the learner and of the learning-teaching process in its various (branches) directed towards helping the child come to terms with society with a maximum of security and satisfaction."

According to Walter B. Kolesnik, "Educational psychology is the study of those facts and principles of psychology which help to explain and improve the process of education."

In the words of Trow, "Educational psychology is the study of psychological aspects of educational situation."

A perusal of the above definitions would indicate that the definitions given by Anderson Kolesnik and 'The Encyclopaedia of Educational Research' provide the true meaning of educational psychology. Other definitions, by and large, put emphasis on 'Study' but do not emphatically state the ultimate aim of studying a subject. A mere study of the behaviour of the learner is not enough unless it is related to the modification of the behaviour towards desired ends.

From these it is concluded that educational psychology is that applied branch of psychology which studies the experiences and behaviours of the learners in relation to educational environment which is mainly provided by the teacher. Therefore, educational psychology becomes a psychology of teaching and learning. Teaching and learning are the main processes of education and the learner is a key figure in the process.

Concept and Meaning

Following points point out the nature of educational psychology. Some of the points overlap.

1. Educational psychology is an applied science.
2. Educational psychology is a social science.
3. Educational psychology is a positive science.
4. Educational psychology is a specific science.
5. Educational psychology is a developing and growing science.
6. Educational psychology is an academic discipline.
7. Educational psychology is not as exact as natural and physical sciences.

Scope of educational psychology is as vast as the scope of education itself. Gates and others have very aptly remarked, "The boundaries of educational psychology are uncertain and changing." The explosition of 'Information Technology'(IT) has been exercising a far-reaching influence on the scope of educational psychology. New and novel situations need new and novel approaches to educational matters. Nevertheless, we may mention the most significant areas of the scope of educational psychology. Here we are listing only the ways of classification.

Classification I: Broad Areas

1. Learner: Growth and Development

(a) Heredity and environment affecting the learner.

(b) General ,growth and development of the learner at different stages of education.

(c) Emotional, intellectual and social development of the learner.

(d) Individual differences of the learners.

(e) Learner's aptitudes, interests and intelligence.

2. Learning

(a) Concept of learning.

(b) Process of learning.

(c) Primary and concomitant learning.

(d) Domains of learning: Cognitive, Affective and Psychomotor.

(e) Learning process

(f) Factors affecting learning.

(g) Transfer of training.

(h) Learning situations.

3. Personality and Adjustment

(a) Emotions.

(b) Mental health of the learner.

(c) Mental health of the teacher.

(d) Character development.

(e) Social interaction.

4. Evaluation and Measurement

   (a) Meaning of the concepts of evaluation and measurement.

   (b) Basic principles of evaluation and measurement.

   (c) Measurement of aptitudes, attitudes and intelligence.

   (d) Measurement of learning.

   (e) Measures of adjustment.

   (f) Applications of the results of measurement and evaluation.

5. Techniques and Methods in Educational Psychology

   (a) Scientific study of educational problems.

   (b) Statistical techniques.

   (c) Implications of research for the classroom teacher.

Classification II: In Terms of Learner and Learning

1. The learner (Pupil).

2. The learning experiences.

3. The learning environment or situation.

4. The learning process.

5. The teaching situation.

6. Evaluation of learning experience.

Classification III: The Educational Psychology Division of the American Psychological Association

1. Human growth and development.
2. Learning.
3. Personality and adjustment.
4. Measurement, evaluation and statistics.
5. Techniques and methods of educational psychologies.

The Learner through out: This includes the study of growth and development of the individual and the concept of maturity in various aspects of personality-physical, mental, social and emotional. Study of learner deals with the influences of his family, social class and peer groups on his personality and behaviour. Social behaviour and social norms of his peer group; emotional health and problem behaviour of the learner are also studied in detail from the mental hygiene point of view. This also includes the study of the abilities, needs and motivational forces, like self-concept, life-goals, values, anxiety of the individual learner as well as the differences that exist among different individuals.

Learning Experiences: This includes providing activities and subjects according to the maturity level of the students.

The Learning Situation: In the learning situation, educational psychology studies such factors as class-room management and discipline, techniques and aids which facilitate learning, methods of teaching, evaluation techniques and practices, guidance and counselling.

The Learning Process: In the learning process, educational psychology deals with the nature of learning and how it takes place. It considers the various theoretical view points as well as experimental evidences to explain the role and nature of reinforcement, forgetting, problem solving, transfer of training and the learning of concepts, skills and attitudes.

The Teaching Situation: Effectiveness of educational psychology becomes relevant only when its methods and findings become a part of educational practices when the teachers apply psychological methods.

Evaluation of Learning Experiences: In recent years, evaluation of learning experiences has assumed great significance in the subject matter of psychology.

What, when and how to teach Questions of Educational Psychology ?

Educational psychologists are more concerned with the answer of these questions. The first question refers to the developmental processes that gradually mature as the child grows up. Similarly the problem of what to teach is important because of its close relationship with the process of maturation. Certain types of learning can be useful to the child only when he has matured sufficiently in certain faculties. We cannot think of teaching mathematics to a three year child, though he may be taught to count simple things. The problem of how to teach is equally important because there are ways and means of teaching which can make the education of a child more effective, meaningful and useful.

Various Aspects

Educational psychology, being functional in its character is very helpful to all sections of society engaged in pursuing different dimensions of education at all levels of education i.e., formal, non-formal and informal.

Educational psychology is of great importance to parents, teachers, guidance workers, career masters, and psychoanalysts etc.

According to W.A. Kelly (1941), educational psychology is helpful in the following ways:

1. It provides a knowledge of the nature of the child.
2. It gives understanding of the nature, aims and purposes of education.
3. It gives understanding of the scientific methods and procedures which have been used in arriving at the facts and principles of educational psychology.
4. It presents the principles and techniques of learning and teaching.
5. It gives training in methods of measuring abilities and achievement in school subjects.
6. It provides a knowledge of the growth and development of children.
7. It assists in the better adjustment of children and helps to prevent maladjustment.
8. It helps to understand the significance and control of emotions.
9. It gives an understanding of the principles and techniques of correct training.

Role in Education

An elementary knowledge of educational psychology would prove very useful to the parents who are undoubtedly the first teachers in the following manners:

1. The knowledge of educational psychology points out to the parents that they should show reasonable amount of love and affection to their children. They should bear in mind the maxim, "Love the child and the child will love you. Hate the child and he will hate you."

2. It helps the parents to understand the process of development and growth of their children.

3. Educational psychology acquaints the parents with the emotional, mental and physical needs of the children.

4. Educational psychology impresses upon the parents of the necessity of providing wholesome environment to the children so that they lead a happy life and are free from anxiety.

5. Educational psychology enables the parents to know that they should not take resource to repression and punishment which adversely affect the mental health of children.

6. Educational psychology enables the parents to observe keenly the behaviour of children. It enables them to control their habits.

7. It helps the parents to understand themselves, their roles and responsibilities towards their children.

The work of the teacher is like that of a gardener to a great extent. The gardener needs the knowledge of the plant life. The teacher also needs the knowledge of the learner. It is the duty of the gardener to ensure that all the plants grow and yield good flowers and fruits and he can do so when he is well-acquainted with all the details about them. The objective of the teacher is to ensure that all the learners under his care and charge develop into happy and healthy personalities and he can do so only when he knows how the learners develop and behave. This knowledge is provided to the teacher by educational psychology.

The work of the teacher may also be compared to that of an artist who must know his material thoroughly if he wants to produce a fine piece of art. What will happen to the artist if he starts his work without fully understanding the kind of material he has to work with. The teacher as an artist, is not only required to know the subject matter but also to know the child's nature and the techniques of moulding his behaviour in accordance with the objectives.

The work of the teacher assume all the more significance and needs more delicacy and expertness than that of the gardener and the artist as here, human beings are involved.

R. A. Davis in 'Applicability and Applications of Psychology with Particular Reference to Classroom Learning' (1943) has pointed out the significance of educational psychology as, "Psychology has made a distinct contribution to education through its analysis of pupil potentialities and differences as revealed by means of various types of psychological tests. It has also contributed directly to the knowledge of pupil growth and maturation during the school years."

G.M. Blair in 'The Psychological Interpretation of Teaching' (1947) has stated the importance of educational psychology to the teacher in these words," Modern teacher, if he is to succeed with his work should be a specialist who understands children, how they grow, develop, learn and adjust. He should be diagnostician, who can discover special difficulties of children and at the same time possesses the requisite skill for carrying forward the necessary remedial work. He should also be performing important educational and vocational guidance functions. No person untrained in the methods of psychology can possibly fulfil the obligations and tasks which are the responsibilities of the teacher."

Basic Issues

Principles and practices of educational psychology are needed by the teacher on account of the following considerations:

Knowledge of John and Latin: Sir John Adams has put it thus in his book 'New Teaching'. The verbs of teaching govern two accusatives, one of the person and another of the thing as, 'the master taught John Latin'." He says that there are two definite subjects-John, the student and Latin the subject which are governed by the verb taught". Now the teacher must understand both John as well as Latin if he wants to make 'teaching' effective. Educational psychology helps him in understanding 'John'. He may be a great scholar of Latin but he will not succeed in teaching Latin to John if he has no knowledge of the mental set up of John. Acquisition of knowledge is now no more the main object of education but it is still very significant in the process of education. Acquisition of knowledge is also a sort of modification in the behaviour of the child. For this purpose the educator will have to consider the mental processes of the child and not only the quality of knowledge which he is going to be put into the living mind.

Knowledge of Individual Differences: No two persons are exactly alike. There is individual difference. Pupils always differ in their level of intelligence, aptitudes, likes and dislikes and in other propensities and potentialities. Different minds are to be trained by the teacher. There are gifted, backward, retarded, talented and handicapped children. All of them should not be treated in the same manner. Knowledge of educational psychology helps the teacher to cater to individual differences of children.

Educational Psychology and Process of Learning: Teaching and learning go side by side. All education depends upon the learning of new responses and the capacity of a human child to learn new responses. Educational psychology discusses the nature of learning theories and types of learning for different age levels and situations. Therefore, knowledge of educational psychology becomes essential to a teacher to study all these problems.

Knowledge of Educational Psychology Provides a Scientific Attitude to the Teachers: The knowledge of psychology can make the teacher more scientific in his educational practices and consequently he will be more objective and methodical in his work.

Psychology Proves Useful in the Methods of Teaching: Educational psychology has discovered many secrets about mental forces. Recent researches made in the field of educational psychology give us valuable suggestions for better methods of teaching and memorizing, for making desirable habits and eradicating anti-social tendencies. Educational psychology tells us how significant play and recreation are for the children and how play-way and project methods turn the work of learning into an interesting play.

Educational Psychology can Change the Outlook and Attitude of the Teacher Towards his Pupils: The knowledge of psychology can change the outlook and attitude of the teacher towards children by understanding them adequately.

Educational Psychology Helps the Teacher in his Own Mental Development: The study of educational psychology can help the teacher to understand himself. He will realise his own merits and weaknesses and make attempts to overcome his weaknesses.

Educational Psychology and Nervous System: The entire education depends on the function of the brain and nervous system. It becomes essential for a teacher to study the nervous system which controls human behaviour. He must have the knowledge of sensory organs which are the gate ways of knowledge.

Educational Psychology and Play: Play is a natural tendency having great educational potentials. Knowledge of educational psychology helps the teacher to provide for a varieties of activities for children.

Educational Psychological Measurements are Very Useful for the Teacher: Educational psychology has made many strides in this respect quite recently. It has produced many reliable tests and instruments of mental measurement. These are proving to be extremely useful in the field of education. We can quite easily measure mental capacities, basic intelligence, temperamental attitudes and special inclinations of children and base educational programmes on these findings. These measurements show that all the children differ in and that every child is a unique being. The teacher can know that children with I.Q. below 90 cannot do well in medical, engineering, administrative or other similar vocations.

But he knows that such young ones are not doomed if they cannot do well in intellectual callings. He can easily explore some other fields where such children can also flourish.

Character Development: Educational psychology helps a lot to the formation and development of character. The teacher comes to know the methods he should adopt in inculcating suitable character traits, and moral principles among the children.

Educational Psychology and Productive Activities: A great stress is being laid these days on work experience and socially useful productive work. Educational psychology helps the teacher to know how various activities in these fields can be used for the fulfilment of the basic needs of children.

Educational Psychology Helps the Teacher in Guidance and Counselling: Students need various types of guidance and counselling. A teacher with the knowledge of educational psychology can render very useful service.

Educational Psychology Helps the Teacher in the Realization of the Aims of Education: The main aim of education is the harmonious and allround development of the educand. Development comes from within and the inner potentialities must be understood and approached for the desired modification in the development of the child. The knowledge of educational psychology helps the teacher to understand the inner potentialities which underlie the behaviour of the child.

QUESTIONS

1. Define educational psychology. State its meaning.

2. "Educational psychology is the science of behaviour." Comment upon this statement.

3. Bring out in detail the scope of educational psychology.

4. "A teacher must have the knowledge of John (student) and Latin (subject matter)." Elucidate this statement.

5. "Educational psychology is the science of education and assists the teacher to understand the development of his pupils." Discuss this statement.

6. State the significance of educational psychology for the class-room teacher.

7. Justify the need of studying educational psychology in the B.Ed. Course.

4

Aims and Principles

Adolescents aged between 10-19 years account for more than one-fifth of the world's population. In India, this age group forms 21.4 percent of the total population. Characterised by distinct physical and social changes, the separate health, education, economic and employment needs of adolescents cannot be ignored. Adolescents are also entitled to enjoy all basic human rights—economic, social, political and cultural—but their inability to exercise these rights places the onus on policy makers and adults to implement separate measures to ensure their rights. Moreover, it is necessary to invest in adolescents as the future leaders and guardians of the nation's development.

The significant role of India's adolescence population in achieving its developmental goals must be recognised. It is, therefore, very necessary to cater to the needs, interests, goals and values of the adolescents.

As observed in Adolescence in India, "A pre-requisite for policy planning and focus is a comprehensive situational analysis of adolescence." The lack of reliable data on the adolescent age group is a major impediment in discussing interests, goals and values of Indian adolescence.

Youth Days

Three main stages of adolescence can be discerned:

Early Adolescence (9-13 years)—Characterised by a spurt of growth and the development of secondary sexual characteristics.

Mid Adolescence (14-15 years)—This stage is distinguished by the development of a separate identity from parents, of new relationships with peer groups and the opposite sex, and of experimentation.

Late Adolescence (16-19 years)—At this stage, adolescents have fully developed physical characteristics (similar to adults), and have formed a distinct identity and have well-formed opinions and ideas.

Groups of Adolescence : Adolescents are generally perceived as a homogenous group, yet they can be stratified on the basis of gender, caste, class geographical location (urban/rural) and religion. Adolescents also include a whole gamut of categories: School and non-school going, drop-outs, sexually exploited children, working adolescents-both paid and unpaid, unmarried adolescents as also married males and females with experience of fatherhood and motherhood.

Analytical Assessment

An overview, based on the secondary data available, confirms the need for a separate focus on the health, education, employment and protection of human rights of adolescents. Reproductive health, in particular, represents the most critical area where an emphasis on the special needs and concerns of adolescents is required. In India, given its predominantly patriarchal set up, ideology of son preference, incidence of early marriage and high rates of maternal mortality, a strong focus on the needs of adolescent girls is warranted. However, both sexes are vulnerable to problems such as those of drug abuse, HIV/AIDS and other infections and sexual abuse.

Values and Objectives

As already observed, there is a lack of reliable and scientific data on this issue. However, it must be accepted that on account of the influence of electronic media, Indian adolescent cannot remain unaffected by globalisation. Nevertheless, following interests, goals and values of Indian adolescent are discernible although it is very difficult to generalise as there are several subgroups on account of the vastness of the country and its plural culture.

Interests: 1. Recreational Interests: (i) Interest in folk dance (ii) Television watching (iii) Celebrating birthdays and attending parties. (iv) Folk dance and music (v) Pop dance and singing (vi) Watching movies (vii) Reading comics and sensational literature (viii) Travelling (ix) Interest in pen-friendship (x) Interest in television games (xi) Watching and Listening Cricket commentaries (xii) Playing cards (xiii) Trends towards for fun gambling (xiv) Interest in smoking as a fashion symbol (xv) Trends towards use of drug and pills. (xvi) Interest in fine arts (xvii) Exchanging jokes (xviii) Interest in drinking, it being status symbol

Religious Interests: (i) Usually sceptical of religious beliefs (ii) Disinterest in the observance of religious rites and ceremonies (iii) In difference to formal religion.

Social Interest: (i) Attending group parties, (ii) Mixing with the opposite sex, (iii) Interest in global matters, (iv) Demonstrating self identity in the group, (v) Group loyalty.

Vocational Interests: (a) Interest in professions related to Commerce, (b) Interest in information technology and especially computers.

Miscellaneous Interest: (i) Conversation in groups (ii) Interest in beautification of the body, (iii) Interest in new things, (iv) Trend towards foreign studies, (v) Trend towards settling in foreign lands, (vi) Heightened sex interest.

Goals: (i) Becoming rich over night. (ii) Getting power and exercising influence. (iii) Capturing political power (iv) Occupying higher posts. (iv) Becoming independent of joint family and having nuclear family.

Values: (1) Re-examination of traditional beliefs and customs and acquiring new ones, (2) Emancipation from home and becoming independent, (3) Knowing everything attitude, (4) Growing gulf between the values of parents and adults, (5) Critical attitude, (6) Indifference to respect for elders, (7) Declining faith in the leaders of all shades.

Various Concerns

Serious problem of 10-14 Year Group: Since adolescents comprise a major part of the reproductive age group, addressing their needs will be critical in determining India's population. An analysis within the age group itself indicates that proportion of 10-14 year olds is greater than the 15-19 year group.

Problem of Gender Discrimination: Any programme for adolescents must recognise the problem of gender discrimination of the adolescents.

Problem of Under Nutrition: If India wishes to achieve the goals of 'Health for All' and adequate 'Nutrition for All', it must attend to the problem of under nutrition among adolescent girls. A sizeable number of adolescent girls are actually malnourished. This will increase the risk of difficulty to child birth.

Problem of Poor Understanding of Reproductive Health: A poor understanding of reproductive health and sexual issues creates several problems in this area.

Problems of High Level of Pre-marital Sexual Activity: In this regard, following trends are noticed:

(i) The magnitude of adolescent sexual activity is significant, and is higher in boys than girls. There is also under-reporting of non-marital relationships by adolescent girls due to fear of social disapproval.

(ii) Men are morely likely to be sexually active and at an earlier age than girls, and attitudes on premarital sexual activity remain conservative. Furthermore, the acceptance of premarital sexual activity is greater among boys than girls.

(iii) Parents and teachers play a minor role in giving information, and are usually reluctant to impart such information. The majority of information on sexual and reproductive issues is obtained from peers (which can sometimes be misleading and inaccurate).

(iv) Commercial sex workers usually serve as partners for first-time sexual encounters.

(v) Contraceptive use is low and rarely used in first-time sexual encounters, including with commercial sex workers. Contraceptive awareness is usually about sterilisation, which is unsuitable for most adolescents. Knowledge of HIV/AIDS, safe sex and preventive behaviour (like use of condoms) is low, across all ages and education levels.

(vi) Knowledge of sexual and reproductive issues is extremely poor. In some studies, 50 percent of female adolescents did not know about mensuration, and the limited knowledge was based on social factors (such as not being permitted to cook) than the actual physio-logical changes.

(vii) There is considerable interest among adolescent boys for information on reproductive health.

(viii) Education did not increase knowledge of sex and reproduction.

(ix) The educational system does not adequately meet the needs for imparting sex education.

(x) Sexual and reproductive decision-making by adolescents is constrained by age and gender factors. Adolescent women have little choice on whom and when to marry, and are usually not in a position to negotiate contraceptive use. This varies slightly with age, with an older wife more likely to make such decisions.

(xi) There is a huge unmet demand for adolescent health facilities, information and counselling services.

Unwanted Pregnancies and Abortions: There is a lack of knowledge of appropriate use of contraceptives. Son preference is another reason.

Maternal Mortality: This is on account of the fact that the body has not yet reached full maturity. Marriage age is very low.

Sexually Transmitted Deceases (STDs), including HIV/AIDS: Young people between the ages of 10 and 25 years make up 50 per cent of all new infections.

Drug Abuse: In India, it is estimated that a substantial number of drug users are in the age group of 12 to 18.

Violence against Women, Sexual Abuse and Trafficking of Girls: Available data indicate that a high incidence of rape occurs in the 10-16 year age group.

Gender Difference in Literacy and Education: The gross enrolment ratio (GER) for girls including adolescent girls lags behind boys. Likewise drop-out rates in the case of adolescent girls are higher than boys.

High Incidence of Unemployment Among Adolescents: Overall, the unemployment rates are almost three times as high for adolescents as that among aged 15 and above.

Depression Leading to Suicide: Every year, suicide is one of the most leading causes of death among them. Each year, 15 to 25 per cent of high school students seriously consider taking this course with depression being the prime motive.

Alcohol and Tobacco Abuse: Alcohol and tobacco abuse is very common among 2.5 to 3 per cent of children between 15 to 20 years of age.

Sex Encounter: In Delhi alone, 15 per cent of children in the age group 15 to 20 have already had their first sexual encounter.

HIV Infections: Sex encounter combined with the lack of awareness at this stage has also increased the possibility of HIV (Human immunodeficiency Virus) infections. India has currently an HIV infection rate of 1.7 per 1000 of which more than 40 per cent is concentrated around teenagers.

Emotional Stress: Family pressures to study and perform better indirectly result in emotional stress for a teenager.

Improper Company: Hanging around with improper friends may also lead to drug abuse, HIV and early pregnancy.

Miscellaneous Issues: Teenagers face numerous issues ranging from pubertal changes pimples, obesity, short height and changes in body structure, to medical problems like asthma, diabetes, thyroid disorders, eating disorders (anorexia) and bed welting.

Concerned Steps

Adolescent Clinic: Dr. Kumar suggests special adolescent clinics. 'Adolescent medicine' a new branch of medical science, might just be the sweet pill in teen's life.

National Policy: There should be a national policy that facilitates establishing adolescent care clinics in hospitals and health centers across the country.

QUESTIONS

1. Give a situational analysis of adolescents in India. State the stages of adolescence in India.

2. Describe the major interests, goal; and values of Indian adolescents. How can these be fulfilled?

3. What are the important problems and issues in the proper development of Indian adolescents? State their educational implications.

4. What type of educational environment is needed to meet the common needs and problems of Indian students during the period of adolescence?

5

Elements at Work

Various Angles

H.C. Mckown has given a very vivid description of individual differences, "In the whole world there are probably no two things alike-no two trees, not two leaves, flowers, blades of grass, rocks, drops, clouds, animals, houses, pianos, books, baseballs or photographs, even though at first glance they appear to be identical. Similarly no two human beings are alike, they differ physically in size, weight, height, colour of eyes and hair texture of skin-and in a thousand other details as well as in thousands of details of mental, social and spiritual life" Not only this, an individual reacts to the same situation in different manners at different times. Mass procedures, no matter, how well-intentioned, fail to accomplish the desired results in educational programmes, unless they are supplemented by adequate attention to the individual needs of the learner. In the words of Charles E. Skinner, "Today we think of individual differences as including any measurable aspect of the total personality." Differences in children may be slight, moderate or extreme.

Types of Individual Differences: Following are the important types of individual differences:

1. *Differences in Physique:* This means tall or short, thin or fat, fair or black, etc.

2. *Differences in Health:* It means healthy or ill, weak or strong.

3. *Differences in Intelligence:* Here the range is very wide-from almost nil intelligence to 140 or above. On the basis of one's I.Q., one can be classified to fall in any of the idiot through genius categories.

4. *Differences with Reference to Achievements:* Pupils differ in achievements in school subjects and their efficiency in vocation.

5. *Differences in Affective Factors:* There are differences in attitude towards ideas, subjects, things and people etc. Likewise differences in interests.

6. *Differences in Motor Ability:* This means control over muscles. The performance of some in some mechanical task is superior and the performance of others is inferior.

7. *Sex Differences:*.Sex differences operate in different ways.

8. *Differences with Reference to Learning Ability and Speed of Learning:* This is evident from daily example. Take a class- room. Some boys learn things quickly-other take days to learn it and some do not learn at all.

9. *Differences with Reference to Race and Nationality:* Many studies lead us to conclude that people belonging to different races and nationalities differ in respect of nature, physical and mental traits, interests and personality etc. It can be intelligence also.

10. *Personality Differences:* Many classifications of personality differences are made. According to Hipprocrates, people are of four types: (a) sanguine, (b) choleric, (c) melancholic, (d) phlegmatic

According to Jung, people can be classified into three types: (a) Introverts, (b) Extroverts, (c) Ambiverts.

Terman has classified people on the basis of intelligence into nine categories-from genius to idiot.

11. *Differences with Respect to Development:* It includes social development, emotional development which includes emotional maturity, emotional stability, etc.

Threefold Broad Classification of Individual Differences

(1)	(2)	(3)
Physical Characteristics	Demographic Characteristics	Cognitive Behaviour
Like appearance, colour, height, size, sex etc.	Like age, caste, socio-economic status etc.	Like thinking, remembering, creating and problem-solving etc.

Important Aspects

Teaching-learning process can be efficient and effective only when individual differences of students are recognised and suitable steps are taken to meet them so that individuals are in a position to develop according to their optimum capacity.

Some students go faster than others and such students may be given double promotion or separate streams formed or some additional work given to them so that their progress is not retarded due to slow learners. Similarly, steps will have to be taken to ensure that the slow learners also make satisfactory progress commensurate with their capacity and ability to work.

A deaf, dumb, blind, undersized, oversized, too fat or too lean learner needs guidance in the selection of such a vocation where his physical defect may not be a handicap and he may be able to earn his living in an honourable manner. Such students need special educational courses. Ordinary schools fail to do justice to them.

There are some students whose parents are very dominating with the result that their children develop inferiority complex. Too lenient parents allow their children to be freelancers and such children suffer from other complexes and develop bad habits. Children of the rich and the poor have altogether different situations to be faced with. The problems are as numerous as the learners.

The programme of guidance is not confined to the selection of subjects, schools, vocations etc. All children need guidance in every aspect of their harmonious development. They need guidance in fields such as recreation, moral and religious, social adjustments, cultural pursuits, physical development, etc.

Democratically, all individuals are equal but physically and psychologically all individuals are unequal and in other words each individual is different from the other. All the same, all are agreed that equal opportunity or equality of opportunity must be provided to every individual for drawing out the best that an individual has so that an individual achieves optimum development. It has been aptly stated by Benjamin S. Bloom, an American educator, "A society which places such great value on education and schooling that it requires the individual to attend school for a long period of time must find the means to make education attractive and meaningful to the individual learner." This implies that education should be individual-centred. But in spite of the loud talk on child-centred or individual-centred education, it is observed that there is very little practical action in this regard.

Undoubtedly, all the students need guidance in one or the other aspect, some need more guidance and others less. Without proper guidance the superior child may go astray, the average one may become backward and the backward may be lost to the society altogether.

Teaching Tactics

In view of the individual differences, it is quite clear that the same curriculum, same methods of teaching and same discipline and in some cases even the same educational institution will not serve the individual needs of children. Ideally speaking each student needs a particular setting and individual instruction with a lot of group interaction. This, however, is not feasible in normal life. At the same time individual differences of children must be catered to. There are seven broad areas, in which a lot of work could be done to take into consideration individual differences. These are:

1. Streaming of students, i.e., making ability groups.
2. Curriculum planning, i.e., providing advanced and ordinary curriculum in different disciplines.
3. Disciplinary treatment.
4. Guidance and counselling.
5. Special schools for the handicapped children.
6. Combining individualised, group and class instruction.
7. Using maxims of teaching and mnemonics.

Following are the general guidelines for meeting individual differences:

1. Courses should be selective to meet the needs of individual students.

2. Opportunities for acquiring manual and mechanical skills should be provided.

3. A wide range of pupil experiences may be provided in the school.

4. Remedial instruction should be made available to such students who need it.

5. Courses should be organised in such a way as bright pupils can learn at their own speed and slow pupils follow their own speed.

6. Guidance regarding co-curricular activities should be provided.

7. Counselling should be provided to students.

8. Assignments should be adapted to the needs of students.

9. Special care should be taken to accept the under-achieving child as a unique individual. His particular needs should be immediately attended to.

10. Efforts may be made to re-establish child's confidence in himself.

11. The teacher should seek the co-operation of other teachers and the parents of the under-achievers.

12. In case of deep-rooted emotional problems which lie at the root of under-achievement, referral may be made to a child guidance clinic after taking the parents into confidence.

13. Students should be taught to recognise their handicaps, and counselled in methods to overcome or compensate for them.

14. Some programme of parents education may be taken up as many problems of the students result from unsatisfactory home conditions.

15. School programme should take into account the needs of those students who are not likely to go to college and those who would join college.

16. The school programme, administration and management should be made flexible enough to allow for adjustment to individual differences.

Earlier Procedures

On account of differences in ability and in previous experiences all children are not at the same readiness (preparation for action) for learning when they enter school or when they learn a new topic or unit in the same subject or when they are promoted to the next class. This makes difference in the new situation because of differences in basic concept formation and the level of knowledge required as foundation on which to build a new lesson.

Thorndike has propounded the Law of Readiness. The law states, "When any conduction unit is not in readiness to conduct, for it to conduct is annoying. When any conduction unit is in readiness to conduct, for it not to do so is annoying."

The law is indicative of learner's state to participate in the learning process. According to Thorndike, readiness is preparation for action. Readiness does not come automatically with maturation. It is a law of preparatory adjustment, not a low about growth. Thorndike termed the neurons and synapses involved in the establishment of a specific bond or connection, a conduction unit. According to this law, for a conduction unit ready to conduct, to do, is satisfying and for it not to do so is annoying.

***Educational Implications*:** Teacher should prepare the minds of the students to be ready to accept the knowledge, skills and aptitudes. For this, he should provide opportunities for those experiences in which students can spontaneously participate. In other words, he should arouse their capacity to link the experiences with their everyday life. 'Simple to complex' is the important maxim. Aptitude tests may be given to the students to find out their readiness to learn.

Dimensions of Individual Differences in the Cognitive Domain: Various dimensions of the cognitive behaviour of the students are as under:

1. Thinking
2. Remembering
3. Analysing
4. Interpreting
5. Reasoning
6. Problem Solving

Identification of Cognitive Differences: Following are the important methods adopted for identifying cognitive differences of students:

1. Intelligence Tests
2. Aptitude Tests
3. Creativity Tests
4. Academic Achievement Tests

Effect of Education

1 Small classes may be organised.

2. Much responsibility may be given to the students for organising their programmes.

3. School marks should not be accepted as the sole evidence of successful student development.

4. Undue reliance should not be placed on tests and measurements.

5. Case histories of each child from kindergarten through higher secondary school must be made available to concerned persons and kept up-to-date.

6. A good system of accessible cumulative records must be developed.

7. Time table should be arranged in a way that the teachers may compile cumulative records and use them.

8. Opportunity to secure advice from specialists in diagnosis of difficulties should be provided.

9. Time for home visits or conferences with parents should be provided.

10. School personnel and parents should accept the statement that honest labour performed to the best of one's ability is worthy of commendation, whether the work be in the shops or offices, factories or farms.

11. Professional service to aid teachers in developing the attitudes, skills and techniques necessary for successful counselling should be provided.

12. Necessary material for testing and recording data needed to understand the individual child's needs, aptitudes and interests be provided.

Using Existing Cognitive Level as Base: Here several maxims of reaching like linking present knowledge with the past and future, direct to indirect or whole to parts may be adopted.

Use of Mnemonics (Aiding the Memory) for Strengthening Memory: For instance for remembering reading, writing, arithmetic, rights, responsibilities and relationships, the term 7 R's may be used. Likewise 4 H's for head, hand, health and heart may be used.

Meaning of Affective Domain of Learning: Affective domain as already mentioned includes interests, attitudes and values. In this domain also, there are wide differences among learners.

Personal Motives

Meaning of the Term Interest: The word interest owes its origin to the Latin word 'intersec' meaning making a difference or its matters. We may, therefore, say that whatever matters to us is of interest to us. Following are some of the definitions of interests:

Crow and Crow state, "Interest may refer to the motivating force that impels us to attend to a person, a thing or an activity."

"An interest is a disposition in its dynamic aspect" according to James Drever.

James M. Sawhrey and Charles W. Telford define interest as, "Favourable attitude towards an object."

McDougall is of the view, "Interest is latent attention and attention is interest in action."

Factors Affecting the Development of Interests: How Interests Emerge? According to "Encyclopedia of Educational Research by Harris, interests of the learners are influenced by the following factors:

(i) Socio-economic status of the family.

(ii) Aptitudes of the learners.

(iii) Personality patterns of the learners.

(iv) Individual differences in general.

The Interest

1. There is an intimate link between interests, wants, drives, motives and basic needs.
2. Interest is a great motivating force and it persuades us to take up various types of activities.
3. There is a close relationship between interest and attention.
4. Some interests are inborn and some are acquired.
5. Our interests dominate us and we interpret everything in the light of our interests.
6. Our interests lead to action and generally yield satisfying results.
7. Strong interests resist fatigue and avoid failure.
8. Interests are superior to our attitudes of mind. An attitude is simply a bent of mind but does not ensure action.
9. Our interests are always shifting.

Broad Types of Interests of Learners: Broad categories are:

(i) Academic interests

(ii) Interests in hobbies etc.

(iii) Play Interests

(iv) Vocational Interests

(v) Sex Interests.

Significant of Interests and Class-room Implications: School work becomes interesting to the student when he finds that it is related to him as an individual and it meets his needs to a considerable extent. He is interested when he realizes that learning is a means to his goals and that the learning experiments will make difference to him personally and when he appreciates that he has a great stake in the results.

Identification of Students Interests: A teacher should identify the interests of the students by using the following measures:

1. Observing their activities.
2. Noting the questions they ask.
3. Keeping in view the topics of their conversation.
4. Take into consideration the books they read.
5. Observing their spontaneous drawings.
6. Noting their wishes.
7. Studying their self-reports of what is of interest to them.
8. Administering interest tests to them.

In order to interest a child in a subject, a teacher must know a lot about the student and about the subject. He must understand the pupils' wants, problems, tendencies, goals and interests at their current stage of development. He should share responsibility with them. Participation of a teacher in a foot-ball game has a great value than being a mere spectator.

One of the ways of arousing interest in class-room activities is to make students participants rather than spectators or members of an audience. A variety of co-curricular activities should be organised so that students can choose activities in which they are interested.

Interest inventories may be used to find out the interests of the students and accordingly steps taken to develop these.

Failure to understand students' interests tends to reduce effectiveness of teaching. The kind of person a student would become is determined to a large extent by the interest developed during the childhood years.

Various Approaches

Meaning and Nature of an Attitude: Anastari has given the meaning of an attitude in these words, "An attitude is often defined as a tendency to react favourably or unfavourably toward a designed class of stimuli, such as a national or a racial group, a custom or an institution."

According to Frank Freeman, "An attitude is a dispositional readiness to respond to certain institutions, persons or objects in a consistent manner which has been learned and has become one's typical mode of response. An attitude has a well-defined object of reference. For example, one's views regarding class of food or drink (such as fish and liquors), sports, maths or democrats are attitudes."

Thurstone states, "Attitude denotes the sum total of a man's inclinations and feelings, prejudice or bias, pre-conceived notions, ideas, fears, threats as conceived about any specific topic. Thus a man's attitude about pacifism means here all that he feels and thinks about peace and war. It is admittedly a subjective and personal affair."

According to the definition given by G. W. Allport, "Attitude is a mental and neutral state of readiness, organised through experience, exerting a directive and dynamic influence upon an individual's response to the objects and situations with which it is related."

1. It is a point of view, or a frame of reference, substantiated or otherwise, true or false which one holds towards an idea, object or person.
2. It includes certain aspects of personality as interests, appreciations and social conduct.
3. An attitude is learnt.
4. An attitude is adopted.
5. An attitude has several aspects such as direction, intensity, generality or specificity.
6. The attitudes of a student are formed as a result of his experience and interaction with real situations.

Components of an Attitude: According to Harrison, an attitude has three components:

1. Beliefs
2. Emotions
3. Behaviour

Types of Attitudes

Positive Characteristics	*Negative Characteristics*
(i) Assisting others	(i) Prejudice
(ii) To be caring	(ii) Entering into arguments and
(iii) To be unselfish	conflicts
(iv) To be at peace with the world	(iii) Tension

Factors Leading to Individual Differences among Learners: These are:

1. Cultural background.
2. Home environment
3. Maturity level of the learners.
4. Neighbourhood environment.
5. Physical surroundings
6. Political environment
7. Religious environment
8. School environment
9. Social environment

Role of the Teacher in Developing Positive Attitudes: Following factors are very helpful in developing positive attitudes in the students

1. Personal example of positive attitude.
2. Friendly, sympathetic but attitude of firmness on the part of the teacher.

3. Understanding the background and needs of the students.

4. Appreciation of individual differences and accordingly adopting disciplinary measures.

5. Making teaching-learning affective.

Measurement of Attitude: The two most frequently used methods for the measurement of social attitude are: "The Methods of Equal Appearing Intervals" developed by Thurstone and "The Method of Summated Ratings" developed by Likert.

Standard of Learning

Meaning of Value: Educators and thinkers differ regarding the precise meaning of the term 'value'. Nevertheless, there is no doubt that values guide our behaviour and conduct, set goals and determine actions towards different events, objects and situations. They are the moving spirit in our lives. The following are some of the important definitions of a value.

A. K.C. Ottaway observes, "Values stand for ideas men live for."

D. H. Parker thinks, "Values belong wholly to the inner world of the mind. The satisfaction of desire is the real value, the thing that serves is only an instrument. A value is always an experience, never a thing or an object."

Kane says, "Values are the ideals, beliefs or norms which a society or the large majority of a society's members hold."

M.T. Ramji writes, "A value is what is desired or what is sought."

T. Parson points out, "Value is an element of a shared symbolic system which serves a criterion or standard for selection among the alternatives of orientation which are intrinsically open in a situation."

Classification of Values: Strictly speaking there are no hard and fast rules to classify values as they are closely interlinked and interrelated.

Values are individual as well as social. Individual values refer to the good of oneself and social values refer to the good of others.

Values may be classified into three categories: biological values, intrinsic values and instrumental values or as instrumental values and terminal values. Plato classified values into three categories-Truth, Goodness and Beauty.

Classification of Values

1.	Aesthetic	–	appreciation of beauty and joy
2.	Emotional	–	courage, endurance, friendliness, harmony and heroism
3.	Material	–	love of money, pleasures of life
4.	Mental	–	impartiality and perseverance
5.	Moral	–	benevolence, gratitude, honesty
6.	Physical	–	beauty, truth, grace, health and strength
7.	Social	–	civic sense, co-operation, courtesy, devotion to duty
8.	Spiritual	–	meditation, pursuit of ultimate reality.

The Values

1. Values can be developed.
2. Environment plays an important role in the development of values.
3. Values held by adults may not necessarily be handed down to the younger generation.
4. Educational experiences, undoubtedly promote certain values and cast others aside.
5. Quality of peer action plays an important role in value development.

Role of the Educational Institutions: Since students spend a good deal of their time in educational institutions, these play an important role in the development of their values.

Following factors should be carefully attended to :

Activity Programme for Developing Values: Following are the important activities to be undertaken by the school in this regard:

1. Community prayer in the school.
2. Cleanliness programme in the school.
3. Community service programmes.
4. Social service programmes in fairs and festivals.
5. First-aid programmes.
6. Celebration of national days and festivals.
7. Dramas, etc. depicting values.

Talks: Emphasis should be laid on the unity of all religions, harmony among communities and national integration.

Personal Examples: The most important aspect of the programme is that the teachers should set examples of good conduct and behaviour which the students may imbibe in themselves.

Concluding Observations: It may be observed that a special responsibility for creating a value-oriented environment lies on the V.I.P.'s, leaders of all shades and all those persons who matter in different walks of life. In fact, by and large, people tend to think that these are the persons responsible for the erosion of values. They must set the highest standards of ethical morality.

The Innovations

Meaning of Creativity: Following definitions point out the meaning, nature and various dimensions of creativity:

Zbigniew Pietrasinski defines creativity as "an activity resulting in new products of a definite social value"

According to Wilson, R.C., Guilford J.P. and Christensen P.R., "The creative process is any process by which something new is produced-an idea or an object including a new form of arrangements of óld elements. The new creations must contribute to the solution of some problem."

Components of Creativity

Ability	*Fluency*	*Flexibility*	*Originality*	*Elaboration*
It is the ability of the individual to see the problem.	It is the ability of the individual to give a number of Successful responses to a given stimulus.	It is the ability of the individual to use different approaches in responding to a stimulus.	It is the capacity of the individual to give original response to a stimulus.	It implies generating new ideas.

In the words of Torrence, creativity is a "process of becoming sensitive to problems, deficiencies, gaps of knowledge, missing elements, disharmonies and so on; identifying the difficulties, searching for solutions, testing and retesting hypotheses and possibly modifying and retesting them and finally communicating results."

According to Drevdhai, J. E., "Creativity is the capacity of a person to produce compositions, products or ideas which are essentially new or novel and previously unknown to the producer."

Different Methods

1. Creativity is a gift of God.
2. Creativity is based on intelligence.
3. Creativity is intuition.
4. Creativity is the process of novelty cell in the brain.
5. Creativity is the presence of 20-22 mental abilities.
6. Creativity lies in the personality of an individual .
7. Creativity is like madness.
8. Creativity is based on heredity.

Why special Stress on the Education of the Creative? Torrance says, "Society is downright savage toward creative thinkers especially when they are young." Suppression of the creativity of the child means learning disabilities, behaviour problems, drop-outs and mental conflicts and above all, a loss to mankind.

Identification of Creativity: We may use both test and non-test techniques for the identification of the gifted.

Guilford and Merrifield have developed test techniques that measure fluency, flexibility, originality, redefinition and sensitivity to problems.

Getzels and Jackson have used five different measures of creativity in their research.

(a) *Word-Association Test:* Students are required to give as many definitions and number of different categories into which they could be placed.

(b) *Uses of Objects Tests:* The student is asked to give as many uses as he can for a common object.

(c) *Hidden Shapes Tests:* A student is required to find more complex form of figure on card in a simple form.

(d) *Three Different Endings:* Here a student is required to suggest three different endings to incomplete short fables.

(e) *Make-up Problems:* A student is required to make-up as many mathematical problems he can on the basis of information given in a complex paragraph.

There are the Minnesota tests of creative thinking, comprising non-verbal tasks like picture construction, creative design, circles and squares etc.

Tornat's check list comprising eighty-four characteristics for identifying the creative children is also very helpful.

Characteristics of a Creative Child: A creative child is :

1. Adventurous.

2. Bold.

3. Complex
4. Dominant, self assertive.
5. Dreamer. But not a day-dreamer.
6. Emotionally sensitive.
7. Independent of judgment.
8. Introvert-Deals with things and not with people.
9. Non-conformist.
10. Psychologically healthy.
11. Resourceful, radical.
12. Risk-taker.
13. Self-accepting
14. Self-assertive
15. Self-controlled.
16. Self-sufficient.
17. Sensitive to environmental stimuli-which means sensitive to loopholes and gaps in the environment.

According to Getzel and Jackson, the characteristics of a creative child are four:

(a) Less popular with teachers.

(b) Independent of judgment.

(c) Unconventional.

(d) Humorous and playful.

A creative child is constantly probing, discovering, imagining, fantasying, asking questions, guessing and wondering.

Actual Problems

School is, in fact the proper place where an organised effort should be made to develop in children the basic foundations of creativity. Deliberate attempts need to be made to develop an environment of creativity.

The teacher can provide certain conditions which will increase the fluency, flexibility, originality and exploration of the students' thinking/ behaviour. The following are the important conditions which can foster students creativity.

1. Create a supportive environment.
2. Adopt a multidisciplinary approach to teaching.
3. Allow the students ask unusual questions.
4. Ask challenging and provocative questions.
5. Assign/suggest activities of an interdisciplinary nature.
6. Develop a spirit of inquiry and to speculate, cultivate a deliberate pace of thinking, etc.
7. Encourage debates, discussions, quizzes etc.
8. Encourage children to experiment, innovate, discover, hypothesise or imagine possible solutions to any pressing issue.
9. Depend upon creative discipline. Do not depend on excessive discipline. It reduce students' creative potential.

10. Love them and let them know it.

11. Provide activities like drama, dance, music etc.

12. Provide materials which develop imagination of the students.

13. Provide opportunities to students for self-initiated learning.

14. Pose open-ended, divergent questions with the focus on alternative responses and novelty, and not on right or wrong.

15. Show consideration to imaginative and unusual ideas of the students.

16. Enthuse pupils that their ideas have values.

17. Use teaching aids that stimulate imagination.

Meaning of Self-concept: Self-concept implies a person's perception or view of himself. Self-concept is what the individual thinks of his actual self. Some psychologists refer to as personal field, behavioural field, life, space, or psychological field. Self-concept plays an important role in the development of personality of an individual. The positive self-concept is likely to enable an individual to lead a happy, contended and well-managed life. His development is optimum. It is, therefore, important that children are trained to learn from the very beginning to develop a positive self-concept which is socially desirable. The idea of self starts growing from the period of infancy and grows during childhood, adolescence and maturity. As the child grows up, he starts feeling that he is separate from others. He slowly begins to learn that certain things belong to him. The part of the environment in which he lives is known as his phenomenal self and the rest of the environment of which he is aware or to which he responds is called phenomenal environment or perceived environment and not self. Following figure adapted from A. Ward Combs and D. Snygg's book, *Individual Behaviour: A Perception Approach to Behaviour* explains these concepts.

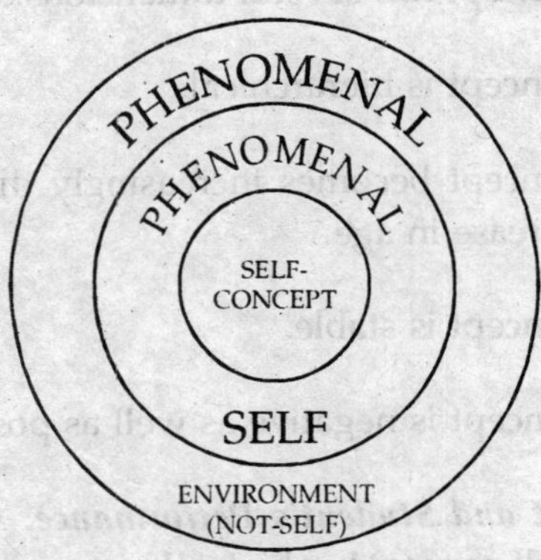

Diagramatic representation of the concept of self-concept

As the child starts advancing he starts feeling that he has a personality and an identity of his own which is different from others. He may be a part of the total environment but it is not his own. Hence there is a line of demarcation between phenomenal self and phenomenal environment as indicated in Figure. It indicates what the individual thinks about himself. Self-concept is the 'me' part of the individual.

The phenomenal self includes all the aspects of the environment with which the individual identifies himself, i.e., the family, the school etc.

Components of Self-concept: Components of self-concept are—beliefs, ideas or perception an individual has about oneself-one's physical, emotional, psychological and social achievements and characteristics.

Self-concept

1. Self-concept is organised. An individual organises a lot of information about himself.

2. Self-concept has several dimensions.

3. Self-concept is hierarchical.

4. Self-concept becomes increasingly differentiated with the increase in age.

5. Self-concept is stable.

6. Self-concept is negative as well as positive.

Self-concept and Student's Performance: A student with a positive or high self-concept has high self-esteem. High self-concept develops self-confidence and poor self-concept hinders initial school adjustment and academic progress also. Students with high concept tend to accept their failure as well as limitations. They are better achievers. They are more determined to achieve their goals. They do not suffer from inferiority complex. They are free from mental sickness and work vigorously and express their ideas and beliefs to others with confidence and conviction. They have the ability to impress others. They are rational in their approach.

Development of Self-concept: Self-concept is based on what children believe their teachers, peers and parents think of them. Positive self-concept is developed through love, encouragement, positive comments and understanding attitude of the teachers and parents. Teachers should adopt suitable strategies and provide opportunities to children to develop their self-concept.

QUESTIONS

1. Explain the meaning of individual differences of students. What is the significance of studying individual

differences? What factors are responsible for these differences?

2. Discuss students differences in terms of interests, attitudes and values. State their educational implications.

3. Discuss teaching strategies to meet individual differences of students in learning.

4. Why is it necessary for a teacher to understand individual differences? Describe the steps to meet the challenges posed by individual differences.

5. Explain the individual differences in cognitive domain. State their implications.

6. What types of individual differences exist in the affective domain? State their educational implications.

7. Give the meaning of readiness and its implications for class-room teacher.

8. What are values? How can these be developed in the students? State the role of the teachers.

9. Who is a creative child? Why should we lay stress on developing creativity? Suggest suitable methods.

10. Explain the term self-concept and its educational implications.

6

Physical Development

A knowledge of the growth and development patterns at each stage is essential for psychological, practical and scientific reasons. Proper acquaintance with the pattern of learner's growth and development would enable a teacher to know to a considerable extent at which age what behaviourable changes occur and when these patterns are usually replaced by more mature patterns. This is important as when too much is expected from the learners and they do not show such results, they develop a feeling of inadequacy. A knowledge of growth and development pattern enables the teachers to adjust the teaching-learning process according to the needs and interests of the learners. The teachers come to know when learners need special guidance. Deviation of the learners from the normal behaviour becomes a cause of anxiety to the teachers. When the pattern of development of behaviour is normal, one stage leads them effectively to the next.

Basic Issues

Following are the general principles of growth and development of individuals:

The Principle of Individual Differences: There are individual differences in the development of children. The difference is mostly in the intellectual capacity of all human beings. Differences in special aptitudes is most marked among children. This is caused by differences in heredity, endowments and environmental differences.

Principle of Continuous Growth and Development Process: The growth and development starts from the moment of conception of the individual in the mother's womb and continues till he reaches his grave. It is a continuous stream of development. Development proceeds by stages but it is a continuous process. Changes in the patterns of body and behaviour take place throughout life. Emergence of each type of behaviour is dependent on the development that has gone before.

Principles of Uneven Tempo of Growth and Development: Growth and development though continuous, yet its rate of development is in fits and starts and not uniform in all times. In the earlier stage it is quick, but slows down in later years of infancy. Again at the stage of puberty, there is a sudden rise in the growth and development.

Principle of Uniformity of Developmental Pattern: Although development has individual differences, yet it follows a definite sequence common to the offsprings of human beings. The outstanding example is that offsprings develop their head first and other parts of the body later on. It is also correct to say that language development in human offsprings has a definite sequence.

Principle of Development from General to Specific Responses: If we examine the different developmental aspects of the child we will find that general activity precedes specific activity in all his/her actions. The movements of the child are of a general nature in the beginning but later on they become specific.

Principle of Inter-relation: It has been observed that the growth and development in various aspects like physical, mental, social, etc. are inter-related and inter-dependent. Growth and development of the child in one aspect leads to the development in other aspects as well. It has been observed that children who are highly intelligent, generally have a robust health, whereas children with a lower intelligence have a weak health and regress in their emotional and social development.

Principle of Developmental Direction: There are two important principles of development: (a) Cephalo-cadal, and (b) Proximo-distal.

Cephalo-cadal: By cephalo-cadal development we mean that it has a longitudinal axis, i.e., that human development is from head to foot. This implies that control of the body as well as improvements in the structure itself, develops first in the head and progresses later to parts further from head. Another examples of this aspect of development is that a child can lift his head by his neck before he can do so by lifting his chest.

Proximo-distal: The proximo-distal tendency means that child develops from the centre of the body, i.e., the spinal chord to the periphery of the body i.e., fingers. In the beginning, the child is able to control his large fundamental muscles and smaller muscles later on. The outstanding example is that the control over fingers comes after control over the arm and the hand.

Principle of Integration: This principle implies that the development of the child is both from general to specific and specific to general. The child while busy in his specific activities arrives at a general rule. Again he tryout his general rule on certain specific activities. Thus, the development of the child integrates both general and specific activities.

Principle of Predictability of Development: We know that every child develops in his own way and develops nearly constantly. It is with this presumption that we can also predict his future range of development. This prediction is only possible in the case of children of average of normal development. We shall not be able to predict in the case of abnormal or highly intelligent children.

Principle of Spiral and not Linear Development: This principle implies that the development of the child is not in a straight line (linear) but is in the form of a cork-screw (spiral). He advances in his development in one period but takes rest in the following period. This enables him to consolidate his development.

The Principle of Struggle: While the child is developing up towards maturity there are conflicting impulses and demands. The child struggles against these in his striving for maturity.

The Principle of Indigenous Motivation: As the child matures in his capacities of doing, thinking and feeling, he has an impulse to put them to use and he does it wholeheartedly. This has been described by Jersild as 'Indigenous Motivation.'

The Principle of Anticipation: The child in his/her process of development also uses his capacity of self-repair. He modifies his behaviour and even habits keeping in view that what he is going 'to become' in future. Thus he consciously anticipates his future direction of development.

The Principle of Interaction of Heredity and Environment: The development of the child is a product of both. This is true at all times and stages of his development.

Involved Factors

A knowledge of principles of growth and development will enlighten the parents and teachers about the potentialities of their children. They should therefore, provide suitable opportunities for the maximum development of their children. For planning and implementing suitable programmes for the all-round development of children, following guidelines may be taken into consideration:

1. Principle of individual differences must always be kept in view.
2. Principle of motivation must be followed by the teachers.
3. Teachers and parents should not place undue demands on the children.
4. Impact of inter-relatedness of growth and development in various aspects must be considered.
5. Parents and teachers should take into account the role of the heredity and environment in development.
6. Principle of 'doing' helps in the development of mental, physical and social skills of the children.
7. Every child needs individual attention.
8. Efforts should be made to develop self confidence in the children that they are capable of achieving optimum development.
9. For proper development, all children need adequate praise and recognition.
10. Children's curiosity should be satisfied to their maximum satisfaction.
11. It should be borne in mind that reasonable amount of repetition is needed to develop skills.
12. Patience on the part of the parents and teachers should be the key note of their endeavour.
13. Each stage in the development of an individual has developmental tasks peculiar to it and these must be taken note of.

14. Observation of children leads, to better understanding on the part of parents and teachers.

15. For developing language appropriate words and phrases should be clearly spoken by parents and teachers.

16. Healthy environment promotes all round development.

17. Consistency, firmness, love and patience on the parts of parents and teachers will go a long way in the wholesome development of children.

18. Healthy human relations established in the earlier stages of life help to set the appropriate pattern of future development.

The Identity

The terms growth and developments are often used interchangeably but they are conceptually different. According to L. D. Crow and A. Crow (1962), growth refers to structural and physiological changes whereas development is concerned with growth as well as those changes in behaviour which result from environment. Usually growth contributes to development but not always.

In general growth refers to change in size and body-bones, muscles etc.

Maturity involves qualitative change.

Development involves a series of progressive, orderly and meaningful changes leading to the goals of maturity.

As the child grows, his mind and body mature and he is able to function at a higher level. Development is a product of maturation and learning.

We refer to the development of 'intelligence' and 'emotions' but growth of 'body and brain'.

The Comparison

Growth	*Development*
1. Growth is used in purely physical terms. It generally refers to an increase in size, length, height and weight of an individual. Changes in the quantitative aspects come into the domain of growth.	Development implies overall changes in shape, form or structure resulting in improved working or functioning. It indicates the changes in the quality or character rather than in quantitative aspects.
2. Growth is one of the aspects of developmental process.	Development is a wider and comprehensive term. It refers to overall changes in the individual. Growth is one of its aspects.
3. Growth describes the changes which takes place in parti-cular aspects of the body and behaviour of an organism.	Development describes the changes in the organism as a whole and does not list the changes in parts.
4. Growth does not continue throughout life. It stops when maturity has been attained.	Development is a continuous process. It goes from womb to tomb. It does not end with the attainment of maturity. The changes, however, small they may be, continue throughout the life span of an individual.
5. The changes produced by growth are the subject of measurement. They may be quantified. For instance, size can be measured in meters and weight in kilos.	Development, as said earlier, implies improvement in functioning and behaviour and hence brings qualitative changes which are difficult to be measured directly. They are assessed through keen observation in behavioural situations.

Contd.

Growth	*Development*
6. Growth may or may not bring development. A child may grow (in terms of weight) by becoming fat but his growth may not bring any functional improvement (qualitative change) or development.	Development is also possible without growth as we see in the cases of some children that they do not gain in terms of height, weight or size but they do experience functional improvement or development in physical, social, emotional or intellectual aspects.

A feeble minded child may have normal physical growth but may lack his mental development. However, as already stated, growth and development are often used interchangeably.

Stages of Growth and Development

Age Groups	*Stage of Development*	*Schooling Stage*
Birth to 2 years	Infancy	
2 years to 6 years	Early childhood	Pre-primary (Nursery/ Kindergarten etc.)
6 years to 14 years	Later childhood	Primary/Elementary
14 years to 18 years	Adolescence	Secondary and senior secondary
18 years to 40 years	Young adulthood	
40 years to 65 years	Mature adulthood	
over 65 years	Aged adulthood	

(Note : Scholars and thinkers differ as regards the age at various stages of development.)

Each stage of development is characterised by a set of somewhat coherent, distinguishing and unique features. Each stage in life has its own problems of adjustment.

The entire development is influenced by the important factors of (i) Heredity and (ii) Environment.

Significant Features

Strictly speaking there is no sharp line of demarcation between one stage of growth and development and another stage. Nevertheless, each stage has certain specific characteristics which must be kept in view while teaching or bringing up children.

Infancy (from Birth to 2 years)

Characteristics: The period is marked by rapid physical growth.

Importance: Modern researches have established that the period of infancy is the foundation on which the future development of the child depends.

Highlighting its importance Ruth Strang of Columbia University remarked "During the first two years of his life he lays the foundation for his future." Dr. F. Good enough, a prominent child psychologist is of the view, "One-half of an individual's mental structure has been attained by the age of three years."

The Impacts

1. The Montessori approach seems to be the ideal approach.
2. The environment in the family should be of affection and love. The child should have the feeling that everybody in the family loves him.
3. Freedom should be given to the child in his movements.

Early Childhood (from 2 Years to 6 Years)

Characteristics: This is the most important and impressionistic period of child's life. He learns his first lesson of citizenship in the home and the school. He develops the instinct of curiosity. He loves make-believe plays.

Time for Learning

This period of a child's life is of great educational significance. It has been correctly held by Watson that "the scope and intensity of learning during this period exceeds that of any other period of development." The following points should be kept in view both by parents and teachers while planning the education of the child at this stage.

1. Provision of Healthy Environment.
2. Rational Treatment.
3. Satisfaction of Curiosity.
4. Learning by Doing.
5. Dynamic Methods of Teaching.

Education may be imparted to children with the help of the Montessori Method which is based on sound psychological principles required for this stage.

This method provides opportunities for the child to develop his five senses as well. This sensory training is only possible at this stage.

Play-way spirit should permeate all learning activities.

Later Childhood (from 6 to 14 Years)

Characteristics: Bodily proportions change. Generally boys are considered superior in games requiring physical strength while girls are superior to boys on the use of fine muscles and in acquiring skills like drawing, painting, sewing etc. According to Watson, "A derivative of anger, annoyance becomes more prominent in later childhood. There is rapid intellectual advancement.

This stage is known as the formative age of the child. He develops his basic outlook, values and ideas. We as parents, teachers and social workers have an important role to play.

The school authorities have a special responsibility towards the development of the child.

1. Child's individuality should be respected.
2. It should be kept in mind that each child is unique.
3. Co-curricular activities should be organised.
4. Group competition may be arranged.
5. Games should be regularly organised.
6. Creative talent should be developed.

Adolescence (from 14 to 18 Years)

Chief Characteristics: (i) There is an outburst of various aspects of development, (ii) It is the period of opposite pattern, (iii) It is the period of preparation for living well in society, (iv) The period is marked by far-reaching sex changes.

Educational Implications: (i) Compulsory physical exercises and games, (ii) Monthly health check-up, (iii) Provision of good library, (iv) Organisation of clubs, (v) Guidance services, (vi) Rational approach by the teacher, (vii) Meeting fears of inadequacy, (viii) No discrimination, (ix) Exercises and educational tours.

Importance of Learning

A knowledge of development patterns at each stage is essential for psychological, practical and scientific reasons. Proper acquaintance with the pattern of human development would enable the teacher to know to a considerable extent at what age what behavioural changes occur and when these patters are usually replaced by more mature patterns. This is important as if too much is expected from students and they do not show such results, they develop a feeling of inadequacy. A knowledge of development pattern enables the teachers to adjust the teaching-learning process according to the needs and interests of the students. The teachers come to know when students need special guidance.

Deviation from normal behaviour becomes a cause of anxiety for the teachers as when the pattern of development is normal, one stage leads them effectively into the next.

Different Phases

Growth rate is rhythmic and regular. Growth rate comes in cycle of waves, "periods" or "phases" of growth. This growth rate is not haphazard and random. According to W.H. Krogman, "The child outgrows in obedience to certain biological laws."

According to studies, there are four distinct periods or phases or rates of growth. Two periods are characterised by slow growth and two by rapid growth.

Growth Rate at Different Stages in Different Parts and Organs of the Body: From birth to two years growth rate is rapid. This is followed by a period of slow growth upto the time of polarity or sexual maturity which usually takes place between the eighth and eleven years. From onward till fifteen or sixteen years, rate of growth is rapid and it is followed by a period of fairly abrupt tapering off the growth to the tune of maturity.

The 'body size' category which includes the skeleton, muscles and internal organs shows more rapid growth during the infancy-early childhood period and the adolescent period than during middle childhood.

The 'lymphatic system' (thymus, lymph nodes, and intestinal lymphoid mass) reaches an adult level by seven years of age and is even large during pre-adolescence before it declines.

Similarly, the 'neural system' (head, brain and spinal cord) is almost fully developed by the age of six. In contrast, the 'reproductive organs' grow very slowly until adolescence at which point they undergo rapid growth.

Rapid Growth

Development tasks are those behaviour patterns at various stages of the lives of individuals which a society expects from them. According to Neugarten, Moore and Lowe, behaviour tasks are expectations regarding age-appropriate behaviour which form an elaborated and pervasive system of norms governing behaviour and interaction in the society Age norms and age expectations operate as prods and brakes upon behaviour. R. J. Havighurst, in 'Human Development and Education' defines a developmental task in these words, "a task which arises at or about a certain period in the life of the individual, successful achievement of which leads to his happiness and to success with later tasks, while failure leads to unhappiness and difficulty with later tasks."

Developmental tasks arise from the following three sources:

1. Developmental tasks such as learning to walk (childhood task) arise mainly as a result of physical maturation.

2. Some developmental tasks develop primarily from the cultural pressures of society.

3. Some developmental tasks grow out of the personal values and aspirations of the individual such as choosing and preparing for a vocation.

Developmental tasks serve the following persons:

(i) Developmental tasks are guidelines which enable the adolescent to know what society expects of him.

(ii) Developmental tasks motivate the adolescent to do what the social group expects him to do.

(iii) Developmental tasks indicates the adolescent what lies ahead and what he will be expected to do when he reaches to next stage of development in his life span.

Developmental tasks during adolescence are as under:

1. Accepting one's role according to one's physique.
2. Gaining emotional and other types of independence from parents and other adults.
3. Establishing new relations with peers of both sexes.
4. Achieving assurance of economic independence.
5. Selecting and preparing for a vocation or profession.
6. Developing attitudes and skills necessary for civic competence.
7. Developing knowledge, attitudes and skills to participate in a democracy.
8. Desiring and achieving socially desirable behaviour.

9. Preparing for a happy married and family life.

10. Building rational and scientific values in harmony with global scenario.

The Difficulties

There are three main hazards or problems in normal development of developing tasks. These are:

(a) Inappropriate expectations of the adolescent himself or the social group to which he belongs.

(b) By passing the stage of development on account of failure to acquire the developmental tasks for that stage.

(c) Hazards arising out of the previous stages.

Role of Textbooks

***Meaning of Curriculum*:** Curriculum is the base on which the subjects, activities and experiences of the adolescents are planned. It is more than the textbooks, more than the subject matter or course of studies. It is totality of all the learning experiences to which the adolescent students are exposed during their stay in the school in the classroom, in the laboratory, in the library, in the workshop, on the farm and the playground. Syllabus is just a part of curriculum. Curriculum is primarily an aid in the developmental tasks. It is a tool, as stated by Cunningham, in the hands of the artist (the teacher), to mould his material (the adolescent) in accordance with the expectations and ideals of the society in his studio (the school).

***Implications for Curriculum Development*:** Following are the implications of the developmental tasks for curriculum development.

1. Curriculum should reflect the societal needs as well adolescent needs.
2. Curriculum should cater to individual differences of adolescents.
3. Curriculum should be diversified.
4. Curriculum should be rich in content.
5. Curriculum should be flexible.
6. Curriculum should provide for a variety of learning experiences related to the society and the adolescent.
7. Curriculum should provide for guidance and counselling.
8. Curriculum should provide for independent learning.
9. Curriculum should provide for project work.
10. Curriculum should include core values of the society.
11. Curriculum should arise out of the past as the present is born out of the past but should be modified according to present needs and should be designed for the future also as the future arises out of the present. In other words it must be functional.

Some of the important pedagogic practices for meeting the developmental tasks are given below:

1. Rich and varied curriculum.
2. Individualised as well as group methods of instruction.
3. Continuous evaluation of the developmental tasks of the adolescents.

4. Provision of co-curricular activities.
5. Introduction of vocational courses and socially useful productive work.
6. Provision for guidance and counselling.

Knowing the Facts

For facilitating the growth and development of the adolescent, it is necessary to understand him properly. This is the most critical period of a student's development with which the teacher has to deal. It is a period of day-dreams, of adventures, of intense affections and stirring of the 'heart'. Some educationists think this period to be a period of great 'stress and strain,' 'storm' and 'strife'.

According to Rabindranath Tagore, "In the world of human affairs there is no worse nuisance than a boy at the age of fourteen. He is neither ornamental nor useful. It is impossible to shower affection on him as a little boy; and he is always getting in the way."

According to William H. Burton, "The adolescent is an odd, awkward, graceful, respectful, selfish, altruistic, idealistic, narrow-minded, sympathetic, cruel individual".

E.A. Peel (1956) is of the view, "the adolescent is beset by problems of divided loyalties, accentuated by the lack of adult privileges and responsibilities. He thus appears excessively aggressive and then excessively shy, excessively affectionate and then quite suddenly detached and cool. These are all problems of the stresses and strains of transition."

Required Things

1. A balance between security and freedom is needed.

2. Adolescents need noble causes in the promulgation of which they may utilize their excess emotion and energy.
3. Separate physical education programmes for adolescent boys and girls need to be planned.
4. Social mixing is considered important at this level.
5. Different types of co-curricular activities are needed for providing new experiences and utilising energy.
6. Sex education on a scientific basis is needed.
7. Unobtrusive adult guidance is needed.

Typical Problems

These may be listed as under:

1. Lack of interest in school work.
2. Lack of proper facilities.
3. Adjustment to emotional problems.
4. Lack of adequate sex guidance.
5. Adjustment with school discipline.
6. Vocational adjustment.

Importance of Schooling

Innumerable opportunities can be provided by the schools to adolescents for making necessary adjustments.

Due Regard to Individual Differences: Adolescents differ as much mentally and emotionally as physically. But we provide little individual attention in schools. Some of them are backward in studies, while some of them are very superior. But they are dragged on the same lines. The backward lag behind still more and this results in emotional disturbance. We must do something to help such unfortunate ones.

Rich and Varied Curriculum: The curriculum in schools often does not relate to the real life of adolescents. Learning in schools is unrelated to their modern needs. It is not according to the requirements of society and that of the students and hence emotional disturbance is created among the students.

Responsibility for Vocational Education: Apprenticeship system provided vocational education in ancient and medieval times. In ancient India vocation was on family basis, the son learnt the vocation by working with the father. It has, therefore, become necessary now for the schools to impart vocational education to students. Moreover far reaching changes have taken place in the economic, commercial, industrial and other areas which need vocational pursuits.

Dynamic Methods of Teaching: Faulty methods of teaching do not develop motivation in the adolescents. Therefore lessons become a drudgery. The adolescents begin to hate the very process of education. There is always tension in their minds. Learning is no more a joyful activity for them.

Improvement the methods of teaching can go a long way in providing emotional security to adolescents. Instructional work can easily be turned into play and then it will be interesting, joyful and at the same time more instructive.

Freedom for Self-development: For the development of a creative mind, freedom for self-development and freedom for activity must be given in a school. "This freedom will not be the licence it is sometimes supposed to be. It will be the controlled freedom of an individual living in a community of which he is one part, and his fellow pupils and teachers are other parts. It will be a freedom from an exaggerated force or undue influence on the part of a teacher; a freedom for the particular pupil to use his particular talents and capabilities and to develop his personality along his own line, under the guidance of the teacher," writes Ryburn.

Creative and Democratic Concept of Discipline: Traditional methods of discipline are faulty. Sometimes schools are considered just like jails and some teachers like jailors. Such discipline is negative. It may serve the purpose superficially but in reality the things are far from being satisfactory.

There should be positive devices of discipline. Discipline should be creative. Children should be made responsible for handling their own affairs as far as it is feasible.

Provision, of Co-curricular Activities: All the children and especially adolescents need provision for the expression of their pent-up emotions and for redirection of their emotional behaviour. In the absence of such provision, emotional stability is not possible. Varied co-curricular activities can solve this problem quite satisfactorily.

Provision of Sex Education: Teachers should provide necessary information about the sex matters and problems. During adolescent period lack of information about sex causes emotional disturbance.

Continuous Evaluation: The present system of examination is faulty. Chance factor counts much in this system. It does not measure the all-round development of the adolescent and causes disturbance. Evaluation should be made continuous and objective.

Satisfaction of the Urge for Practical Activity: Dr. Zakir Husain observes, "The future Indian school will not perpetuate the stupid tyranny of requiring its boys and girls, bursting with active energy, to sit silent and sombre, brooding over books and swallow irrelevant, unwanted, unassimilated information getting passively educated by others. The prevalence of a certain peculiarity, namely, urge for practical activity, makes this stage comparatively easy for the organizer of education and a fairly uniform type of school based on hand work can serve the needs of the vast majority of children."

Healthy Physical Conditions in the Schools: Poor physical conditions in the school bring fatigue and boredom to the adolescents. They are very soon fed up with the school and its activities. Lack of recreational activities is also responsible for emotional disturbance. The school authorities should be careful in this respect also.

Role of the Teacher in the Developmental Tasks of the Adolescent: The role of the teacher in this respect is very important. It is a great factor in the wholesome emotional development of the adolescent. He should control his own emotional expression and manifestations in the presence of adolescents, otherwise he would prove himself contagious.

Following are the important ways at the disposal of the teacher for the development of adolescents in the school.

Equal Treatment: The school is responsible for the education of the poor students as well as the rich ones. Resources of poor students should be studied individually and effort should be made to meet their monetary needs in connection with their education. Simple living should be a guiding principle in all the educational institutions.

Providing Emotional Security: Some teachers themselves need emotional stability. Such emotionally unbalanced teachers prove contagious for the adolescents. They are themselves a prey to inferiority-complex, persistent worries or over-excited emotions. They are generally irritable and provocative. For the balanced emotional development of adolescents, teachers themselves should be emotionally developed. "Example is better then precept" is a famous saying which aptly applies to the teacher.

Role of Love in Schools: In most of the schools, teaching is based on fear. Children know that they will be caned if they are not successful in studies. They get heavy home task which is often impossible to complete without help and guidance which is not available at home. They sleep at night with the dreams of canes. They wake up in the morning with fear and constant worry. Under such circumstances emotional tranquility is not possible.

There is famous saying 'Love the child and the child will love you. Hate the child and he will hate you.' Love should be the basis of all work.

QUESTIONS

1. Distinguish between growth and development. Why is it necessary for a teacher to understand the process of growth and development?
2. What is development? State the principles of growth and development. What is their implications for the teacher?
3. Describe the stages of growth and development along-with their educational implications.
4. What is growth rate? Explain the meaning of growth curve and its characteristics with the help of drawing a growth curve.
5. Explain the meaning of developmental tasks. Mention these tasks during the adolescence period. Suggest their curriculum implications.

6. What type of pedagogic practices, class organisation and school organisation would you suggest for meeting the developmental tasks of the adolescents?

7. "Adolescence is a period of conflicts and dilemmas". Discuss the implications of the above statement. Also analyze the role of school in providing a suitable environment for development of positive sense of identity in adolescents.

8. "Physical development in adolescence has psychological implications". Discuss these implications highlighting the role of guidance programme in schools related to the area mentioned above.

7

Making Children Learn

The Meaning

Learning is a term used for a relatively permanent change in behaviour or response as a result of practice, training for experience. As a result of learning some change takes place in the individual; now he can do what he could not do earlier. The outcomes of learning from learning activities may be attitudes, skills, social competence and abstract and creating thinking. Learning is an enrichment of experience.

Schools are set up for making children and thus learning occupies the central place in the school programme.

Following definitions of learning would help us to have a comprehensive view of learning :

1. For Boaz, "Learning is a process by which the individual acquires various habits, knowledge and attitudes that are necessary to meet the demand of life in general."

2. Commins and Fagin define learning in these words, "Learning as a sequence of mental events or conditions leading to changes in the learner?"

3. In the words of Crow and Crow, "Learning involves the acquisition of habits, knowledge and attitudes."

4. Encyclopaedia of Educational Research records, "Learning refers to the growth of interests, knowledge and skills and to transfer of these to new situations."

5. Gates defines learning in these words, "Learning is the modification of behaviour through experience and training."

6. In the views of Gooch, "Learning as we measure it is more or less a permanent change in behaviour which occurs under the motivational conditions of practice."

7. In the words of Hilgard, "Learning is the process by which an activity originates or is changed through reacting to an encountered situation, provided that the characteristics of the change in activity cannot be explained on the basis of native tendencies, maturation or temporary states of organism."

8. According to Hunder and Hilgard, "Learning is the process by which behaviour (in the broader sense) is originated or changed through training procedures (whether in the natural environment or in the laboratory)."

9. According to Munn, "To learn is to modify behaviour and experience."

10. Peal, E. A. states, "Learning is a change in the individual following upon changes in the environment.

11. Skinner views are "Learning as acquisition and retention."

12. Travers I. F. writes, "Learning is a process that results in the modification of behaviour."

13. According to Wordsworth, R. S., "Any activity can be called learning so far as it develops the individual (in any respect, good or bad) and makes his behaviour and experience different from what that would otherwise have been."

Main Features

1. Learning is acquiring new behaviour.
2. Learning is adjustment in behaviour.
3. Learning is change in behaviour.
4. Learning is doing.
5. Learning is a life-long process.
6. Learning is pre-planned.
7. Learning is purposeful.
8. Learning and maturation have positive connection.
9. Learning is related to environment.
10. Learning and intelligence are correlated.
11. Learning exposes 'new vistas' of knowledge.
12. Learning is universal i.e., both human beings and animals learn. Of course, human beings have a rational

will of their own. They are, thus in a position to get the maximum from the environment.

13. Learning is organising experience.

14. Learning affects the behaviour of the learner.

15. Learning is both individual and social.

16. Learning is affected by physiological, psychological and environmental factors.

17. Learning involves psychological, motor and affective activities.

Goals in Learning: Following are the broad categories:

1. Acquisition of knowledge. This includes (a) Perception, (b) Conception, and (c) Association learning.

2. Acquisition of skills.

3. Acquisition of attitudes, ideals and values.

The Procedure

Learning process in general includes the following:

(i) Acquisition of new experiences.

(ii) Retention of old experiences in the form of impressions.

(iii) Development and modification of experience.

(iv) Growth and increase in these experiences.

(v) Creation of new experiences.

(vi) Synthesis and organisation of the old and the new experiences, resulting in a novel pattern called learning.

Fagin (1958) states that learning is a sequence of mental events or conditions leading to changes in the learner. As a sequence of events, the learning process is as under:

(1) The individual has needs and is therefore in a state of readiness to respond. These are antecedent conditions within the learner. (2) He meets a learning situation or problem. A new interpretation is required because previously learned responses are not adequate for reaching the goal and satisfying his need. He encounters something new or unexpected, and searches for a different response. (3) He interprets the situation with reference to his goals, and tries a response or responses which seem to satisfy his need. The way he perceives the situation and the response he makes depends both on his 'readiness' and on external conditions of the situation. (4) If his response leads to devised goals or satisfaction, he will tend to interpret and respond to similar future situations in the same way. If not, he keeps on trying and reinterpreting until satisfying consequences are attained. The learning process is this whole sequence.

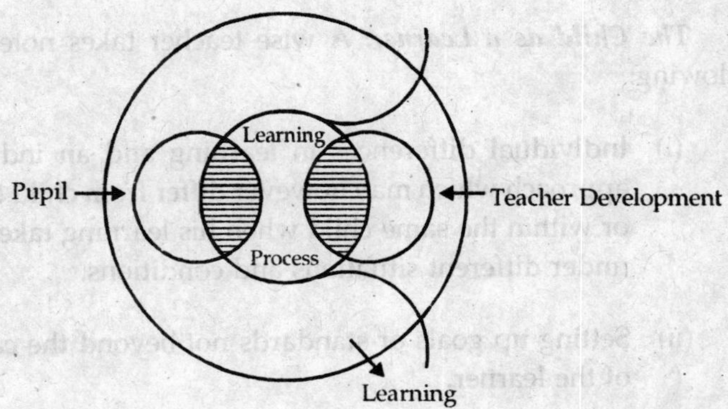

Learning Process

Learning cannot be visualised without teaching. They are inter-related. One cannot exist without the other. To have a proper perspective of the learning process, we must consider it in the teaching-learning situation: teacher, student, learning and the interaction. The teacher creates the learning situation. The process is the interaction between student and teacher. Teaching and learning relationship or interaction may be explained with the help of a diagram.

The Teacher: The teacher has to be an 'inducer of change'.

The Environment: The teacher at the very outset must set the stage or environment for effective study of the pupils.

(i) A definite place of study.

(ii) Favourable physical conditions for learning such as proper light, adequate space and ventilation, etc.

(iii) A definite time schedule for study-what to study, when to study and how to study.

(iv) A clear idea of the purpose of study.

The Child as a Learner: A wise teacher takes note of the following:

(i) Individual differences in learning and an individual approach which may however differ from child to child or within the same child when his learning takes place under different situations and conditions.

(ii) Setting up goals or standards not beyond the capacity of the learner.

(iii) Keeping in view that the previous experience of the learner is fundamental in the process of learning.

(iv) Awareness of the fact that knowledge of one's own performance, mistakes and information of successful result helps in learning.

(v) Knowing that the active participation by the learner is essential in learning.

(vi) Realising that motivation is a powerful influence in determining effective learning.

(vii) Realising that a motivated learner can acquire knowledge and understanding more quickly than one who is not motivated.

(viii) Keeping in view that excessive motivation may sometimes be less effective in some kinds of learning. In some instances it may result in 'pushing' the child too much disregarding his abilities.

(ix) Knowing that learning depends on the mental set or the mood of the learner. The teacher has to find out whether the learner is ready for the task or not. If not, what are the ways and means to make him ready for the purpose.

(x) Believing that emotion of the learner is a powerful factor in learning and the teacher must learn how to use this to his greatest advantage. In this respect the good interpersonal relationships in the class-room as well as in the school should not be neglected by the teachers.

(xi) Having faith that good study habits of the individual also promote learning.

Subject Matter and Its Presentation: In the course of formal and informal teaching, a resourceful teacher plans and directs pupil experiences which lead to effective learning. The study of the learning process enables the teacher to make the following deductions, with the help of which he tries to affect purposeful learning in pupils:

1. by following certain well-tried principles and maxims of teaching to guide the pupil's learning activities;

2. by considering the maturity and the capacity of the learner;
3. by employing fruitful motivational devices;
4. by directing and modifying perception of the learner;
5. by using practice most effectively;
6. by removing emotional disturbances; and
7. by directing teaching towards transfer.

Factors at Work

The teacher would make learning effective, if he attends to the following elements carefully.

1. Who is to leant or whom to teach? The child is to learn and therefore his interests, abilities and aptitudes have to be taken note of. It must be remembered' that he is an active being. Individual differences have to be attended to.

2. Who is to teach or from whom to learn? The teacher is to teach. He should, therefore, present a good model of teaching.

3. Why to teach or why to learn? Education should not be taken in terms of traditional 3 R's i.e. reading, writing and arithmetic, but in terms of 7 R's i.e., reading, writing, arithmetic, recreation, rights, responsibilities and relationships.

4. What to teach or what to learn? This includes the acquisition of the knowledge, skills and behaviour.

5. How to teach? The teacher must be well versed with the technology of teaching.

6. How to learn? The teacher and the learner must fully understand that learning takes place through mutual co-operation. A learner learns maximum when he is motivated. The teacher, therefore has to provide motivational situations so that the learner is at his best. He has to be fully conversant with learning theories and teaching strategies.

7. When to teach or when to learn? This is concerned with creating motivational situations for the learner.

8. Where to teach or where to learn? The school should not be taken the only place of imparting or receiving education. It is one of the agencies of education; of course the most important one.

Chart Showing Broad Kinds of Learning

1	2	3	4	5
Prime or Conscious Learning	Concomitant or Unconscious Learning	Developmental Learning	General Learning	Hierarchical Learning

It is very difficult to classify learning into clear-cut categories because one category overlaps the other.

Prime and Concomitant Learning: As a matter of fact there are only two broad categories of learning i.e., Prime learning and concomitant learning.

Prime learning is deliberate, formal as well as non formal, purposeful and systematised. It includes all types of learning except concomitant learning. All aspects of the entire instructional programme i.e., curriculum, textbooks, methods of teaching and evaluation etc. are related to prime learning. Most of the changes in behaviour take place through prime learning.

Concomitant learning is that learning which comes in a casual manner without any direct intention to learn but on some occasions it becomes very powerful. Concomitant learning in a broad sense takes place under indirect influence of the home, the school and the society. Students learn so many things in the school in a casual manner. It is sometimes called incidental learning. We are reminded of the learning of King Roburt Brace from the efforts of a spider. After making several unsuccessful attempts, ultimately it achieved its objective. The King, who had been unsuccessful in defeating his enemies, picked up courage like the spider again and succeeded. It was not deliberate learning.

It is said that a student gets one-fourth of his learning from his teacher (Prime learning), another from his intellect (prime learning), another fourth from his fellow students (prime learning) and the rest (major part of this learning is concomitant) through his general experience in various situations.

Basic Issues

1. Different types of learning experiences should be provided to satisfy the needs of each and every learner as notable 'differences' exist between individuals.

2. Learning experiences should be provided for natural integration of feeling, doing and thinking as the learner is a living 'organism', a unitary integrated whole.

3. Rich learning experiences should be provided to meet the needs of the learner as he always seeks to maintain equilibrium or balance by satisfying his needs.

4. The setting of learning should be purposive or goal-oriented as the learner is a goal seeking organism to satisfy his needs.

5. The learning situations should provide freedom to make creative contribution as the learner is an active, behaving and exploring individual.

6. While providing learning experiences for the learner, family background and individuality of the learner should be taken into account as the learner is a social being and needs social environment.

7. The learner needs sympathy and guidance for his personality development as he is quite immature.

8. Learning activities should be based on co-operative group work so as to develop the socialised personality of the learner.

9. Bright students can learn things quickly than the dull ones.

10. A motivated pupil learns more readily than one who is not motivated.

11. Learning through reward or success motivation is more effective than punishment or failure.

12. Learning goals should be neither too high nor too low.

13. The personality of a teacher is a great contributory factor in teaching-learning.

14. Active participation of the learner is more effective than passive reception.

15. Meaningful materials and meaningful tasks are learned more quickly.

16. Moderate practice and repetition is very useful for durable learning.

17. Effective audio-visual aids contribute to make learning effective and inspirational.

18. Transfer of learning will be better if learner himself discovers relationship between new and old tasks.

19. Optimal learning takes place when appropriate teaching strategies are adopted.

School's Atmosphere

Learning is influenced by various conditions of life at home and school. As for home conditions are considered i.e., heredity and other influences of the home, very little can be done in the school to modify these. However, schools can ensure that students are given adequate opportunities to develop their hereditary endowment.

The schools should take the following steps to promote learning in the learners to their optimum levels.

Healthful Physical Conditions in the School: Unsuitable furniture in the class-room (i.e., students' desks and chairs and blackboards etc.), bad ventilation, over crowding etc. affect the rate of learning and the general response of the learners.

Teachers' health, voice and speech etc. also affect learning.

Therefore, all possible attempts should be made to provide healthy physical environment.

Stimulation and the Role of the Teacher: Best learning takes place when the teacher is successful in arousing the interest of the student. "The guidance of the teacher is mainly a matter of giving the right kind of stimulus to help him to learn the right things in the right way," writes Ryburn.

Factors Influencing Learning

Health of the child	*Personal Factors*	*Environmental Factors*	*Relationships*	*Media Influence*	*Methods of Learning*	*Methods of Teaching*	*Maxims of Teaching*
1. Physical development	1. Sensation and perception	1. Natural surroundings	1. Teachers	1. Print Media	1. Whole vs. Part Learning	1. Lecturing	1. From known to unknown
2. Postures	2. Fatigue and Boredom	2. Social surroundings	2. Parents	2. Non-print Media	2. Mediating Method	2. Demonstration	2. Easy to difficult
3. General health	3. Maturation	3. Cultural surroundings	3. Peers		3. Space vs. Unspaced Method	3. Individual Practical Work	3. Simple to complex
	4. Emotional condition	4. Home environment			4. Recitals	4. Individual in workshop	4. Concrete to abstract
	5. Needs	5. Class-room environment			5. Memory Systems	5. Field Trips	5. Indefinite to definite
	6. Intelligence	6. School environment			6. Laws of Association	6. Projects	6. Particular to general
	7. Motivation	7. Political environment				7. Discussion	7. Empirical to rational
	8. Attention					8. Conference Seminar etc.	8. Deductive-inductive
	9. Aptitude					9. Assignments	9. Psychological to logical
	10. Attitude					10. Tutorial (Individual)	
						11. Programmed Instruction	
						12. Teaching Machines	
						13. Electronic Media	
						14. Audio visual Aids	

Goals Set Before the Pupils: A definite goal should be set before each child according to the standard expected of him. Immediate goals should be set before small children and distant goals for older ones. It must be remembered that the goals should be very clear and the children must understand these goals.

Complacency in the pupil should be avoided and in no case the pupil should feel that there is nothing more which he should learn and that there is no scope for improvement. R. Strang writes, "A little learning is a dangerous thing insofar as it may make a child content with what he has accomplished. The child's felt need for a skill is decreased once he has obtained enough proficiency to accomplish his immediate purpose. It is important, therefore, that as soon as the child begins to acquire skills, he should set for himself suitable specific standards of accuracy and precision.

Association of Things: Thorndike points out that things which we want to go together should be put together. Many different things should be brought together as a part of one process. Then it becomes easier to make the students understand their connection. We have discussed at various places that things can be associated in a number of ways.

Guidance and Instruction: Suitable guidance should be given to the students in selecting the best response to the environment. Demonstration is very helpful to teach various skills.

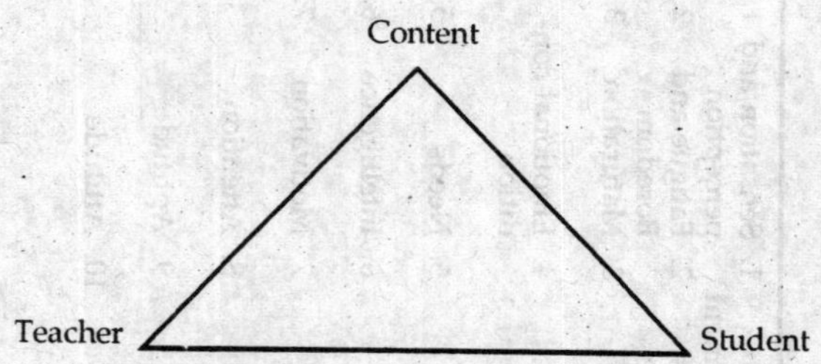

Conditions related to Content, Teacher and Student

Emotional Conditions: Children should be praised when they show good results. This gives them encouragement to show all the more better results and they develop confidence, hope, self-reliance and self-respect. Sympathetic attitude on the part of the teachers gives stimulus and a sense of security to the students. We should discard our habits of fault-finding. This develops fear and feelings of insecurity and of inferiority.

Result of a Total Situation: Learning is affected by the whole situation. It is not always possible to estimate the result of one individual factor. Learning is fruitful and permanent if the total situation is related to life.

In fact total situation includes all the factors that we have enumerated above. Learning is influenced both by heredity and environment. There is a lot that can be done by the teachers to facilitate learning.

Summary: Internal class-room factors which affect learning and improvement are (1) Goals or Purposes (2) Motivation (3) Interest (4) Attention (5) Drill or Practice (6) Boredom or Fatigue (7) Aptitude (8) Attitude (9) Emotional factors- Instincts (10) Speed, Accuracy and Retention (11) Age (12) Learning activities provided by the teacher (13) Testing (14) Guidance.

Encouraging Factors

Meaning of Motivation: The word motivation has been derived from the Latin word 'motum' which means to move, motor and motion. Motivation is an internal force which accelerates a response or behaviour. Some learners learn the same subject matter or task more efficiently than others, some find it more rewarding and interesting than others; and some enjoy it more than others. At any given time learners vary in the extent to which they are willing to direct their energies to the attainment of goals, due to difference in motivation.

Intrinsic Motivation: It comes into display when the resolution of tension is to be found in mastering the learning task itself. The material learned provides its own reward. For example, the student who studies the construction of model dams diligently so that he can make a model, is experiencing a kind of intrinsic motivation.

Extrinsic Motivation: It occurs when a student pursues a learning task for reasons which are external. When a student engages himself in the construction of model dams because he thinks it will please his father, who is an ex-engineer, this becomes a case of intrinsic motivation. Motivation is probably a function of an interactive situation where reward to a particular action acts as an incentive. Some of the common forms of extrinsic motivation are:

(a) Purposive goals

(b) Knowledge of results

(c) Punishments and rewards

(d) Praise and blame

(e) Rivalry.

Ways of Children: The teaching-learning process aims at maximum learning in a minimum period of time. It is, therefore, necessary that children should be properly motivated and the teacher should be conversant with important ways of motivating children. Important techniques of motivating children are:

1. Using learners-centred approach in teaching-learning process.

2. Linking new knowledge with previous knowledge.

3. Using activity methods of learning.

4. Employing group methods of learning.
5. Providing stimulating physical and psychological environment in the class-room.
6. Making appropriate use of praise and blame.
7. Making right use of rewards and punishments.
8. Developing an attitude and experience of success-students should feel that they are progressing in learning.
9. Creating an environment of mutual interest and cooperation i.e., involvement of learners in the learning process.
10. Maintaining an emotionally balanced mental state- by the teacher himself.

Generation Factor

Meaning of Heredity: By the heredity of an individual we mean all those inborn physical and mental traits that he inherits from his parents and ancestors. Every child comes into this world with certain physical and mental features which he got from his parents. He is born with a body and mind which developed from the fertilized ovum he got from his mother and father. His limbs and organs grow from the same. His mental tendencies are also based on the same.

According to Woodsworth "Heredity covers all the factors that are present in the individual when he began life not at birth, but at the time of conception about nine months before birth."

Meaning of Environment: By environment we mean all those physical and mental factors that affect and influence the development of the child. The home, the family, the neighbourhood, the companions, the school, the teachers, the political and religion agencies, the society in general, the temperament and other mental traits of parents and other elders, the economic, social and cultural status of the parents-all influence the development of the individual. No individual is the same at maturity as he was born. The environment changed him. Everything that influences the child apart from himself from what he inherited from his parents is his environment.

E.G. Boring, H.S. Longeld and H.P. state "The environment is everything that affects the individual except his genes."

In the words of R.S. Woodsworth and D.G. Marques, "Environment covers all the outside factors that have acted on the individual since he began life."

Psychologists View: Many psychologists are of the view that "the inborn nature is the chief factor in development and it solely determines the possibilities to which the child can be educated." They do not find any weight in the influence of environment. They give all importance to nature which determines the development of the young ones.

Another school of thought believes otherwise. It gives all credit to nurture. The adherents of this school think that a child may be developed to any level according to the breeding. They claim to make Gandhis and Jawahars of any babies given into their charge from birth provided the children live in the selected environment for a long time.

Isolated examples in support of both the views are cited. The problem is very important for education. If heredity is everything, then there is no sense in providing schools with adequate equipment and healthy psychological and physical environment. In the words of Wordsworth, "Shall the gardener pin his hope on careful cultivation of the soil or the selection of the best seed?" Answer is very clear. Emphatically both determine the quality of harvest.

The much-mentioned slogan 'heredity versus environment' is misconception. We should talk of 'heredity in the environment.' Both heredity and environment are essential for development. Hence any trait of the individual is the 'product' of heredity and environment. The individual does not equal heredity + environment but does equal heredity x environment i.e., O (organism or individual) = H (Heredity) x E (Environment). Heredity sets the probable biological limit, whereas environment determines the level up to which the development is possible. Every development is due to an interaction of heredity and environment.

Personality may be compared to a rectangle. Heredity makes the base while environment the altitude. A rectangle cannot exit without either of the two.

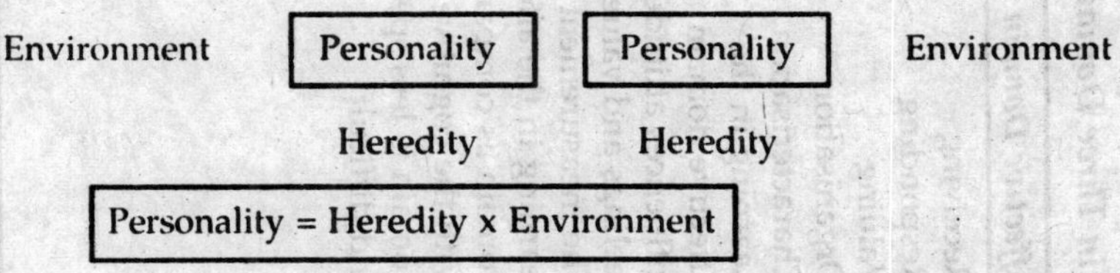

Sometimes heredity plays a major role in the development of personality and sometimes environment. However, both play their roles. In case both, the base i.e. the heredity and the altitude, the environment are inferior, we shall have Jukes and Kalikaks as offsprings.

Scope and Sphere

There are three major domains of learning as given below:

Domain	*Nature of the Domain*
1. Cognitive Domain	It is related to knowing or intellectual abilities.
2. Affective Domain	It is concerned with emotions, feelings and values.
3. Psychomotor Domain	It relates to learning of skills.

Main Three Domains

Knowledge Domain	*Affective Domain*	*Psychomotor Domain*
1. Knowledge 2. Comprehension It relates to student's ability of giving: (a) Meaning of a concept, definition or principle (b) Interpretation i.e., seeing inter-relations (c) Extrapolation i.e., drawing conclusions 3. Application 4. Analysis 5. Synthesis 6. Evaluation The highest form of learning is problem solving. The measurement in the cognitive domain as compared with the affective domain is easy and specific.	(a) Receiving (b) Responding (c) Valuing (d) Organisation (e) Characterisation (1) Learning in the affective domain influences attitudes/ feelings and values (2) The measurement of learning in the affective domain as compared with the cognitive domain is less specific and difficult	(i) Gross body movements (ii) Co-ordinated movements (iii) Non-verbal communication (iv) Speech behaviour or (1) Initiation (2) Manipulation (3) Precision (4) Articulation (5) Naturalisation (mechanisation and inter nalisation), Articul ation implies co-ordi nation of action performed with efficiency in terms of time, speed and case. Naturalisation implies performance in skill with natural case and almost without conscious effort so that it is like a habit.

Aims of Teaching

Cognitive Domain in Economics: To acquire the knowledge (information) of facts, terms, concepts, conventions and trends, principles and generalizations, assumptions, hypotheses, problems, process, etc., in Economics.

Behavioural Outcomes: To demonstrate the achievement of the above objective, the pupil:

(a) recalls facts, terms, concepts, principles, trends etc.

(b) recognises facts, terms, concepts principles, trends etc.

(c) reads information from various forms of representation of data, i.e., maps, charts, diagrams, graph, etc.

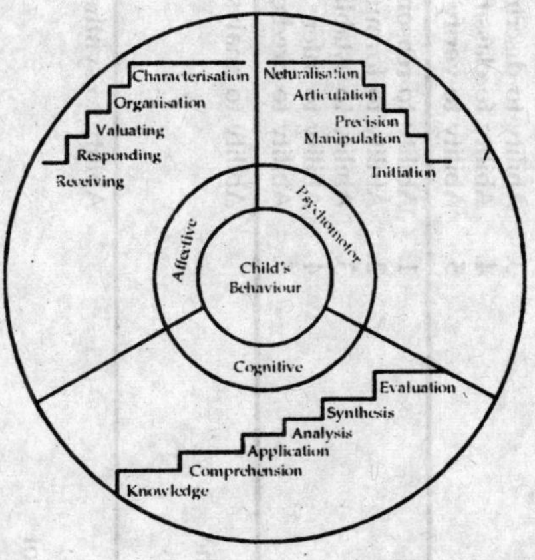

Domains of Learning

Affective Domain in Economics: To develop desirable positive attitudes necessary for developing a broader outlook.

Behavioural Outcomes: To demonstrate the achievement of the above objective, the pupil:

Cognitive Domain and Educational Implications

	Objectives	*Mental Process or Abilities*	*Level (Lowest level to highest level)*
1.	Knowledge-imparting information	1. Ability to recall 2. Ability to recognise	
2.	Comprehension-making content clear	1. Ability to see relationship 2. Ability to cite examples 3. Ability to discriminate 4. Ability to classify 5. Ability to verify	
3.	Application-enabling the learners understand the use of theoretical statements in practical situations.	1. Ability to reason 2. Ability to formulate 3. Ability to establish 4. Ability to infer 5. Ability to predict	
4.	Analysis—enabling the students to breakdown the matter into its constituent parts for comparison etc.	Ability to analyse	
5.	Synthesis-enabling the learners to combine elements in components of learned material to form new structured wholes.	Ability to synthesise	
6.	Evaluation-enabling the learners to make judgements (quantitative and qualitative) about the extent to which material satisfies criteria.	Ability to evaluate	

(a) respects the views, opinions and problems of others and displays sympathy and fellow-feeling towards them:

(i) shows tolerance.

(ii) controls emotions and displays restraint.

(iii) discusses issues of disagreement with others impartially.

(b) unhesitatingly mixes with people of different economic strata.

Psychomotor Domain in Economics: To acquire practical skills essential for the study of Economics.

Behavioural Outcomes: To demonstrate the achievement of the above objective, the pupil:

(a) draws maps, charts, tables, diagrams, graphs, etc., from the given data.

(b) translates data from one form of presentation to another.

(c) prepare models.

Implications for Domains

1. Teaching should provide learning experiences for mutual integration of feeling, doing and thinking.

2. Teaching should provide learning experiences in meeting the individual needs of learners.

3. Teaching should provide purposive setting of learning or goal oriented learning. Teaching should provide appropriate guidance to learner to achieve his goal.

4. Teaching situations should provide freedom to develop creative powers.

5. Teaching should provide different learning experiences for satisfying the needs of each and every learner.

6. Teaching should be organised in such a way that the family background and the individuality of the learner are taken into account. A suitable social environment of group work should be provided.

7. Teaching should be based on sympathetic guidance to the learner.

8. The entire range of class-room inter-action should be the co-operative group process so as to develop social attitudes in the learners.

Family vs School

Cognitive growth and development is influenced by both, the heredity and environment. Very little can be done to change the hereditary influence. But a good deal can be done by the parents, the teachers and the school to provide a healthy environment for the child. The cultural and social experiences, learning opportunities and discipline which he gets for the developmental process as he advances, contribute significantly towards his mental growth and development.

Cognitive organisation means presenting and exhibiting the intellectual grasp of the subject by the teacher. This implies the art and science of presenting ideas and information meaningfully and effectively so that clear, stable and unambiguous meanings emerge and are retained over a longer period of time.

External Conditions include the arrangement and the time when the stimulus event is to be presented.

Eight Phases of an Act of Cognitive Learning: Gagne describes eight phases of an act of learning. These are in the order of their occurrence.

Phase	*Brief Description*
Motivation	The child strives to achieve some goal and is rewarded when he reaches it.
Attending	The child attends and perceives the stimulus.
Acquisition	The essential incident of learning takes place. The knowledge is coded for storage in the nervous system.
Retention	Memories are stored up in the nervous system.
Recall	The memory store is searched and the learned entity is recalled.
Generalization	The acquired knowledge is applied on a new situation. There may or may not be a transfer of learning.
Performance	There is change in behaviour. It implies that learning has taken place.
Feedback	Thus is the last phase of learning. It is achieved through the reinforcement process. The feedback shows the achievement of the child.

Internal Conditions include, attention, motivation, and the previous knowledge of the child.

Gagne is of the view that we should first look at the internal capabilities of the child. Later on the external which includes the stimulus situation of the learner.

Gagne held that before any new higher capability is learnt by the learner we should try to find out his lower capabilities. It is these which may be a part of the new and higher capability. It is on the basis of these subordinate learning's that a higher capability is learnt.

Attitudes: The attitudes, emotions and values which the children develop in school play a very significant role in their personalities.

Attitudes relate to what one thinks or believes about a thing. They influence behaviour. People have varying attitudes to things, groups and persons.

Anastasi defines an attitude, "as a tendency to react favourably or unfavourably toward a designated class of stimuli, such as a national or a racial group, a custom or an institution."

Thurstone states, "Attitude denotes the sum-total of a man's inclinations and feelings, prejudices or bias, pre-conceived notions, ideas, fears, threats, and conceived notions about any specific notion."

An attitude has a well-defined object of reference. For example, one's views regarding type of food or drink, sports, maths and of peace are attitudes.

An attitude can be learnt and developed.

Values: A value is the worth or importance that an individual places on something. When one values a thing, one strives for it. An individual may work for money, for knowledge, for assisting others, depending on his values. Similarly an individual may try to be honest, brave or courageous etc. if he values these qualities. When an individual achieves his values, he feels happy. When he fails to achieve them, he feels unhappy. A person who values honesty, will be unhappy if he is not able to live up to his standard of honesty. Thus like attitudes, values also influence personality.

It must be fully appreciated that the learners or the students acquire attitudes and values from the teachers as well as their peers. Students tend to take over the thinking and ideals of their teachers. Consciously and unconsciously they imitate their teachers.

If teachers are to influence students, some measure of identification by the students with them is necessary. Students also identify with groups or institutions.

Students will identify with those teachers who are affectionate, cheerful sympathetic, enterprising, etc. and concerned with their welfare in all aspects. The students will identify with those teachers who provide security to them.

Hierarchical Order of the Affective Domain

Objective	*Feelings, Attitudes and Values*	*Level Almost Hierariehal level (Lowest level to highest level)*
1. Receiving	Attending and awareness	↓
2. Responding	Feeling, movement and change	↓
3. Valuing	Worth, utility and cause effect relationship	↓
4. Organising	Judging, integrating and categorising	↓
5. Characterisation	Sustained use of new values and commitment.	↓

Teachers, if they want to develop wholesome attitudes, emotions, interests and values in their students, must set good examples before them. It must be remembered that moralisation has little impact on students.

Meaning of Psychomotor Learning: All forms of learning which involve both understanding and training of muscles are called psychomotor learning. It involves learning a number of skills. Psychomotor learning includes (i) Gross body movements. (ii) Coordinated movements (iii) Non-verbal communication (iii) Speech behaviour (Initiation, manipulation, precision, articulation, naturalisation) (iv) Articulation implies coordination of action performed with efficiency in terms of time, speed and case. Naturalisation implies performance in skill with natural ease and almost without conscious effort so that it is like a habit.

Reading, writing, drawing maps, charts, diagrams, graphs etc; preparing models, walking, running, cycling, swimming, performing experiments and handling tools etc. are example of skills learning.

Hierarchical Order of the Skills of Psychomotor Domains

Objective	*Level*
1. Imitation	↓
2. Manipulation	↓
3. Precision	↓
4. Articulation	↓
5. Naturalisation (Highest Level of Efficiency)	↓

Educational Implifications of Psychomotor Learning

Verbal Instructions or Preparation: Verbal instructions should be given very clearly. With small children verbal instructions should be very brief. With adults verbal instructions may be more detailed. It is not necessary that verbal instructions should be given only in the beginning. They can be given whenever needed. This step may also include statement of aim.

Modelling or Presentation: Practical demonstration of the work to be done may be given. The teacher may demonstrate how to hold the pen and how to move it to write a certain letter. A very important aspect of modelling in handwriting is the presentation of the letters which a child to copy. This work may be done on the blackboard by the teacher. Instructions may also be given simultaneously while demonstrating the action.

Physical Manipulation or Practice: Sometimes it is helpful to physically guide the child's limbs. In teaching to write, a teacher may hold and guide a child's hand. A dance teacher may help a child to place hands and feet in the correct position. The teacher may go from child to child and guide and correct.

Application/Encouragement: The acquisition of a skill is not effective if it is not applied or put to use. For example if the students have learnt how to draw a particular design, they should be asked to draw similar other designs. Children should be encouraged so that they go ahead in performing the skill with confidence.

To conclude, it may be observed that smooth and automatic performance with accuracy and speed would result when three elements are present i.e., effective presentation by the teacher and confidence and practice by the learner.

QUESTIONS

1. What is learning? Explain learning process.

2. What is learning? State the factors on which effective learning depends. Explain the role of the teacher in this regard.

3. State the role of psychological principles in learning.

4. State the conditions affecting learning.

5. What is motivation? State its place in learning. What methods should a teacher adopt to motivate students in the teaching-learning process?

6. Explain the role of heredity and environment in the growth, development and learning of students.

7. Explain the difference between primary learning and concomitant learning. State their respective place in student's learning.

8. Mention the three domains of learning and their major areas of learning.

9. Give examples of instructional objectives and their behaviour outcomes in the three domains of learning. State the teaching implications for all domains.

10. Give the characteristics of cognitive domain and educational implications.

11. Explain the affective domain and its educational implications.

12. State the meaning of psychomotor domain and its educational implications.

8

The Right Context

Particular Approaches

With a view to understand the behavioural approach to learning, it is important to understand behaviour. By behaviour we mean an activity of an organism that can be observed and measured by another person or organism.

The behaviouristic approach describes learning as a connection between stimulus and response. This approach stresses that learning begins with natural responses (reflexes) and new behaviours result from the acquisition of new bonds of stimulus and response through experiences.

The work of Ivan Pavlov (1849-1936), a Russian thinker and his famous experiment with the salivating dog became the starting point of behaviourism. Watson (1878-1958) and Skinner (1904-1980) have given more stress on objectivity in behaviours. Skinner conducted his experiments on rats and pigeons. His approach is known as operant conditioning. An operant is a set of acts that are performed by an organism while doing something.

Once a desirable response occurs in behaviour, it is reinforced with a suitable reinforcer.

Main Features

1. Learning brings about changes in behaviour.
2. Learning is the result of continual interaction of the individual with the environment.
3. The behaviouristic changes are objectively observable.
4. Chief emphasis of the behaviourists is on environment.
5. The behaviourists attach more importance to environment than heredity.
6. Behaviour is understood by conditioning.
7. Conditioning is composed of stimulus-response links (S-R links).
8. An objective and scientific method can be used successfully to study the phenomenon of conditioning and behaviour.
9. The chief method of learning is conditioning.
10. By virtue of similarity, contrast or contiguity (closeness of occurrence in time or situation), one unit of knowledge gets associated with a new unit of knowledge.

Contribution of Behaviourism: Following are the chief contributions of behaviourism to education:

1. It points out that all behaviour is learnt in the process of interaction with environment. So the teachers must provide appropriate environment.

2. It emphasises the importance of environment and its impact on human growth.

3. It has indicated the importance of motivation. The teacher can make his teaching effective only when the learners are motivated.

4. Behaviourism has given new methods and techniques of understanding the learner's behaviour.

5. It has contributed to the understanding of the emotions of the child. This requires that the teacher himself should present a model of emotionally developed individual.

6. It has given new methodology of teaching known as 'programmed learning' which has been successfully employed in several countries.

7. It has led to the development of new approaches, methods and techniques of dealing with maladjustment in children.

8. It has brought psychology out from the controversy of mentalistic approach to human behaviour.

9. The teacher should define learning objectives very specifically in terms of behaviour.

10. The order of arrangement of objectives should be graded i.e. simple to complex.

11. The role of rewards plays a significant role in learning.

12. According to behaviouristic approach, punishment should be avoided.

13. It has greatly contributed to the psychology of learning.

The Shortcomings

1. It is criticised on the ground that the results of experiments conducted on animals regarding behaviour are not applicable to human beings who live in a social environment.

2. The approach dehumanises the learning process as it emphasises the mechanisation of the mental process.

3. The approach gives no consideration to the elements of curiosity, creativity and spontaneity of human beings.

4. The approach attempts to explain emotions thoughts and actions solely on the basis of overt behaviour.

5. The approach does not give heredity its due importance in the development of behaviour.

6. The approach is artificial in nature as it does not deal with the depth of mind.

7. The approach considers the human being as a machine.

Other Approaches

Meaning of Cognitive Approach: Cognitive approach to learning involves the ability to construct mental images, involving thought, reasoning, memory and language. An individual constructs images by observing the surroundings, understanding them and internalising them in a mental process.

The child gains knowledge through a variety of experiences. Cognitive activity consists of active process in perception, memory and reason. These involve class instruction, books, pictures and motion pictures. Formation of correct concepts is very essential in cognitive development from the very beginning.

Bruner points out that cognitive development occurs in three phases: (i) Enactive (doing), (ii) Ikonic (object models or pictures), and (iii) Symbolic (signs and symbols). For instance, a young child, cognising what an orange means would be touching or holding or tasting it (enactive model). Later as he grows up, he sees pictures or models of it (Ikonic model). Later on, gradually he deciphers the word 'orange' (symbolic model).

Jean Piaget considers that cognitive development, intellectual development and development of intelligence are more or less synonymous. According to him, cognitive development implies how knowledge is acquired and developed through successive stages and at various age levels.

Factors Facilitating Cognitive Development: Cognitive development is facilitated both by heredity and its interaction with the environment. In a broad sense, internal readiness, environmental experiences, social experience and equilibrium are the important elements which facilitate cognitive development. Piaget asserts that learning is a function of development.

Intelligence is regarded as a way of behaving. Behaving is reflected in an individual's 'adaptation' to the environment. Adaptation takes place through the interaction of 'assimilation' and 'accommodation.' An intelligent behaviour requires a balance between assimilation and accommodation. This balance is called 'equilibrium.'

'Assimilation' implies incorporation of something from the environment. New ideas, concepts and stimuli are taken in and incorporated into one's 'existing set of scheme.' A scheme is the organised pattern of behaviour which the child develops when he is engaged in any activity. For example, when a child is engaged in sucking, there is a certain pattern of movements of the cheeks, lips, and hands. When a child is confronted with a new object, he will try to understand the new object by applying his old scheme to it. He grasps. He adapts himself to a new object by assimilating it. His old scheme does not change in the process.

'Accommodation' involves modification or change in some elements of an old scheme or learning a new scheme which is more appropriate for the new object. A baby who has already got a scheme of sucking mother's breast accommodates to the object placed in the mouth-finger, nipple, pencil, a toy—depending on its shape, form and the size. The baby develops a new scheme or modified scheme. This is called 'accommodation'.

Thus a baby assimilates when he understands and perceives the new in the light of his old perceptions. A baby forms a new scheme when he modifies or changes his old perceptions to suit the new. This implies adjusting or accommodating. In this way a baby forms new structures or new schemes and consequently develops cognivity.

Different Phases

Following are the four stages of cognitive development and their related accomplishment:

Sensory Motor Stage: It covers the period from birth to two years. This stage is marked by sensation. Simple learning occurs but the child does not think at this stage. These early sensory motor experiences have a great bearing on his later perceptual and intellectual abilities.

Pre-Operational Stage: It is roughly between two years and six years. A major characteristic of this stage is that it is egocentric, which means that the child is primarily concerned with himself. He expresses his needs. He also tries to establish relationships with his parents, siblings, other children and adults in the neighbourhood.

Concrete Operational Stage: This stage is usually between the age of six and eleven or twelve. At this stage, the child develops logical operations from simple associations. He is concerned with the integration and stability of his cognitive system. He can add, subtract, multiply and divide. He is also in a position to classify concrete objects. These operations are called 'concrete' because they relate directly to objects. These operations do not involve abstract thinking.

Formal Operational Stage: This stage covers the period between eleven or twelve and fourteen or fifteen. The child is in a position to free himself from the concrete operations related directly to objects and to groups. The child is capable of reasoning with propositions removed from the concrete. He also develops an experimental spirit.

Difficulties Ahead

1. Poor environmental stimulation.
2. Poor hereditary environment.
3. Lack of proper attention, assimilation etc. on the part of the learners.
4. Defective teaching-learning material.
5. Low level of learner's intelligence.

Factors at Work

Integration of Cognitive, Affective and Psychomotor Skills: There are three aspects of behaviour—Cognitive, psychomotor and affective. Cognitive relates to knowledge aspect, psychomotor to physical and health, and affective to emotions and ideals. Each aspect represents one of the aspects of behaviour. A teacher to be effective must have a judicious blend of all these three aspects. He must have the mastery of the subject-matter and the methods so as to impart information and knowledge to the students in an effective manner. He must be physically sound. He should also cater to the physical and health development of the students.

Practical Side

The child should be extensively exposed to situations wherein he make use of his sense organs and motor parts. He should be provided opportunities for narrating, observing, imagining, thinking, reasoning. questioning, doing independent work, manipulating and improvising etc. The following activities should be planned for facilitating the mental growth of the child.

1. Story making, telling, writing and listening.
2. Picture competition.
3. Essay writing involving imagination.
4. Assembling parts of some dismantled object.
5. Modelling.
6. Quiz questions.
7. Debates and elocution contests.
8. Problem-solving opportunities.

Human Experience

***Meaning of Humanistic Approach to Learning*:** The word humanistic is derived from the Latin Word 'Homo' meaning 'human being'. Thus humanistic approach gives a central place to the human being in learning. It is comparatively a new approach to learning. It makes use of terms like belongingness, co-existence, creativity, mental health and values etc. Above all it emphasises 'self-development'. This approach is based on understanding the needs of the learners and this is the first step towards the fulfilment of learning objectives. Its watchwords are 'better learner', a 'better human being' and 'well-adjusted human being'.

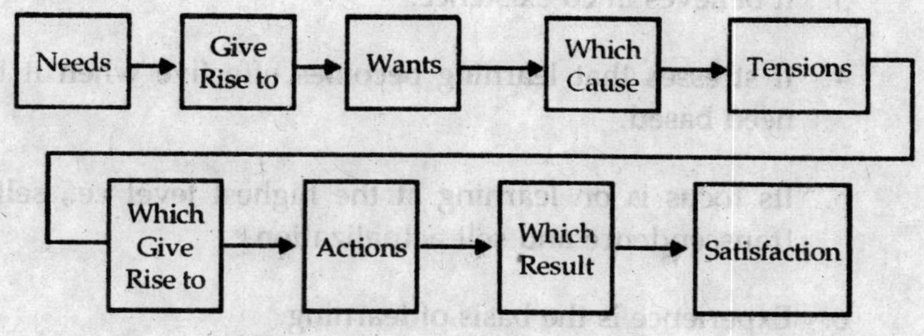

Motivational Cycle

C.R. Rogers (1902-1972) and A.H. Maslow (1916-1970) are the chief exponents of the humanistic approach to learning.

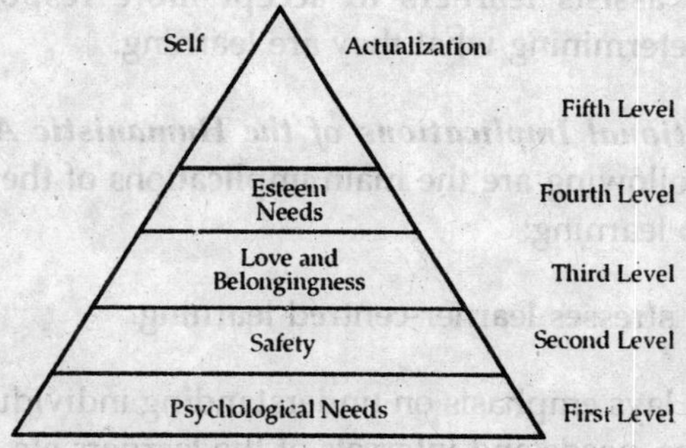

A Schematic Representation of Maslow's Hierarchy of Motivation

Main Characteristics of Humanistic Approach: Important characteristics of humanistic approach to learning are given below:

1. Welfare of all human beings is its main concern.
2. This approach lays emphasis on learning in natural environment of co-operation, equality, freedom, love and peace rather than of physical values, like money, wealth etc.

3. It believes in co-existence.

4. It stresses that learning becomes effective when it is need based.

5. Its focus is on learning at the highest level i.e., self-transcendence and self-actualization.

6. Experience is the basis of learning.

7. It emphasises self-motivation for better learning.

8. It aims at increasing the learner's self-direction and independence.

9. It assists learners to accept more responsibility in determining what they are learning.

Educational Implications of the Humanistic Approach to Learning: Following are the main implications of the humanistic approach to learning:

1. It stresses learner-centred learning.

2. It lays emphasis on understanding individual differences, needs and interests of the learners etc.

3. It envisages active learning on the part of the learner.

4. It highlights the importance of self-discipline and self-control.

5. It considers the teacher as a friend, guide and helper to the learner.

6. It enjoins upon the teachers to involve students in the process of learning.

The Limits

1. It relatively ignores the significance of passive listening (a good deal of learning takes place even in passive listening) on the part of the learners.

2. It tends to develop individualistic attitudes and relatively ignores social development of the learner.

QUESTIONS

1. State the meaning of behaviouristic approach to learning. Mention its salient characteristics. Explain its contribution to learning.

2. What do you understand by cognitive approach to learning in the context of Piaget's views? State the various stages of cognitive development and related accomplishment at each stage. What are the suggestive activities for facilitating cognitive development?

3. Give the main characteristics of humanistic approach to learning. Explain its educational implications.

4. What are the various approaches to learning?

5. "A teacher to be effective must have an ideal blend of various approaches to learning." Elucidate this statement.

9

Process of Assessment

The Measurement

On several occasions, the terms measurement, evaluation and assessment have been used as synonyms. In this context, reference is made to 'A Critical Dictionary of Education' (1982) which states, "Educational discourse has many words that relate to the broad task of judging the worth of a person, programme, or a piece of work, including 'evaluating', 'measuring', 'assessing', 'appraising', 'examining', 'testing', 'marking', 'grading', and 'scoring'. Such words, are often confused."

The terms evaluation and assessment are explained in 'The Dictionary of Education' (1982) in these words, "Evaluation is often used interchangeably with assessment. This is because there is a considerable overlap in their meanings. Both involve measurements designed to describe the amount of certain attributes. There is a tendency, however, for evaluation to be used in a more general way, involving a wide range of measures with a great acceptance of subjective judgements. There is also a tendency for evaluation to be used more when the subject of evaluation is not a person (or group of persons) but the success of a course of teaching or method of teaching. Assessment is therefore used more usually in situations where the procedures involve more objective instruments and when these instruments are measuring personal attributes."

These three concepts have been explained in 'The International Dictionary of Education' (1977) as : Evaluation is "Value judgement on an observation, performance test or indeed any data whether directly measured or inferred."

Assessment in education is the "process by which one attempts to mea sure the quality and quantity of learning and teaching using various assessment techniques, assignments, projects, objective type tests".

Measurement is "an act of finding dimensions of any object and the quality found by each act."

In 'The International Encyclopaedia of Education' (1985), M. Q. Panton has explained these terms as: Measurement implies "assigning a numerical quantity. Measurement may be included in an assessment or evaluation." "Assessment should be reserved for application to people. It covers activities included in grading (formal and non-formal, examining, certifying, and so on. Student's achievement on a particular course may be assessed. An applicant's attitude for a particular job may be assessed. A teacher's competence may be assessed."

As regards evaluation, it states, "In general it would seem preferable to reserve the term educational evaluation for application to abstract entities such as programmes, curricular and organisational variables. Just as assessment may be characterized as a routine activity in which most educators will be involved, evaluation is an activity primarily for those engaged in research and development."

William Wiesma and Stephan G. Jurs in their publication 'Measurement and Testing' (1990) observe, "For all practical purposes assessment and measurement can be considered synonymous. Evaluation is a process that includes measurement." Mathematically, evaluation may be stated as

"Evaluation = Quantitative description of learner's achievement + Qualitative description of learner's abilities + Value judgements about achievements and abilities."

The Distinction

According to Wrightstone, "Evaluation is a relatively new technical term introduced to design a more comprehensive concept of measurement that is implied in conventional tests and examinations." In examination and measurement the emphasis is upon the academic subjects only whereas evaluation includes all the changes that take place in the development of a balanced personality and measures the qualities of head, hand, health and heart of an individual.

In the words of Clara M. Brown, "Evaluation is essential in the never ending cycle of formulating goals, measuring progress towards them and determining the new goals which emerge as a result of new warning. Evaluation involves measurement which means objective quantitative evidence. But it broader than measurement and implies that considerations have been given to certain values, standards, and that interpretation of the evidence has been made in the light of the particular situation."

Bradifield and Murdock explain the difference between measurement and evaluation in these words, "Measurement is the process of assigning symbols to dimensions of phenomena in order to characterise the status of a phenomenon as precisely as possible. Evaluation is the assignment of symbols to phenomenon in order to characterise the worth or value of a phenomenon usually with reference to some social, cultural or scientific standard."

The difference between measurement and evaluation may be explained with the help of an example. It we take a type learner, he is examined for typing. The result indicates that he typed 40 words per minute with 5 errors. This is measurement. The main phenomenon here is typing. Speed and accuracy is the result of typing, which are measured. 40 words and 5 errors are symbols, through which his typing ability is measured. Now if the results of this learner is compared with other learners and he is given 'B' grade, then this process is evaluation.

The difference between evaluation and measurement may also be explained with the help of the following examples:

1. A teacher measures Sohan's height 185 cm. He evaluates the height when he says that Sohan is 'long'.

2. A teacher measures Mohan's achievement in History to be 50 per cent. He evaluates his achievement when he says that Mohan's achievement in History is 'Satisfactory'.

3. A teacher measures the size of a class-room and finds that is 4 m x 3 m. He evaluates the class-room dimensions when he reports that the class-room is 'too small' for 40 students.

4. Rohit and Rahul study in the same class. In the first test they obtain 50 and 70 marks respectively in English. In the second test, both of them obtain 80 marks. Now in the second measurement (test scores), achievement in English is the same, yet the evaluation will differ, when the teacher states that the rate of progress of Rohit is comparatively better than that of Rahul.

The above mentioned examples tend to clarify the difference between measurement and evaluation. But in several situations it is not so easy to identify measurement and evaluation separately. This happens in situations when evaluation becomes a natural process after measurement without giving much thought.

As a matter of fact evaluation is a process of qualitative judgement. Thus it is also a kind of measurement. The only difference is that measurement is objective while evaluation is mostly subjective.

Assessment has a narrow meaning than evaluation but broader meaning than measurement. Evaluation involves assessment and measurement. It is a wider term and includes assessment and measurement also.

The Objectives

***Definitions of Evaluation*:** Chester T. McNernly observes, "The purpose of any programme of evaluation is to discover the needs of the individuals being evaluated and then to design learning experiences that will solve these needs.... Evaluation is an important and delicate process not only from the standpoint of determining the needs and growth of programmes and individuals but also from the standpoint of what it does to the individuals being evaluated.... An evaluation cannot adequately be made by using a single check list, an isolated anecdotal record, or a battery of examinations, a complete evaluation will require the use of many techniques."

Shane and McSwam conceive evaluation, "as a process or inquiry based upon criteria cooperatively prepared and concerned with the study, interpretation, and guidance of socially desirable changes in the developmental behaviour of children. It is a process within the child as a result of which he responds to the psychological interpretations he makes of his school-community environment."

According to Good, "Evaluation is a process of ascertaining or judging the value or amount of something by careful appraisal. 'Values' imply the outcome of the learning activity whereas 'amount' signifies the acquisition of knowledge and skill. It means that evaluation concerns itself with scholastic achievement as well as with behaviour changes."

Thomas M. Briggs and Joseph Justman write that evaluation is 'a process by which the values of an enterprise are ascertained.'

Wiles defines evaluation as, "Evaluation is a process of making judgements that are to be used as a basis for planning. It consists of establishing goals, collecting evidence concerning growth or lack of growth toward goals, making judgements about the evidence, and revising procedures and goals in the light of the judgements. It is a procedure for improving the product, the process, and even the goals themselves."

C. E. Beeby describes evaluation as, "The systematic collection and interpretation of evidence leading as a part of process to a judgement of value with a view to action."

In simple language evaluation may be described as a process by means of which changes in behaviour of children are studied and guided towards pre-determined objectives.

The primary aim of evaluation is to bring about improvement in the teaching- learning process so that the learner develops his potentials to the optimum level. Following are the broader aims of evaluation:

To Evaluate the Achievement of the Students: The abilities and the achievements of the students must be evaluated. Evaluations are conducted to discover whether or not the learner has been able to acquire the required knowledge, skill and attitude.

To Measure Personality: Evaluation is used to test the power of clear thinking, quickness of mind, calmness and perseverance of the students.

To Find out the Efficiency of Teachers and of the School: Evaluations provide a suitable occasion for the authorities to judge the efficiency of the teachers. The efficiency of the institution is also judged. They provide a proper occasion to the teachers to know whether or not their methods of teaching-learning are appropriate.

To Help in Diagnosis: Evaluation helps to discover the specific weak points of an individual or class and thus gives an opportunity to the teachers as well as to the taught to remove these defects.

To Act as Incentives: Stimulation to work hard is provided to the students through the system of evaluation. Some objectives are placed before the students and for the realisation of those objectives, the students develop in them the habits of constant hard work.

To Help in Prognosis: Evaluation has a prognostic value also. With this device, the aptitudes of the students are determined.

To Give Uniformity of Standard: The external evaluation facilitates the problem of uniformity of standards attained by the students of the different institutions.

To Help in Grouping: Evaluation facilitates the work of grouping individuals for the purposes of teaching by bringing those together who have more or less the same attainment.

To Measure Fitness for Admission to Higher Courses: Evaluation is designed to determine the capacity and fitness of the candidates to pursue higher courses of general or professional study or training. Evaluations which serve this purpose are called Entrance or Qualifying Examinations.

To Help in Selection by Competition: Evaluation is also conducted to select the best candidates for appointment to public services or for awarding prizes and scholarships.

Whatever be the definition of evaluation, it must serve the following objectives:

1. Assist learners in their learning.
2. Diagnose learning difficulties of learners.
3. Determine readiness for new learning experiences.
4. Assist learners in their problems of adjustment.
5. Prepare reports of learner's achievement.
6. Assist teachers in adopting proper strategies of teaching-learning.
7. Fulfil class-room objectives of instruction.

Practical Aspects

1. To make provision for guiding the growth of individual pupils.
2. To diagnose the weaknesses and strengths of pupils.
3. To locate areas where remedial measures are needed.
4. To provide a basis for a modification of the curriculum and courses.
5. To provide a basis for the introduction of experiences to meet the needs of individuals and group of pupils.
6. To motivate pupils towards better attainment and growth.
7. To test the efficiency of teachers in providing learning experiences and the effectiveness of instruction and class-room activities.
8. To improve instruction.

9. To bring out the inherent capabilities of a pupil, such as attitudes, habits, appreciation and understanding, manipulative skills in addition to conventional acquisition of knowledge.

The Ingredients

1. Specifying learning outcomes.

2. Collection of evidence about pupil's growth through reliable data gathering devices.

3. Analysis and interpretation of performance or pupil's growth.

4. Diagnostic appraisal i.e., indicating the level of performance rather than the judgement on the performance.

5. Redefining and readjusting the instructional objectives on the basis of feedback.

Main Features

A publication of the NCERT entitled Reforming Examinations: Some Emerging Concepts, lists the following generalisations:

1. Evaluation is a function of the learner and instruction and, therefore, good evaluation is one which is done by the teacher, of the taught as an individual.

2. Evaluation provides quality control at every stage of the teaching-learning process and, therefore, evaluation would be treated as an integral part of the teaching-learning process.

3. Since evaluation provides feed-back about the rate of pupil's learning and the effectiveness of instruction,

evaluation should be done unit-wise after teaching every unit.

4. As the purpose of teaching is learning by students, focus of teachers' evaluation should be on improvement of pupils' achievement and not on judging their achievement. Therefore, diagnostic testing and remedial teaching should go side by side.

5. Pupil's achievement is the outcome of the integrated process of learning within a given set of conditions. Evaluation of pupils' learning should, therefore, be also integrated with regard to both the process and product of learning.

6. Keeping in view explosion of knowledge, the new curriculum stresses the learnability aspect more than the knowledge aspect. Emphasis in evaluation should, therefore, shift from testing of rote memory to that of problem solving abilities and attitude development.

7. For appraisal of the total development of the learner, it is essential that evaluation should not be limited to scholastic achievement alone, but it should encompass all aspects of pupils' development. As such evaluation techniques will have to be extended beyond written and practical examinations to include oral testing, observations, checklists, rating scales and interviews.

8. Since independent learning by students is considered an important method of learning in the new curriculum, self- assessment by pupils of their own learning should be practised in the evaluation system of an institution, so that cooperative assessment of the teacher and the learner is encouraged.

9. Since it is impossible to achieve 100 percent or even near to 100 percent reliability of the various tools used for evaluating pupils, it is desirable that students should be classified broadly into 5 to 7 grades rather than using 101 point scale as at present.

10. As every pupil learns at this own rate, he should be judged in terms of his own capacities and goals and not in terms of the standards of his class, institution or the board of secondary education. As such passing of a student in all the subjects at a time cannot be considered essential.

11. The grades of every pupil indicate only his level of performance which may be satisfactory or unsatisfactory in terms of his own standard. Thus, a grade howsoever low it may be, cannot be taken as failure but as an indicator of his present level of achievement.

12. Given more time and proper remedial teaching a student can improve his achievement. Therefore, a student should get the opportunity of improving his grade in one or more subjects, if he so desires.

13. The more accurately and meaningfully the evidence about pupils' growth in different aspects of his development is reported to students, teachers, parents, employers and institutes of higher learning, the more appropriate and reliable would be the decision taken for classification, certification and selection of students for different purposes. Therefore, regular recording of pupil performance in various areas of development is a perquisite to every evaluation programme.

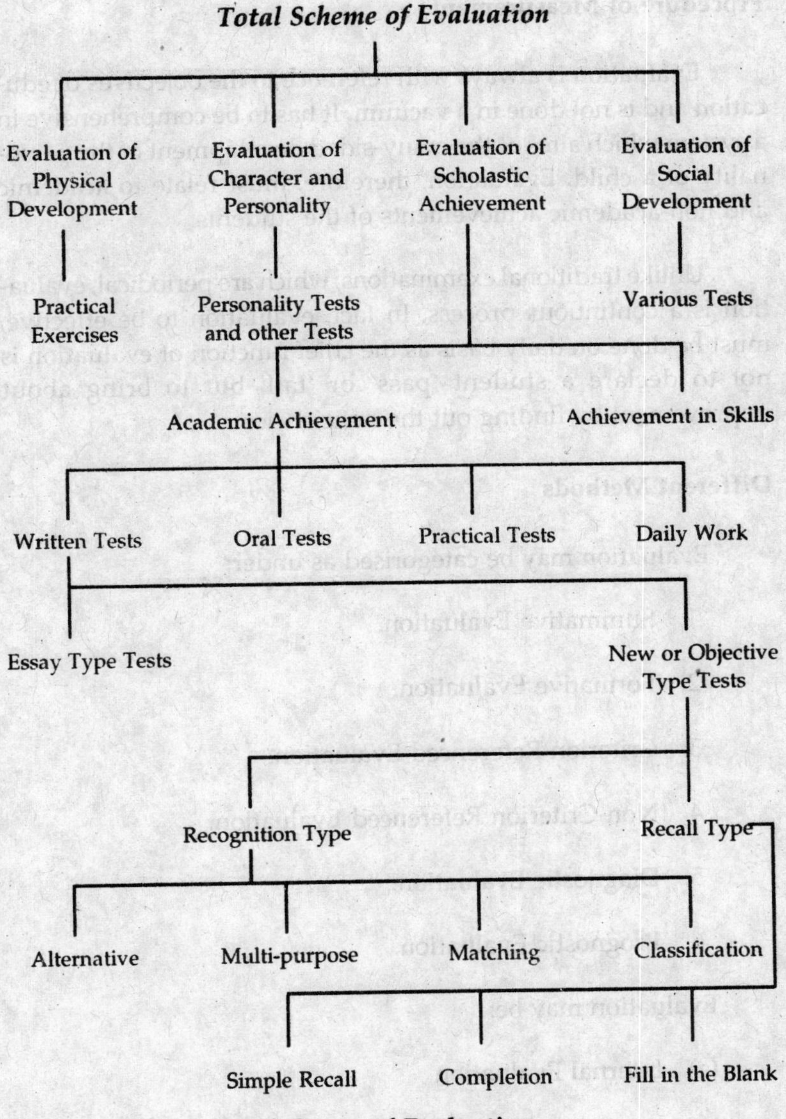

Scheme of Evaluation

Procedure of Measurement

Evaluation is always with reference to the objectives of education and is not done in a vacuum. It has to be comprehensive in a system which aims at the many-sided development of the personality of a child. Evaluation, therefore, must relate to academic and non-academic achievements of the students.

Unlike traditional examinations; which are periodical, evaluation is a continuous process. In fact, evaluation to be effective, must be done on daily basis as the chief function of evaluation is not to declare a student 'pass' or 'fail' but to bring about improvement by finding out the deficiencies.

Different Methods

Evaluation may be categorised as under:

1. Summative Evaluation.
2. Formative Evaluation.
3. Criterion Referenced Evaluation.
4. Non-Criterion Referenced Evaluation.
5. Diagnostic Evaluation.
6. Prognostic Evaluation.

Evaluation may be:

(a) Internal Evaluation

(b) External Evaluation.

(c) Combined Internal-External Evaluation.

***Meaning of Summative Evaluation*:** Following definitions throw light on the meaning of summative evaluation.

1. Gronlund, N.E. observes, "Summative evaluation typically comes at the end of a course (or unit) of instruction. It is designed to determine the extent to which the instructional objectives have been achieved and is used primarily for assigning course grades or certifying pupil mastery of the intended learning outcomes."

2. According to Nikto, A.J. "Summative evaluation describes judgements about the merits of an already completed programme, procedure or product."

3. W. Wiersma and S.G. Juts state, "Summative evaluation is done at the conclusion of instruction and measures the extent to which students have attained the desired outcomes."

Characteristics and Main Features: A perusal of the above definitions shows that the summative evaluation has the following chief elements:

(i) Summative evaluation is done at the end or completion of a particular instructional programme whose duration may vary from a semester to whole year.

(ii) Summative evaluation checks whether there has been learning or not. If the answer is yes, then what is the quantity and quality of the learning in relation to predetermined objectives?

(iii) The instructional programme should be for the attainment of some objectives.

(iv) It lends to the use of well-defined evaluation designs.

(v) It focuses on analysis.

(vi) It provides descriptive analysis.

(vii) It tends to stress local effects.

(viii) It is concerned with broad range of issues.

(ix) Its instruments are reliable and valid.

(x) For this evaluation, there are external examinations as well as teacher-made tests and rating scales etc.

Meaning and Definition

(i) In the views of R.L. Ebel and D.A. Frisbie (1986), "Formative evaluation is conducted to monitor the instructional process, to determine whether learning is taking place as planned."

(ii) W. Wiersma and S.G. Jurs write, "Formative evaluation occurs over a period of time and monitors student progress."

(iii) According to N. E. Gronlund, "Formative evaluation is used to monitor learning progress during instruction and to provide continuous feedback to both pupil and teacher concerning learning successes and failures. Feedback to pupils reinforces successful learning and identifies the learning errors that need correction. Feedback to the teacher provides information for modifying instruction and prescribing group and individual remedial work."

(iv) In the words of A. J. Nikto, "Formative evaluation is concerned with judgements made during the design and/or development of a programme which are directed towards modifying, forming or otherwise improving the programme before it is completed."

The Characteristics

(i) It is used to monitor the learning experiences of the students during the period of instruction.

(ii) It aims at providing continuous feed-back to both teacher and student concerning learning success or failure during the teaching-learning process.

(iii) Feed-back provides specific learning errors and correction.

(iv) Feed-back to students provides reinforcement.

(v) Feed-back to the teachers provides information as to whether any modifications are necessary in his strategies of teaching.

(vi) Formative evaluation involves assessment of class-work, homework, oral questions and quizzes etc.

(vii) Formative evaluation uses mostly teacher-made tests.

(viii) Formative evaluation is used for assessing student learning progress during instruction.

(ix) Results of formative evaluation are not used for assigning course grades.

(x) Formative evaluation is done during an instructional programme.

(xi) The instructional programme aims at the attainment of certain objectives during the implementation of the programme also.

(xii) Formative evaluation is done to monitor learning and modifying the programme if needed before its completion.

(xiii) Its design is exploratory and flexible.

(xiv) It seeks to identify influential variables.

(xv) It requires analysis of instructional material for mapping the hierarchical structure of the learning tasks and actual teaching of the course for a certain period.

In this book *'Evaluation Thesaurus'* M. Seriven, who is the originator of the terms summative and formative evaluation, explains the difference in these words, "The formative evaluation is conducted during the development or improvement of a product (or person). It is an evaluation for in-house staff and normally remains in-house but it may be done by an internal or an external evaluator (preferably a combination). Summative evaluation, on the other hand, is conducted after completion of a programme (or a course of study) and for the benefit of some external audience or decision maker (e.g., funding agency or future possible users) though it may be done by an internal or an external evaluator or by a combination."

Gloria, Hitchok and others (1986) state the difference between the summative and formative evaluation in these words, "It is fairly straight forward to produce an 'ideal' type of either a summative or a formative profile. It is far more difficult to combine the two into one unified system. The underlying philosophies of the two appear difficult to reconcile."

Alkin (1974) pointed out that a formative evaluation study uses a great variety of instruments which are either locally developed or standardized, it relies on observation and informal data collection devices, mostly locally chosen. In contrast, summative evaluation studies tend to use well defined evaluation designs, as unobtrusive and non-reactive as possible, they are comparative and concerned with a broad range of issues, for example, implications, policies, costs, competing options. The instruments used in summative evaluation are publicly accepted, reliable and valid instruments, reflecting concerns of the sponsor and of the decision maker.

Following are the main differences between these two types of evaluation:

1. Summative evaluation is the terminal assessment of performance at the end of instruction but formative evaluation is the assessment made during the instructional phase to inform the teacher about progress in learning and what more is to be done.

2. The summative evaluation limits the use of profiles and record of achievement but they are regularly used in formative evaluation.

3. The main consideration in summative evaluation is the determination of the extent to which the examinee has mastered the knowledge and skills associated with a course. On the other hand, the main consideration in formative evaluation is to reveal the processes by which the examinee achieved these outcomes.

4. In summative evaluation, the assessment is done to test learning outcomes against a set of objective criteria without revealing the details of the route to the teacher which the student followed in reaching that point. Formative evaluation takes the form of a dialogue between the student and teacher in which the task is determined by both.

5. Summative evaluation relates to the worthwhileness of the instructional programme which has already been completed. Formative evaluation, on the other hand relates to worthwhileness of the instructional programme which is still going on and can be modified.

6. A formative evaluator is partisan of the instructional sequence and makes all possible efforts to make teaching learning better. A summative evaluator is non partisan and uncommitted who passes judgment on the teaching-learning endeavour.

7. Formative evaluation is in-house evaluation while summative evaluation is mostly done by outside agencies.

8. Formative evaluation is day to day evaluation and is intended to bring about improvement. Public examinations and annual tests and semester tests come under the category of summative evaluation.

9. In a broad sense, all class-room assessments which are not used for grading purpose whether these are home assignments, questioning during teaching, class-room observations of students responses, and informal tools come under the category of formative evaluation. As for judgement (pass/fail) of scoring, summative evaluation is used.

Various Kinds of Tests

Meaning of Criterion-referenced Test (CRT): The CRT aims at measuring the achievement of a learner on a certain domain to find out his level of achievement in that domain. It has little to do with the achievement level of other learners (examinees). Some of the important definitions of CRT are :

1. In the words of Gronlund, N.E. (1985), criterion-referenced test is "a test designed to provide a measure of

performance that is interpretable in terms of a clearly defined and delimited domain of learning tasks."

2. Sex Gilbert (1989) writes, "Criterion-referenced tests relate a student's score on an achievement test to a domain knowledge rather than to another student's score."

3. Poham, W.J. and Husek, T.R. in their paper, "Implications of Criterion-referenced Measurement" published in Journal of Educational Measurement Vol. VI (1969), define criterion-referenced measures as, "Those which are used to ascertain an individual's status with respect to some criterion i.e., performance standard. It is because the individual is compared with some established criterion, rather than other individuals, that these measures are described as criterion-referenced. The meaning of an individual score is not dependent on comparison with other testees. We want to know what the individual can do, not how much he stands in comparison to others."

The Characteristics

1. Its main objective is to measure student's achievement of curriculum based skills.
2. It is prepared for a particular grade or course level.
3. It has balanced representation of goals and objectives.
4. It is used to evaluate the curriculum plan instruction progress and group student's interaction.
5. It can be administered before and after instruction.
6. It is generally reported in the form of:

(i) Minimum scores for partial and total mastery of main skill areas.

(ii) Number of correct items.

(iii) Percent of correct items.

(iv) Derived scores based on correct items and other factors.

The Uses

(i) to discover the inadequacies in learner's learning and assist the weaker section of learners to reach the level of other students through a regular programme of remedial instruction.

(ii) to identify the master learners and non-master learners in class.

(iii) to find out the level of attainment of various objectives of instruction.

(iv) to find out the level at which a particular concept has been learnt.

(v) to better placement of concepts at different grade levels.

(vi) to make instructional decisions of what to do with a learner in individually prescribed instruction programme.

The Limitations

1. Criterion-referenced test tells only whether a learner has reached proficiency in a task area but does not show how good or poor is the learner's level of ability.

2. Tasks included in the criterion-referenced test may be highly influenced by a given teacher's interests or biases, leading to general validity problem.

3. Only some areas readily lend themselves for listing specific behavioural objectives around which criterion-referenced test can be built and this may be a obstructing element for teachers.

4. Criterion-referenced tests are important for only a small fraction of important educational achievements. On the contrary, promotion and assessment of various skills is a very important function of the school and it requires norm-referenced testing.

The Interpretation

1. Interpretation should be based on what the items actually measure.

2. There should be sufficient items for each type of interpretation.

In case there are less than 10 items, they should be combined with other items through lengthening content items.

3. The test should contain easy as well difficult items otherwise it would be difficult to describe what low achievers could do.

Ronal Hambelton and Daniel Eignor (1978) have suggested the following guidelines.

Determination of Objectives

1. The purposes of the test should be stated clearly and concisely.

2. Objectives should be written in such a way that each item could be identified with one objective.

3. There should be appropriate rationale for the inclusion of each objective in the test.

4. The set of objectives of the test should be a true representative of content domain.

5. The class-room teacher should be in a position to adapt the test to meet local situation.

Construction and Inclusion of Test Items

1. The set of test items should measure an objective for which it has been included in the test.

2. The test items should be valid indicators of the objectives for which they have been prepared.

3. The test items should be in appropriate form to measure the objectives for which they have been selected.

4. A heterogeneous sample should be used in the test items.

5. Item analysis should be used to detect flawed items.

6. The item review process should be described.

7. The test items should be free from any bias.

8. The test items should be free from technical flaws.

Management Side

1. The test manual should specify the role and responsibilities of the examiner.

2. The test administrator should have adequate information relating to the purpose, time limits, answer sheets and scoring of test.

3. The directions of the test should be clear.

4. The test should be easy to score.

The Layout

1. Test booklet should be attractively printed.

2. The layout of test booklet should be convenient for examiners.

The Authenticity

1. The test length should be sufficient enough to find out test score reliability.

2. The sample of examinees used in finding out reliability should be adequate and representative.

3. The reliability information should be provided in the test for each intended use of the test score.

4. The reliability information provided in the test should be appropriate for the use of the score of the test.

The Scores

1. There should be a rationale for the selection of the method for determining cut-off scores.

2. There should be evidence for the validity of the chosen cut-off marks.

The Sanctity

1. The validity evidence should be adequate for the intended use of the test score.

2. The test manual should provide an appropriate discussion on the factor affecting the validity of the scores.

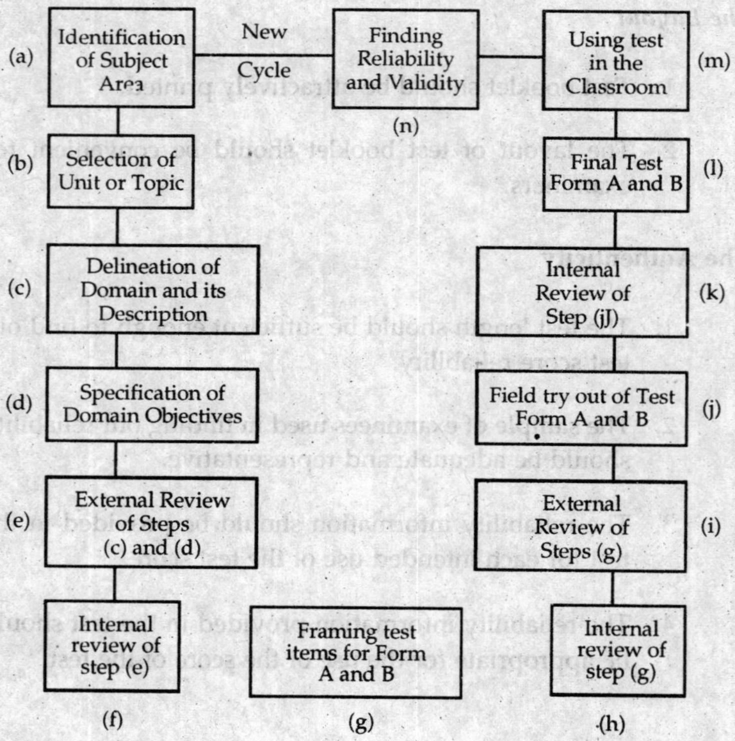

Various Steps in Development

Source: Singh, Pritam, Criterion-referenced Testing: A Monograph (NCERT, New Delhi, 1983)

Meaning of Norm-referenced Test (NRT): Norm-referenced Test is used primarily for comparing achievement of an examinee to that of a large representative group of examinees at the same grade level. The representative group is known as the 'Norm Group'. Norm group may be made up of examinees at the local level, district level, state level or national level. Since the development of norm-referenced tests is expensive and time consuming, they are produced by commercial test publishers.

NRT is defined as under:

Bormuth (1970) writes that a norm-referenced test is designed "to measure the growth in a student's attainment and to compare his level of attainment with the levels reached by other students and norm group."

N. R. Gronlund defines Norm-referenced Test as "a test designed to provide a measure of performance that is interpretable in terms of an individuals relative standing in some known group."

The Characteristics

1. Its basic objective is to measure student's achievement in curriculum based skills.

2. It is prepared for a particular grade level.

3. It is administered after instruction.

4. It is used for forming homogeneous or heterogeneous class groups.

5. It classifies achievement as above average, average or below average for a given grade.

6. It is generally reported in the form of Percentile Rank, Linear Standard Score, Normalized Standard Score and Grade Equivalent Score.

The Uses

N. Vasantha Ram Kumar and K. N. Lalithamal (1990), state the following uses of NRT:

1. to make differential prediction in aptitude testing;
2. to get a reliable rank ordering of the pupils with respect to the achievement we are measuring;
3. to identify the pupils who have mastered the essentials of the course more than others;
4. to select the best of the applicants for a particular programme;
5. to find out how effective a programme is in comparison to other possible programmes.

The Limitations

According to the above mentioned authors, some of the criticisms raised against these tests are:

1. Test items that are answered correctly by most of the pupils are not included in these tests because of their inadequate contribution to response variance. They will be the items that deal with important concepts of course content.
2. There is lack of congruence between what the test measures and what is stressed in a local curriculum.
3. Norm-referencing promotes unhealthy competition and is injurious to self-concepts of low scoring students.

***Process for the Development of NRT*:** L.M. Carey (1988) has described the following stages for the development of NRT.

Design Stage: It is done through:

(i) Curriculum analysis.

(ii) Selecting objectives to be measured

(iii) Analysing objectives for determining pre-requisite skills.

(iv) Developing table of specifications for test.

(v) Determining specifications for items.

Development Stage: This consists of:

(i) Writing items according to specifications.

(ii) Developing needed art work and illustrations.

(iii) Writing response directions and examples.

(iv) Writing administrative directions.

(v) Reviewing items, illustrations and directions.

(vi) Developing test lay-out.

(vii) Developing simple test.

Conducting Field Test: At this stage, test is tried out through:

(i) Selecting representative group.

(ii) Administering test.

(iii) Scoring.

(iv) Analysing information.

(v) Analysing data and selecting items.

(vi) Developing final test form.

Developing Test Norm: Norms of the test are developed through:

(i) Describing characteristics of population.

(ii) Selecting representative norm group.

(iii) Administering test to norm group.

(iv) Scoring.

(v) Converting raw scores to standard scores.

(vi) Creating norm tables.

Writing Test Manual: The test manual is written through:

(i) Describing the design process and skills measured.

(ii) Describing the field test process.

(iii) Describing the development process.

(iv) Describing criteria used to select items.

(v) Describing norm group selection procedure.

(vi) Describing norm group characteristics.

(vii) Describing test characteristics-reliability and standard error of measurement.

(viii) Describing standard administrative procedures.

(ix) Describing scoring procedures and derivation of standard scores.

(x) Describing score interpretation procedures.

Differences in NRT and CRT

NRT	*CRT*
1. It stresses discrimination among individuals.	1. It stresses what examinees can do and what they cannot do.
2. NRT covers a large domain of learning task with just a few items measuring each specific measuring each specific task.	2. It focuses on a delimited domain of learning tasks with a relatively large number of items
3. It contains items of average difficulty.	3. It contains easy as well as items.
4. A student is tested after each unit (usually large) of the new material presented.	4. A student is tested after each unit for mastery of objectives.
5. A student is assigned the marks or grades to indicate his performance.	5. A student is allowed to proceed to the new material if mastery is obtained.
6. A student is allowed to go to the next unit along with the whole class.	6. A student is given remedial instruction if the material presented is not mastered.
7. A student is presented with the new materials of the next unit.	7. A student is tested again after remedial work to check for mastery of the material.
8. A student is tested for the new material and assigned marks.	8. A student is tested for mastery of objectives.

The Similarities

1. Achievement domain is measured in both.
2. Same types of items can be used in both.
3. Same rules are followed for writing items in both excepting the item of difficulty.

4. Validity and reliability are needed in both.

5. Sample of test items should be relevant and representative in both.

Overall Impact

A norm-referenced test typically attempts to measure a more general category of competencies (for examples, reading, comprehension), knowledge (for example, familiarity with the unitary government system) or aptitude (for example, problem solving potential).

A criterion-referenced test, on the other hand, typically focuses on a more specific domain of examinee behaviours. A 100-item on referenced test may be needed to cover the entire range of a learner's reading comprehension skills as against five separate twenty-item criterion-referenced test focusing only on five well defined skills within the overall realm of reading comprehension.

CRT and NRT are used to measure the attain-ment of the learner. The fundamental distinction between NRT and CRT is based on the manner in which one interprets the results of the learner's test performance. In the case of NRT one interprets learner's test performance according to the performance of 'others'. In case of CRT, one interprets learner's performance in relation to well defined norms of knowledge, skills; attitudes and the like.

Meaning of Diagnostic Evaluation/Testing: A diagnostic test has been defined by English and English (1958) in these words, "One designed to locate the particular source of a person's difficulties in learning especially in school subjects."

Importance of Diagnostic Evaluation: Diagnostic evaluation provides the feed-back to the teachers as well as to the students regarding their strengths and weaknesses. It helps teachers to modify their teaching-learning strategies so as to make them more effective in the light of the feedback. Diagnostic evaluation is an integral part of overall evaluation.

The Uses

(i) Diagnostic tests serve as guides to the attainment of the students.

(ii) Diagnostic tests serve as guides to locate the attainments of difficulties of the students.

(iii) Diagnostic tests help in isolating difficulties of students individually.

(iv) Diagnostic tests help to group students for remedial or special coaching.

Development of Diagnostic Testing: Essential Points: Following points should be kept in view by the teacher and the tester while planning diagnostic evaluation:

1. The diagnostic tests should be prepared in accordance with the specific tasks regarding a particular subject or area of a subject, for instance diagnostic tests for comprehension and spelling etc. would be quite different.

2. There should be a large number of items/questions covering various aspects of the relevant subject matter for which test is designed.

3. Variety of questions like very short type and the multiple type should be included in the diagnostic test.

4. On a particular skill to be evaluated a large number of items should be included in the test.

5. Scoring should be easier and quicker.

6. The nature of the questions should be such as they can be administered.

7. Several equivalent forms of diagnostic tests may be prepared.

8. Different kinds of tests may be made use of on students of different abilities.

Administering the Diagnostic Test: The following points need to be kept in view:

1. Confidence of the learners must be won by the teacher and the learners assume that the test is to assist them in the improvement of their learning rather than declaring them pass or fail.

2. The environment in which the test is administered should be made as related as possible.

3. Students should be seated comfortably.

4. Students should be asked not to consult each other while taking the test.

5. If any student is unable to follow any item, he should be allowed to seek a clarification from the teacher.

6. The teacher may insist that the students taking the test should attempt all questions.

7. Time schedule may not be forced strictly. If any student takes a little more time, he may be allowed to do so.

Follow up: After finding out the strengthens and weaknesses of the students, the teacher may modify his teaching strategies so as to make himself more effective. Students can also benefit from the result of evaluation.

Diagnostic Tests	*Achievement Tests*
1. Diagnostic tests are normally for below average students.	1. Achievement tests are meant for all students.
2. Diagnostic tests are used to identify difficulties and weaknesses of the students.	2. Achievements tests are used to evaluate the achievement level of the students.
3. Diagnostic tests lead to remedial teaching or special coaching.	3. Achievement tests are used to compare the achievements of students and also for grading.
4. Diagnostic tests concentrate on difficult content areas.	4. Achievement tests relate to the entire unit/course covered.
5. Diagnostic tests are not usually used to evaluate the efficiency of the teachers and the teaching learning process.	5. Achievements tests, at various occasions, are used to determine the effectiveness of the teachers and the teaching-learning process.

The Areas

1. Achievement of the students in specific subjects.
2. Achievement of the students in specific areas of a subject or subjects.
3. General educational achievement.
4. Intelligence.
5. Personality.

QUESTIONS

1. Explain the difference between measurement, evaluation and assessment. Why do we prefer the term evaluation?

2. Explain the term evaluation. Why is it needed? State its chief characteristics.

3. What is continuous and comprehensive evaluation? Explain it in detail.

4. Prepare a comprehensive and total scheme of evaluation.

5. Explain CRT. State its characteristics. Describe its merits and demerits.

6. State the meaning and characteristics of Non-Referenced Evaluation. Describe its uses and limitations.

7. Compare Criterion Referenced Evaluation and Non-Criterion-referenced Evaluation. Which of the two would you prefer?

8. State the meaning of summative evaluation and formative evaluation. Explain their distinction.

9. What is the meaning of diagnostic evaluation? State how this type of evaluation helps to overcome learning deficiency.

10. Explain the difference between diagnostic evaluation and achievement evaluation.

10

Tests for Evaluation

Meaning of an Intelligence Test: An intelligence test is that test which is used to measure the intelligence of the learners. The Intelligence Quotient (I.Q.) becomes the basis.

Intelligence has been viewed differently by scholars. More than one hundred definitions of intelligence are found in the educational literature. However, in general, intelligence is considered as the global capacity of an individual to think rationally, to act purposefully and to deal effectively with the environment. All the inventions of the world would be attributed to persons of high intelligence. The individuals differ in intelligence. Differences in individuals in the level of general intellectual ability and the cognitive process are found on account of difference in intelligence to a great extent.

Intelligence is measured through a complicated process involving a comparison and establishing a relationship between chronological age (C.A.) and mental age (M.A.). This relationship is expressed by the term intelligence quotient (I.Q.) When the mental age is divided by CA and the quotient is multiplied by 100, the result is I.Q.

$$I.Q. = \frac{M.A.}{C.A.} \times 100$$

Several tests are available to measure the I.Q. of the individuals.

The Utility

Intelligence tests are very useful for the following purposes:

Knowing Individual Differences among Learners: Dr. V.V. Kamat has classified Indian children as under:

Category	*Range of I.Q.*
Near genius or genius	140 and above
Extraordinary	130-139.9
Very Superior	120-129.9
Superior	110-119.9
Average or normal	99-109.9
Backward	80-98.9
Very backward	70-79.9
Borderline	60-69.9
Morons	40-59.9
Imbeciles	20-39.9
Idiots	Below 20

Grouping in the Class: Sometimes grouping in the class is done on the basis of intelligence test results.

Class-room Teaching: Intelligence tests enable the teacher to know the general mental level of the students and accordingly he adopts his teaching techniques.

Identification of Slow Learners and the Gifted: Intelligence tests help to identify learners in their capacity to learn. Accordingly enrichment programmes are provided to the gifted and compensatory/remedial education to the slow learners.

Selection to Courses: Different subjects require different degrees of intelligence. Some call for a higher order of intelligence and the others of a lower order.

A nation-wide study in the U.S.A. gave the following Median I.Q. of the high school students in different courses:

Course	*Median I.Q.*
Technical	114
Scientific	108
Academic	106
Commerce	104
Trade	92

Burt found the following correlations between:

Intelligence and arithmetic (Problems)	.65
Intelligence and the compositor	.63
Intelligence and reading	.56
Intelligence and spelling	.52
Intelligence and writing	.21
Intelligence and hard work	.18
Intelligence and drawing	.15

This implies that children of high I.Q. are superior in abstract thinking than those of low I.Q.

Selection in Occupations: Burt draws up the following provisional scheme for occupational classification according to the degree of intelligence occupations require:

S.No.	*Occupation*	*I.Q. Require*
1.	Higher professional and administrative work-Lawyer, physician, architect, teacher (University and Secondary level)	150
2.	Lower professional technical and executive work	130 to 150
3.	Clerical and highly skilled work—short hand, typist, bank clerk, salesman, electrician, nurse.	115 to 130
4.	Skilled work-tailor, dressmaker, carpenter, cashier, printer.	100 to 115
5.	Semi-skilled repetitive work-barber, welder, miner, painter, banker	85 to 100
6.	Unskilled repetitive work-manual labour	70 to 85
7.	Casual labour-simplest routine work	50 to 75

Promotion: Intelligence tests are used for the promotion of students to the next class.

Selection of Students to a School: In good schools there is always rush for admission. All the applicants though eligible for admission cannot be admitted. It then becomes necessary to adopt some additional methods of selection. Intelligence tests help to meet out this difficulty to a considerable extent. By administering these tests, authorities pick out the innately brighter boys.

The Discovery of Unusual Cases: The lack of intelligence may be the main cause of abnormal behaviour. The intelligence tests help to find out cases of abnormal behaviour.

Intelligence and Success in College: Gates and others think that an I.Q. of at least 120 is needed to do acceptable college work in a first class college with an average expenditure of time and energy.

Help in Diagnosis of Backwardness: Ordinary scholastic examinations fail to discover 'educable abilities'. The failure of a child in the examination is no indication that he lacks intelligence. This failure may be due to defective methods of teaching or it may be due to some temperamental or physical obstacles which might have stood in the way of the child. There may not be any fault with the intelligence of the child, only it has not been allowed to work itself out.

Award of Scholarships: Various public scholarships are awarded on the basis of the results secured through intelligence tests. The Government of India selects some students for the award of scholarships for studying in Public Schools on the basis of the intelligence and achievement tests.

Evaluation of Methods and Materials of Instruction: Intelligence Tests are helpful in evaluating the results of the experiments conducted by a school in the relative importance of the different methods of instruction i.e., achievement obtained with different text-books or with a certain text-book as contrasted with extensive reading material not confined to any one book.

Assessment of Teacher's Work: When the achievement of the pupils in a subject does not correspond to the scores of intelligence tests, it gives indication to the fact that the subject has not been properly taught by the teacher and properly understood by the students.

Limitations of Intelligence Tests: It would be a great mistake to think that these tests are all in all in measuring the various aspects of the learner's personality. Intelligence is one of the factors. Too much reliance cannot be made on this evaluation tool. It is to be used in conjunction with other tools. Following are the important limitations of intelligence tests:

1. Intelligence tests seek to measure intelligence which in itself is not a clear concept. Psychologists differ radically on the meaning and nature of intelligence.

2. Intelligence tests fail to measure the depth, strength, weakness and quality of an individual relating to his emotional stability.

3. Intelligence tests fail to evaluate the ethical, moral and spiritual qualities of an individual.

4. Intelligence tests fail to take into account the environmental factors. The tests may include items/material with which the children of certain socio-economic groups have more experience then those of the weaker sections.

5. Use of intelligence tests needs a good deal of care and caution on the past of the test user.

Testing Success

***Definition and Meaning of an Achievement Test*:** An achievement test is an instrument or tool to evaluate relative achievement of the learners. It occupies an indispensable place in the teaching-learning process. The following definitions enable us to have a comprehensive view of achievement tests.

In his book 'Modern Educational Measurement', W. James Pophan provides the nature of achievement tests: "Tests in the cognitive or psychomotor realms are often focused on an examinee's attainment at a given time; these tests are usually referred to as achievement tests."

In the words of Thorndike and Hagen, "The type of ability test that describes what a person has learned to do is called an achievement test." Gronlund defines an achievement test as, "a systematic procedure for determining the amount a student has learned through instruction."

N. E. Gronlund and R. L. Linn, in their publication 'Measurement and Evaluation in Teaching' have observed, "There typically have been norm-referenced tests that measure pupil's level of achievement in various content and skill areas by comparing their test performance with the performance of other pupils in some general reference group."

Classification of Achievement Tests

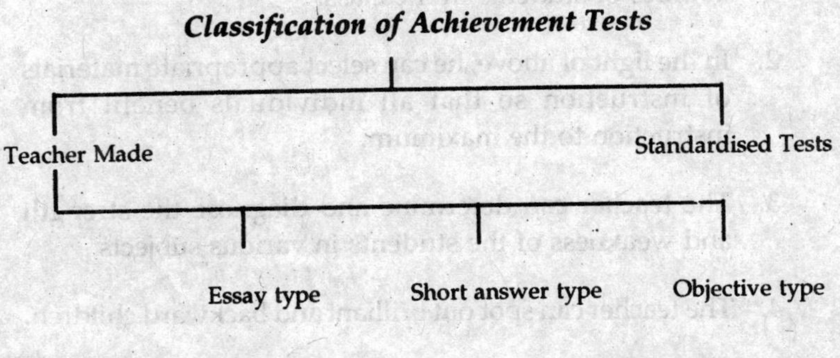

Classification of Objective Type Achievement Tests

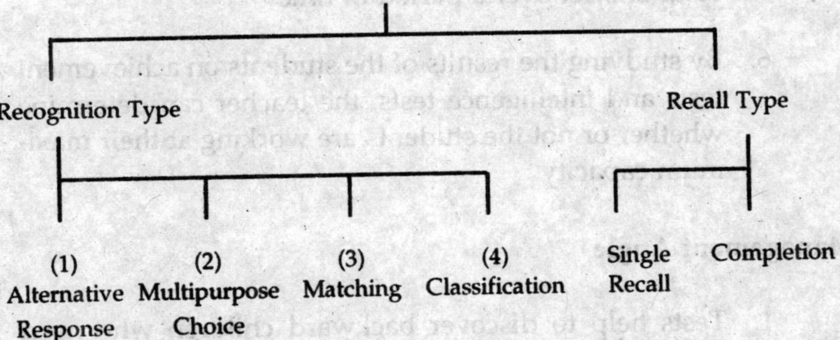

Major Objectives

These can be used for the following purposes:

1. To diagnose student's strength and weakness.
2. To motivate students.
3. To report to the parents.
4. To predict future progress.
5. To reflect teacher's effectiveness.

The Uses

1. The teacher comes to know about the general range of abilities of students in the class.

2. In the light of above, he can select appropriate materials of instruction so that all individuals benefit from instruction to the maximum.

3. The teacher can determine and diagnose the strength and weakness of the students in various subjects.

4. The teacher can spot out brilliant and backward children.

5. He can determine the progress of the group in a particular subject over a period of time.

6. By studying the results of the students on achievement tests and intelligence tests, the teacher can determine whether or not the students are working at their maximum capacity.

Management Angle

1. Tests help to discover backward children who need help and to plan for remedial instruction for such students.

2. Tests help to select talented pupils for special classes and courses.

3. Tests help to decide proper classification of students.

4. Tests help to get a better understanding of the needs and abilities of pupils.

5. Tests help to select students for the award of special merits or scholarships.

6. Tests help to group pupils in a class so that students are put in such a way that individual differences are as slight as possible.

7. Tests help the parents in recognising the strengths and weaknesses of their children so that they direct their energies on suitable goals only and do not put heavy demands on them.

8. Tests help to determine the efficiency of one school with the others.

9. Tests help to determine the general level of achievement of a class and thus judge the teaching efficiency of the teacher. The level of achievement of a class may be judged on the basis of the achievement of the class in the beginning and at the end of the school year.

10. Tests help to discover the type of learning experiences that will achieve these objectives with the best possible results.

11. To evaluate, revise and improve the curriculum in the light of these results.

12. Tests help to evaluate the extent to which the objectives of education are being achieved.

13. Tests help to classify school objectives.

Students' Angle

1. Students come to know about their strengths and weaknesses.

2. Students are motivated to work hard for removing their deficiencies.

The Bright Side

1. It should contain a sufficient member of test items for each measured behaviour.
2. A good achievement test is tried out and selected on the basis of its difficulty level and discriminating power.
3. It should be divided into different knowledge and skill area according to behaviours to be measured.
4. Its instructions in regard to its administering and scoring are so clear that they become standardized for different users.
5. It should have a description of measured behaviour.
6. It provides equivalent and comparable forms of the test.
7. It is accompanied by norms which are developed at various levels and on various age groups.
8. It includes a test manual for its administering and scoring.

Broad Classification of Achievement Tests: Tests vary according to form, type and use etc. Yoakaya and Simpson give the following classification of tests.

1. Form : (a) Oral Examinations. (b) Written Examinations.
2. Purposes: (a) Prognostic. (b) Diagnostic. (c) Power. (d) Speed. (e) Accuracy. (f) Quality. (g) Range.
3. Organization: (a) Essay. (b) Objective.
4. Period or Time of Administering: (a) Daily. (b) Weekly. (c) Monthly. (d) Term (e) Year.

5. Duration: (a) Short. (b) Long.

6. Methods of Scoring and Interpreting Results: (i) Standardized. (ii) Non-standardized.

7. Abilities Involved: (i) Appreciation. (ii) Comprehension. (iii) Judgement. (iv) Organization. (v) Retention. (vi) Speed. etc.

8. Nature of Material included: (a) Reading. (b) Writing. (c) Spelling. etc.

9. Mental Functions Involved: (a) Association. (b) Memory (c) Recall (d) Recognition. (e) Problem Solving.

10. Types of Response Involved: A. (i) Alternate Response (ii) Yes-No (iii) Plus-minus.

    Multiple Response: (i) Best Answer (ii) Correct Answer. (iii) Completion (iv) Matching. (v) Identification. (vi) Enumeration. (vii) Essay.

Test for Intelligence

By an achievement test we mean test of academic achievement such as English or Hindi etc. An achievement test is a measure of learning itself and an intelligence test is a measure of learning capacity. An achievement test attempts to measure the standard of education whereas intelligence test attempts to measure educability.

The development of an individual in the future is likely to be along the lines of tests for specific aptitude rather than test of general intelligence. Dunlop writes, "The more 'general' the intelligence test the less its value. By increasing the specificity, we add to its value."

The Standards

Meaning of a Rating Scale: A rating scale is a method by which we systematize the expression of opinion concerning a trait. The ratings are done by parents, teachers, a board of interviewers and judges and by the self as well.

There are two characteristics of a rating scale. (1) Description of the characteristics to be rated, and (2) Some methods by which the quality, frequency or importance of each item to be rated may be given. These rating scales give an idea of the personality of an individual.

By a rating is meant the judgement of one person by another. "Rating is, in essence, directed observation," writes Ruth Strang. A. S. Barr and others state, "Rating is a term applied to expression of opinion or judgement regarding some situation, object or character. Opinions are usually expressed on a scale or values. Rating techniques are devices by which such judgements may be quantified."

Descriptive Rating Scale: The rater puts a check (V) in the blank before the characteristic or trait which is described in words or a phrase.

Examples: Has this pupil initiative?

- Shows marked originality.
- Willing to take initiative.
- Quite inventive.
- On the whole unenterprising.
- Very dependent on others.

***Numerical Scale*:** Here numbers are assigned to each trait. If it is a seven-point scale, the number 7 represents the maximum amount of that trait in the individual; 4 represents the average amount. Instead of 7 point scale we can have 9 point or 5 point or 3 point scale. A nine point scale may be:

1. Most pleasant
2. Extremely pleasant
3. Moderately pleasant
4. Mildly pleasant
5. Indifferent
6. Mildly unpleasant
7. Moderately unpleasant
8. Extremely unpleasant
9. Most unpleasant.

The Graphic Scale: This is similar to the descriptive scale and the difference lies only in the way it is written. This is also called "Behavioural Statement Scale." The following two examples may be noted:

(a) *Example*: Responsibility for completing work.

Very high	High	Average	Low	Very Low

(b) *Example*: Social attitude.

Anti-social	Self-centred	Has no positive attitude	Usually considerate of others	Strongly altruistic

The Percentage or Group Scale: Here the rater is asked to give the percentage of the group that possesses the trait on which the individual is rated. For example-for rating the self-confidence of an individual, the rater may check one of the following:

Falls in the top 1 per cent.

Falls in the top 10 per cent, but not in the top one per cent.

In the top 25% but not in the top 10%.

In the top 50% but not in the top 25%.

In the lower half, but not in the bottom 25%.

In the bottom 25%, but not in the bottom 10%.

In the bottom 10%, but not in the bottom 1 per cent.

In the bottom 1 per cent.

Man to Man Scale: An individual is asked to rate the ratee by comparing him to the person mentioned on the Scale and assign the ratee his position. For example A B C D E are the persons who have been already rated as very persistent, not easily stopped, working quite steadily, somewhat changeable, give up easily.

Example: Is he generally a persistence person?

A	B	C	D	E

Because of subjectivity element, the use of this type is very limited.

Graphic Scale: In this scale a straight line is shown vertically or horizontally with various clues to help the rater. An example of such a scale is given below.

1	2	3	4	5
Very effective	Slightly effective	Average ineffective	Slightly ineffective	Very

Rating by Cumulative Points: The weights of +1 and -1 are assigned to every favourable and unfavourable attribute, characteristic or trait.

Standard Scale: This type of scale is used in evaluating the quality of handwriting on the basis of some pre-established scale values.

Advantages of Rating Scales

1. Helpful in writing reports to parents.
2. Helpful in filling out admission blanks for colleges.
3. Helpful in finding out students needs.
4. Helpful in making recommendations to the employers.
5. Helpful in supplementing other sources of understanding about the child.
6. Rating scales especially are quite interesting to the raters, especially the graphic.

The Limitations

1. Some characteristics are more difficult to rate.
2. Subjective element is present.
3. Lack of opportunities to rate students.
4. Raters tend to be generally generous.

The teachers or the counsellor may rate each individual on each quality on a three-point, four-point or five-point scale. In a five-point scale, the description of the qualities of an individual may be 'Outstanding', 'Very Good', 'Good', 'Average' and 'Poor'.

1. The specific trait or mode of behaviour must be defined properly. For example, we want to rate a child's originality in performing a task. First of all we must formulate a definition of 'originality' and then try to rate it.

2. The scale should be clearly defined, i.e., we are rating at a three, four or five-point scale.

3. The trait to be treated should be readily observable.

4. Uniform standards of rating scale should be observed.

5. The rater should observe the rates in different situations involving the trait to be rated. This will bring reliability to the judgement of the rater.

6. The number of characteristics to be rated should be limited.

7. In the rating scale card, some space may be provided for the rater to write some supplementary material.

8. The directions of using the rating scales should be clear and comprehensive.

9. Several judges may be employed to increase the reliability of any rating scale.

10. Well-informed and experienced persons should be selected for rating.

Generosity Error: Sometimes raters would not like to run down their own people by giving them low ratings. The result is that high rating is given in almost all cases. Such an error is known as 'generosity error'.

Stringency Error: The opposite of generosity error may be called stringency error. Some raters have a tendency to rate all individuals low.

The Halo Error: 'Halo' means a tendency to rate in terms of general impressions about the rates formed on the basis of some previous performance.

The Error of Central Tendency: There is a tendency in some observers to rate all or most of the raters near the mid-point of the scale. They would like to put most of the ratees as 'Average' etc.

The Logical Error: Such an errors occurs when the characteristic or the trait to be rated is misunderstood.

Tool's Definition

The characteristics of a good tool of evaluation may be classified as under:

Characteristics of a Good Tool of Evaluation

Practical or Practicability of Test	*Texchinal*
This includes	This comprises
1. Acceptability	(i) Discrimination
2. Cost effectiveness	(ii) Item suitability
3. Ease of administration	(iii) Norms
4. Ease of scoring	(iv) Objectivity
5. Ease of interpretation	(v) Predictability
6. Face validity	(vi) Reliability
7. Fairness	(vii) Standardization
8. Meaningfulness of test scores	(viii) Validity
9. Time elementality	
10. Utility	

Meaning of Reliability of a Test: A test is said to be reliable if it gives the same results whenever it is repeated. If there is no variation in a pupil's score obtained in a test today and obtained after a sufficient long time, the test is said to be reliable. The test should alsc give the same result, if it is applied by different persons who follow the set instructions. With a view to have a comprehensive idea of reliability, we may mention a few definitions of reliability.

According to Frank S. Freeman, "The term reliability refers to the extent to which it gives consistent result on testing and retesting."

In the words of Anatsai, "The reliability of a test refers to the consistency of score obtained by the same individual on different occasions or with different sets of equivalent items."

L.J. Cronback regards reliability as "consistency throughout a series of measurements."

To Ross, "Reliability means consistency." Ross has further observed, "The ideal test tells the truth consistently."

Nature of Reliability: Gronland is of the view that while considering reliability, following points may be taken note of:

1. Reliability pertains to the results obtained with an evaluation tool and not to the tool itself.

2. An estimate of reliability always relates to a particular type of consistency.

3. Reliability is a necessary condition but not a sufficient condition for validity.

4. Reliability is basically statistical in nature.

Factors Influencing the Reliability of an Evaluation Tool/Test

Intrinsic Factors	*Extrinsic Factors*
Factors which lie within the test itself.	Factors which are outside the test itself.
(i) Length of the test.	(a) Group variability.
(ii) Homogeneity of items of the test.	(b) Guessing and chance errors.
(iii) Difficulty value of items.	(c) Environmental factors
(iv) Discriminative items	(d) Momentary changes
(v) Scores reliability.	

Length of the Test: In some tests, total test as well as sub-test scores are given. The reliability of the whole test is generally higher in comparison with that of the sub-tests. This is because the whole test has more items, i.e., it is longer. Spearman-Brown formula may be used to calculate reliability after increasing test length.

Variability of the Group: If the range of the sample group is wide, the reliability coefficients obtained would also be high. A homogeneous range would provide low coefficients.

Ability Level of Students: Reliability is related to the ability level of students. Some tests have high reliability for older students and low reliability for younger ones, because older students have better understanding level.

Scoring Technique: There is higher possibility of mistakes if scoring is done by hand. These mistakes may be in checking answers, as well as totalling. If tests are machine-scored, there would be less number of mistakes and reliability would be higher.

Guessing: There are great individual differences in guessing capacity of students and therefore, it leads to some unreliability in test scores. A larger number of true false items results in more guessing and so it increases unreliability.

Method of Test Construction: The nature and form of test items, their difficulty, extent of dependence of one item on another, objectivity of scoring, sampling, nature of the group on which the test has been standardized influence test reliability. An increase in the number of alternate-responses would increase reliability.

Testing Conditions: Results obtained from the administration of the test in a quiet place, say testing room/classroom would not be same as obtained at an open place or in the hall. Likewise the attitude of the examiner as well as of the students also influences reliability of the test. Cheating or the absence of it is also likely to influence results.

Chance Fluctuations or Momentary Distractions: Sudden stomache or headache, broken pen or pencil, concern about family may also affect reliability.

Various Procedures

Following are the methods for determining the reliability of a test.

1. Test-Retest
2. Equivalent Form
3. Split-half
4. Inter-item Consistency

Test-Retest Method: For establishing reliability through this method, the same test is administered twice to the same group of students/learners/subjects with a given time intervals between the two administrations of the test. With the help of these two sets of scores, correlation is computed. This correlation coefficient provides a measure of reliability. It indicates how stable the test results are over the given period of time. Thus this correlation coefficient can also be referred to as a correlation of stability.

There are certain assumptions made when we compute a coefficient of stability.

First, the characteristics being measured by the test are stable over time.

Second, practice or forgetting does not affect significantly the trait being measured by the test.

Third, no differential learning should occur between the two administrations of the test.

Equivalent Form Method: Determination of reliability by means of equivalent form method involves the use of two different but equivalent forms of the test. These forms are also called alternative or parallel forms. Equivalent forms cover the same content, use same types of items, instructions, time limits and formats of equal difficulty. The two forms of the test are administered to the same group of students/learners/subjects in close succession or with minimum time lag. The correlation coefficient is computed from the two sets of scores. This correlation coefficient provides a measure of equivalence. It indicates the degree to which both forms of the test measure the same aspects of behaviour. Inconsistencies in scores in this method can be attributed to difference in content sampling or item sampling. Long intervals between the two administrations will lower the reliability.

***Interpretation of a Reliability Co-efficient*:** There are three considerations which must be kept in mind while interpreting reliability. First, the reliability of a test as estimated by one technique in one situation and with one example will not be the same as an estimate obtained with a different technique, in a different situation, or with a different sample.

Second, a reliability co-efficient situation is only an estimate of the magnitude of inconsistency in test scores and it does not indicate the causes of inconsistency.

Third, reliability is not the be-all and end-all of a measuring tool. It is not an end in itself rather a step on a way to that goal.

Reliability is a pre-requisite of validity. Reliability is a matter of stability of test scores whereas validity is the correlation of the test with certain outside independent criteria.

Factors which can Decrease the Reliability of a Test

(i) Homogeneous grouping of students

(ii) Guessing.

(iii) Poor testing environment.

(iv) Items having high difficult value.

(v) Items having low discriminating power.

Meaning of Validity of a Test: Before understanding the meaning of the validity of a test, we may mention a few definitions of validity.

In the words of Thorndike, "A measurement procedure is valid in so far as it correlates with some measurement of success in the job which it is being used as a predictor."

Leo. J. Cronbach says "Validity is the extent to which a test measures what it purports to measure."

Gates defines validity of a test as, "A test is valid when it measures truly and accurately the ability or quality one wants to appraise."

Boring and others believe, "The degree to which the test actually succeeds in measuring what it sets one to measure is called validity."

Gronlund states, "Validity refers to the extent to which the results of an evaluation procedure serve the particular uses for which they are intended."

Stanley and Hopkins have observed, "The validity of a measure is how well it fulfils the function for which it is being used the degree to which it is capable of achieving certain aims." Validity is chiefly a concern for the 'basic honesty' of the test or the tool in the sense of doing what one promises to do. To be precise validity implies how well a tool measures what it intends to measure.

Nature of Validity: Following points regarding the nature of validity may be noted:

(i) Validity is a matter of degree. It is best considered in terms of categories that specify degree such as higher validity, moderate validity and low validity.

(ii) The validity pertains to the results of a test or evaluation instrument and not to the instrument itself. We sometimes speak of the validity of a test for the sake of convenience but it is more appropriate to speak of the validity of the test results or more specifically of the validity of the interpretation to be made from the results.

(iii) No test can be said to have 'high' or 'low' validity in the abstract. Its validity must be determined with reference to the particular use for which the test is being considered.

(iv) The validity of a test cannot be reported in general terms.

Types of Validity

(1)	(2)	(3)	(4)	(5)
Content validity	Criterion related validity (a) Concurrent (b) Predictive	Construct validity	Face validity	Factorial validity

Content Validity: Content validity is the most important criterion for the usefulness of a test/tool. It is especially important in the case of an achievement test. Content validity relates to the process of matching the test items with the instructional objectives. The content validity relates to the degree to which a test samples the content area which is to be measured. All major aspects of the content area must be adequately covered by the test items and they must be in the correct proportions.

Criterion-Related Validity: Criterion-related validity implies the extent to which a tool performance is related to some other valued measure of performance.

(i) *Concurrent Validity:* It means correlating the test scores with another set of criterion scores.

(ii) *Predictive Validity:* It refers to the extent to which a test can predict the future performance of the students/learners. This type of validity is important for those tests which are used for classification and selection purposes. The degree to which a test can predict the future performance of the individuals depends upon the degree of relationships between the two variables-the test and the criterion. The higher the relationship between these variables, the greater will be the predictive validity of a test. The most important and difficult task in this method is to determine the criterion which is the index of future performance. Predictive value is reported through a coefficient of correlation obtained when predictor and the criterion data are correlated.

Construct Validity: Construct validity refers to the extent to which a test reflects presumed to underlie the test performance and also the extent to which it is based on the theories regarding these constructs.

Face Validity: Face validity refers not to what the test measures but what the test 'appears to measure'.

Factorial Validity: According to Guliford, the factorial validity is the clearest description of what an evaluation/measurement tool measures. The relationship of the different factors with the whole test is called factorial validity.

(i) An admission test to B. Ed. course to select suitable candidates-Criteria related (Predictive).

(ii) A test given at the end of the academic year of +2 course to measure how much the learners have achieved of the course-Content Validity.

(iii) A test designed to be comparably similar in structure and content to another test-Criteria related (concurrent).

(iv) A test designed to measure intelligence among a group corresponding to the variation in age—Construct Validity.

Different Attitude

There are mainly two approaches to find out the validity of a test— (1) Logical Validity, and (2) Empirical Validity.

Logical Validity: When one attempts to judge precisely as to what the test measures, one makes logical analysis. Logic is based on consistency of thought. There are two methods of finding logical validity.

(a) *Deductive Validity*: Deduction is from general judgement to particular judgement. When trying to find out deductive validity of a test, one tries to see as to whether the test corresponds to the definition of the trait intended to be measured. The traits should be objectively defined, e.g., in a test of vocabulary knowledge for 8th grade, the word knowledge and vocabulary must be well defined, as:

Knowledge = ability to give definition

Vocabulary = words commonly used in 8th grade textbook.

Inductive Validity: When one proceeds from particular to general, one adopts an inductive method. In this method we assign the name to the trait on the basis of the test and find the validity and instead of seeing whether a test measures a particular trait, we see what it measures.

Proficiency in Certain Areas of Knowledge: There are some tests in which irrelevant factors are included, which influence the test scores.

Cultural Factors: The logical validity is affected by cultural factors.

Response Set: Mental set is a state which causes one to obtain different scores at different times if the same test is presented in different ways, i.e., change in order of items in battery of a multiple choice items, e.g., Seashore test.

Representativeness of the Topic: A test should include items relative to the topic.

Empirical Validity (Statistical Validity): When the validity of a test is determined by correlating it with criterion, the validity is known to be statistical validity. The extent of the correlation indicates how well the test predicts the criterion against which it is tested.

Factors Affecting Validity

Factors in the tools itself.	*Functioning content and teaching procedure.*	*Factors in test administration and scoring.*	*Factors in the pupils' responses.*	*Nature of the group and criterion.*
These include: (i) Lack of clear directions (ii) Too difficult reading vocabulary and sentence Structures (iii) Inappropriate level of difficulty of the test items (iv) Test items not properly constructed (v) Too short a test (vi) Inappropriate arrangement of items (vii) Scope for guessing	Effective teaching-learning. Students need to have previous experience of the solution of such problems	Physical and Psychological conditions during testing time	Students motivation to take the test	Effects of age, sex, educational and cultural background

Practical Aspects

Objectivity refers to the extent the opinion or judgement of the scorer is eliminated from the scoring process. Objectivity is high in most of the standardized tests of achievement, aptitude, creativity and intelligence, etc. The test items are of objective type-fill in the blanks, multiple choice, true-false, etc. Objectivity is usually attained by

(i) stating the items precisely and specifically.

(ii) requiring short and specific answers.

(iii) scoring the test by the use of a previously determined scoring key or providing specific guidelines for scoring.

Predictability of an Evaluation Tool: The test should be such as can give a forecast of the possibilities of the future achievement of the students.

Following factors determine the practibility of a good tool of evaluation:

Administrative Case: A test which is simple to apply and contains complete directions will always be a good test.

Acceptability: A good test must be acceptable to all the persons and in all the circumstances and situations, e.g., the Binet-Simon Intelligence Test. This is a test which is acceptable to all the individuals of any grade in all the situations.

Cost Effective: As far as possible, a good test should be economical not only from money point of view, but from the point of time and effort required by the testing procedure.

Face Validity: It implies how worthwhile a test will appear to testee, who takes it and to other layman who will see the results. For example, the medicine prescribed by a doctor will not be so effective, if the patient has less of faith in prescription.

Similarly, testee will be resentful and distressful, if the test does not appear to be worthwhile to him.

Interpretation Ease: A good test is one, which could easily be interpreted by the class teacher and the tester himself.

Meaningfulness of Test Scores: A test must provide clues to the objectives for which it is administered.

Purposefulness: One must search for a test that fits the decisions to be made. It is unrealistic to evaluate a test in abstract. The test manual should be approached with a definite measurement problem in mind, e.g., selecting students for a course in humanities or sciences or a special branch in these fields.

Scoring Ease: Scoring would be easy if items have been objectively constructed and the scoring procedure adopted is also objective. In the test itself, separate space should be provided for scoring. Scoring may be done by hand as well as by machines. So stencil-scoring, punch-card scoring or any other method may be used.

Time Saving: The time available for testing is usually very short, as tests requiring longer time are not easily accepted. It is, therefore, better to prefer shorter tests other things being equal. The reliability and validity of a test, does not always depend on its length. Shortening tests to a very few items will destroy their value but not much is gained by lengthening tests beyond 100 items. Hence, this fact should be kept in mind while considering the time factor.

QUESTIONS

1. State the importance of tools of evaluation. Classify them.
2. Explain observation as a tool of evaluation. Stale its merits and limitations.

3. State the significance of interview as a tool of evaluation.
4. Explain the meaning and significance of self-reporting techniques in evaluation. State their limitations.
5. Define an intelligence test. What are its types? State the uses and limitations of intelligence tests.
6. Discuss the importance of achievement tests in evaluation.
7. Explain the characteristics of an achievement test.
8. State the difference between an achievement test and an intelligence test.
9. Define rating scales. State their types, uses and limitations.
10. What is meant by the reliability of a test of evaluation? State factors influencing reliability. Describe the method of determining reliability.
11. What is meant by the validity of a test of evaluation? State the factors affecting validity.
12. Write a short note on the practicability and objectivity of an evaluation tool.

11

Measurement Equipments

Evaluation tools play a significant role in the cognitive and non-cognitive development of students. Without the tools, the effectiveness of the educational programme cannot be assured. In fact, in broad terms of evaluation, tools are needed in all aspects of education. Evaluation cannot be done in a vacuum. It is always with reference to the objectives of a particular system of education. The traditional system of examination in India owes its origin to the objectives as laid down by Macaulay and as the objective of education was to produce a class of clerks, the examination system was also meant to serve that end. Our traditional type of examination, thus, is one-sided and concerned with the academic subjects only and entirely ignores the non-academic aspects. Here, too, it fails to measure scientifically and objectively the achievements of the students.

Basic Principles

Schematically the concept of educational evaluation may be presented by showing relationship among objectives, content [subject-matter, learning activities and evaluation procedures (testing)].

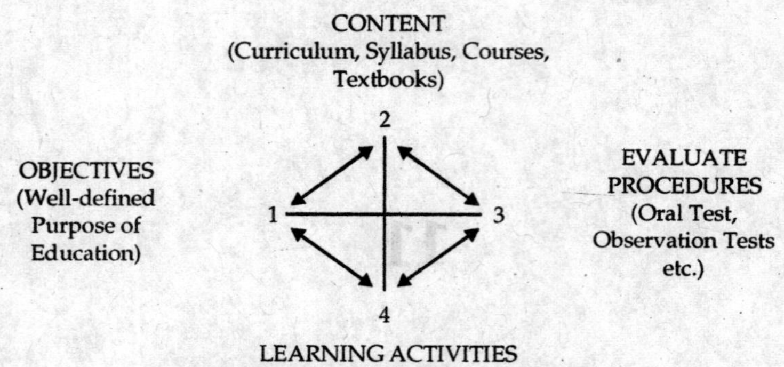

Schematic View

The inter-relationships of these four aspects of evaluation clearly indicate that the process of evaluation is a continuous one and involves continual appraisal of objectives of the teaching-learning process and of the testing procedures used by the class-room teacher.

The inter-relation of objectives, instruction or the learning experiences and evaluation in a programme of teaching may be expressed through Fig.

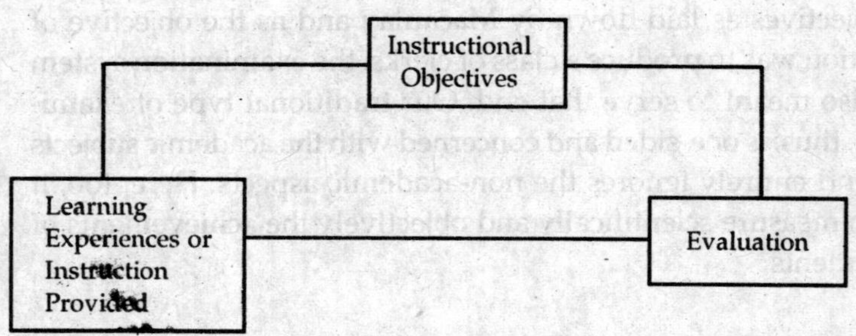

Interrelationship of Objectives

It is, therefore, very essential that tools of evaluation should be as reliable, valid and perfect as they can be.

Classification of Tools of Evaluation

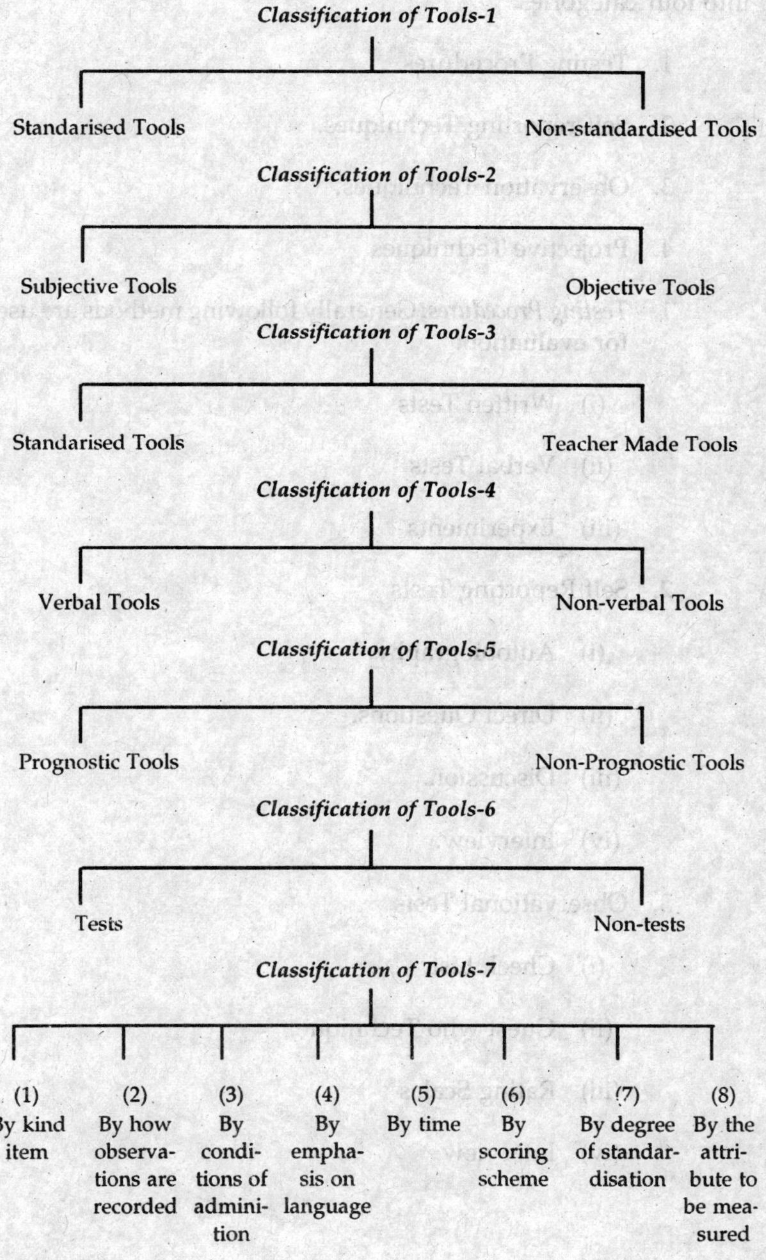

The tools and techniques of evaluation can be categorized into four categories.

1. Testing Procedures.

2. Self-reporting Techniques.

3. Observation Techniques.

4. Projective Techniques.

1. *Testing Procedures:* Generally following methods are used for evaluation:

    (i) Written Tests

    (ii) Verbal Tests

    (iii) Experiments

2. Self Reporting Tests

    (i) Autobiography.

    (ii) Direct Questions.

    (iii) Discussion.

    (iv) Interview.

3. Observational Tests

    (i) Check List.

    (ii) Guest who Technique.

    (iii) Rating Scales

    (iv) Interview.

4. Projective Tools
   - (i) Doll Play
   - (ii) Rorschach Test
   - (iii) Sentence Completion
   - (iv) TAT (Thematic Apperception Test)

Relative Importance of Specific Tools

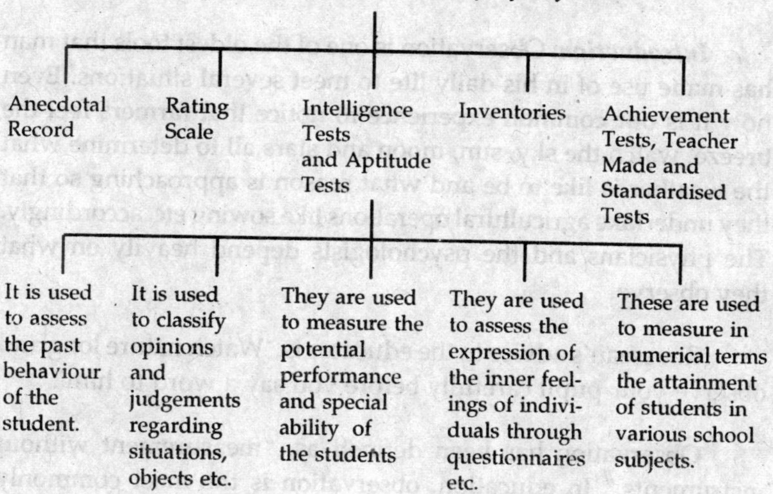

Following are the commonly used tools in evaluation :

1. Achievement Tests.
2. Anecdotal Records.
3. Aptitude Tests.
4. Attitude and Behaviour Testing Tools.
5. Autobiographical Method.
6. Case History.

7. Intelligence Tests.
8. Interview.
9. Personality Tests.
10. Projective Tools
11. Pupil's Dairy
12. Questionnaires and Check Lists
13. Rating Scales.
14. Sociometric Tools

***Introduction*:** Observation is one of the oldest tools that man has made use of in his daily life to meet several situations. Even now it is our common experience to notice that farmers feel the breeze, watch the sky, sun, moon and stars all to determine what the weather is like to be and what season is approaching so that they undertake agricultural operations like sowing etc. accordingly. The physicians and the psychologists depend heavily on what they observe.

Rousseau's advice to the educator is, 'Watch nature long and observe your pupil carefully before you say a word to him'.

Observation has been defined as, "measurement without instruments." In education, observation is the most commonly employed of all measurement techniques. In the present as well as in the past, students have been labelled as good, fair or poor in the achievement and lazy or diligent in study etc., on the basis of observation. Similarly, teachers have listened to speeches and ranked students 1, 2, 3 and so on.

Requisite of Good Observation: The subjective element is very prominent in observation. To eliminate the subjective element, reliance should be placed on a large number of individual observations or on the observations made by a large number of observers.

Behaviour is a reflection of personality. It must be observed very carefully, intelligently and scientifically as observation of behaviour has been recognised as basic to other techniques.

As a tool good observation is based on:

I. Proper planning.

II. Proper execution.

III. Proper recording.

IV. Proper interpretation.

Making Schemes

1. Specific activities or units of behaviour to be observed must be clearly defined.

2. An appropriate group of subjects be selected to observe.

3. Scope of observation-whether individual or group-should be decided.

4. The length of each observation period, number of periods and interval between periods should be decided.

5. The form of recording should be suitably determined.

6. The instruments to be used should be carefully decided.

7. Physical position of the observer should be duly demarcated.

8. Proper tools for recording observation should be kept handy.

9. Various terms may be studied carefully.

The Implementation

An expert execution demands skill and resourcefulness on the part of the investigators. This depends upon:

(i) Proper arrangement of special conditions for the subjects.

(ii) Assuring proper physical position for observing.

(iii) Focussing attention on the units of behaviour or the specific activities under observation.

(iv) Observing discreetly the length and number of periods and intervals decided upon.

(v) Proper handling of the recording instrument being used.

(vi) Utilizing well the training received in terms of expertness.

Devices Used in Observation

(i) Check lists.

(ii) Rating scale.

(iii) Score cards.

(iv) Blank form of tally frequencies.

The Recording

Generally two methods are employed for recording observation. Which of the two methods to use depends upon the nature of the activities or behaviour of the group to be observed. The skill of the observer also plays an important role in deciding upon the method.

The first method is to record the observation simultaneously. It is useful in the sense that a time-gap may distort facts. However, at times, this may not be feasible when the action or activity performed is very swift. Moreover, this is likely to distract the subjects.

Facts may be recorded soon after the observation is over. This is helpful as this does not distract the mind of the subjects. The investigator may not be able to recall facts accurately after the interval of a few minutes.

The Interpretation

Records of observation should be interpreted cautiously and judiciously after taking into consideration various limitations of planning and processes etc. involved in observation.

Recording Devices: Following are the major devices of observation:

1. Check lists.
2. Rating scales.
3. Score cards.

Effective Observation

1. Sampling to be observed should be adequate.
2. Traits to be observed should be defined as accurately as possible.
3. Methods of recording should be simplified.
4. Too many variables may not be observed at a time.
5. Length of observation should be adequate.

6. Length of each observation period, interval between periods and number of periods should be clearly stated.
7. Conditions of observation should remain constant.
8. Observers should be fully equipped.
9. Interpretations should be carefully made.

Types of Observation

Participant Observation	*Non-participant Observation*
1. The observer becomes more or less a member of the group which is under observation.	1. The observer takes a position so that his presence does not disturb the movements/ activities of the group.
2. The observer plays a dual role i.e., observer as well as participant. of the group in detail.	2. It is very helpful in recording and studying the behaviour of the members.
3. He may assume the role of an attentive listener or a full fledged participant.	3. Non-participant observation is used in the case of abnormal individuals, infants and children.
4. It is a flexible type of observation.	
5. It gives more reliable results.	
6. It is economical and helps in finding out delicate hidden and minute facts.	

The Good Observer

1. Alertness.
2. Ability to discriminate
3. Freedom from preconception.

4. Emotional balance.
5. Good eyesight.
6. Right perception.
7. Good speed of recording.
8. Ability to sift fact from fiction.

The Merits

1. Being a record of the actual behaviour of the child, it is more reliable and objective.
2. It is a study of an individual in a natural situation and is therefore more useful than the restricted study in a test situation.
3. This method can be used with children of all ages; of course, the younger the child, the easier it is to observe him. This method has been found very useful with shy children.
4. It can be used with a little training and almost all teachers can use it. It does not require any special tool or equipment.
5. It can be used in every situation.
6. It is adaptable both to individuals and groups.

The Demerits

1. There is a great scope for personal prejudices and bias of the observer.

2. Records may not be written with hundred per cent accuracy as the observation is recorded after the actions of the observed. There is some time-lag.

3. The observer may get only a small sample of student behaviour. It is very difficult to observe everything that a student does or says. As far as possible, observations should be collected from several teachers.

4. It reveals the overt behaviour only-behaviour that is expressed and not that is within.

Meaning of an Interview: Interview as an evaluation tool is a person-to-person relationship in which the interviewer tries to evaluate the learning outcomes of the learner. Interviews are used for a variety of purposes in evaluation.

1. It aims at getting some information about the home and environmental situation of the learner so as to find out whether the environmental situation is conducive to learning.

2. It aims at evaluating several personality traits of the learner.

3. It aims at finding out the learning difficulties of the students and to adapt teaching-learning accordingly.

4. It aims at evaluating the achievement of the learner with a view to select him for a particular course of a vocation.

5. The counselling interview aims at helping the learner to gain insight into his problems and assisting him in solving these.

Focal Points in Interviewing

1. Why The interviewer should be very clear in his mind for the purpose of interview.
2. Who is to interview? The interviewer must be clear in his mind of his strengths and weaknesses.
3. Whom-He should understand the learner thoroughly.
4. How-He should know the technique of interviewing.
5. Where-Suitable place should be selected for this purpose.
6. When-Proper motivation should be developed.
7. What to ask—He should prepare his questions thoughtfully.

Limitations of an Interview

1. An interview is subjective.
2. Some learners are very shy and they do not respond enthusiastically to the interview.
3. An interview does not evaluate the written ability of the learner.
4. An interview needs a lot of time.

Self-reporting

Meaning of Self-reporting Techniques: Self-reporting techniques of evaluation are those techniques which are used in evaluation to find out the reaction of the respondents (students) to items concerning their characteristics or behaviour. The students generally are required to express their likes, dislikes, fears, hopes, ideas about religious beliefs and sex etc. Their expressions reflect the way in which they cope with their own needs and demands of the environment they encounter with.

Significance of Self-reporting Techniques: Broadly speaking, self-reporting techniques are commonly used for measuring the following traits of the students:

1. Adjustment
2. Attitude
3. Interest
4. Personality
5. Diverse traits

Examples of Self-reporting Techniques: These are as under:

(a) Check list

(b) Questionnaire

(c) Rating scale.

Important Self-reporting Instruments: These are:

1. Edward's Personal Preference Schedule
2. The Minnesota Multiphasic Personality Inventory (MMPI)
3. Minnesota Teacher Attitude Inventory (MTAI)
4. Woodworth Personal Datasheet

The Limitations

(i) Being subjective in nature, they are likely to have a biased element.

(ii) The respondents may attempt to present themselves as most favourable by giving fake or untrue responses.

Precautions to be Taken in the Use of Self-reporting Techniques

1. After rearranging the items, techniques may be again used to find out the responses of the students after a short-interval.

2. 'Lie' scales may be used to check deceiving tendency.

3. 'Forced Second Technique' may be used in which a student is given a choice to be exercised for performance which appears to be equally good or bad, e.g., who has exercised greater influence in developing your value system-your mother or father?

4. Information obtained through self-reporting techniques may be supplemented to the information obtained through other means.

5. More than one self-reporting technique may be used.

6. Norms for local population may be established.

7. Standardised inventories should be used.

8. Only due faith should be placed in this type of technique.

9. Only those techniques should be used in which the teacher has received reasonable amount of training.

10. In administering and interpreting the information, help of trained professionals may be obtained.

12

Organising Examinations

The Process

Several procedures are suggested by experts in the construction of an achievement test. Procedure suggested by Gronlund and Linn (1990) seems to be the most appropriate. It includes the following steps:

1. Determining the purposes of testing.
2. Developing the test specifications.
3. Selecting appropriate type of items.
4. Preparing relevant test items.
5. Assembling the test.
6. Administering the test.
7. Scoring the test.

8. Appraising the test.

9. Using the test results.

Determining the Purpose of the Test: According to purpose, tests may be divided into the following five categories:

(i) Pre-testing which includes

(a) Readiness pre-test

(b) Placement pre-test

(ii) Testing during placement

(c) Formative test

(d) Diagnostic test

(e) End testing-summative test

Developing Test Specifications: Specifications of the test includes:

(a) A list of instructional objectives.

(b) An outline of the course contact.

(c) A two-way chart.

Selecting Appropriate Types of Questions: There should be a balanced selection of essay type, short-answer type and objective type questions.

Preparing Relevant Test Items: This includes the following steps:

(a) Matching the test items with the learning outcome.

(b) Selecting most representative items.

(c) Preparing test items which are of proper difficulty level.

(d) Avoiding all possible barriers in test items which prevent examinees from responding.

(e) Avoiding providing any clues to answers which may help examinees to answer correctly even if they lack the necessary achievement.

Assembling the Test: After preparing relevant test items, the test constructor should follow the process as indicated below:

(a) Writing each item on a separate card.

(b) Reviewing the test items by the test constructor himself and also by some other teacher.

(c) Arranging the test items according to well defined criteria.

(d) Providing proper instructions to the examinees.

Administering the Tests: Following suggestions are made while administering the test:

(a) Long announcements before or during the test should not be made.

(b) Instructions, if any, should be given in writing so that uniformity is maintained and all the examinees get the same opportunities.

(c) The test administrators should not respond to the individual problems of the examinees, otherwise any hint on their part may provide unfair chance to some examinees.

(d) Test should be administered in an appropriate physical and psychological environment.

***Scoring the Test*:** Scoring may be done mechanically or manually; depending upon the situation.

***Appraising the Test or Item-analysis*:** After scoring, the test should be appraised for each item.

Using the Test Results: Test results are used primarily for the following purposes:

(a) For making decisions about the promotion of students to the next higher grade.

(b) For bringing about improvement in teaching methods and techniques.

In Black and White

The blue print, sometimes also called the design of the achievement includes the following elements:

1. Identifying Instructional Objectives.
2. Weightage to Instructional Objectives/Learning Outcomes.
3. Weightage to Content/Subject Units.
4. Weightage to type of items/questions.
5. Weightage to Scheme of Options.
6. Preparation of Marking Scheme.
7. Item Analysis.

Weightage to Objectives

S.No.	Objectives	Marks	% Marks
1.	Knowledge	30	30%
2.	Understanding	45	45%
3.	Application	15	15%
4.	Skill	10	10%
	Total	**100**	**100**

Weightage to Content

% Content	Total
Topic No. 1	20
Topic No. 2	20
Topic No. 3	18
Topic No. 4	14
Topic No. 5	16
Topic No. 6	12
Total	**100**

Weightage to Forms of Questions

S.No.	Form of Question	Marks for each Question	No. of Questions	Total Marks	%
1.	L.A.	8	4	32	32%
2.	S.A.I.	5	8	40	40%
3.	S.A.II.	2	9	18	18%
4.	Map	5	2	10	10%
	Total		23	100	

Note: The expected length of the answers under different types of questions would be as follows:

S.No.	*Type/ Forms of Question*	*Marks for each Question*	*No. of Questions*	*Expected length of each Question*	**Expected time for each Question (in minutes)*
1.	L.A.	8	4	upto 250 words	17 x 4 = 68
2.	S.A. I.	5	8	upto 100 words	8 x 8 = 64
3.	S.A. II.	2	9	20 to 30 words	3 x 9 = 27
4.	Map	5	2	10	5x2=10
					169 min.
					11 min. for revision
					180 min

L.A. = (Longer Answer Type Questions)	4
S.A. I. = (Short Answer I Type Questions)	8
S.A. II = (Short Answer II Type Questions)	9
Maps	2
Total	**23**

*This is only an approximation. Though students are advised to be as near the approximation as possible, the actual length, however, may vary. As the total time is calculated on the basis of the number of questions required to be answered and the length of their anticipated answers, it would, therefore, be advisable for the candidates to budget their time properly by cutting out the superfluous length and be within the expected limits.

1. There will be no overall option in the form of 'Do any ten questions or so'.

2. Internal choice (either/or type) on a very selective basis may be given in long answer questions testing higher mental abilities.

3. The alternate question given by way of choice should be based on the same objective and the same unit. It would

have the same anticipated difficulty level and length of answer.

Weightage to Difficulty Level of Questions:

S.No.	***Estimated Difficulty Level***	***Percentage***
1.	Easy (C)	15%
2.	Average (B)	70%
3.	Difficult (A)	15%

Note: A question may vary in difficulty level from individual to individual, as such the approximation in respect of each question will be made by the Paper Setter on the basis of general anticipation from the group as a whole taking the examination. This provision is only to make the paper balanced in its weight rather than to determine the pattern of marking at any stage.

Broad hints regarding points to be covered and the marks to be awarded are issued to the examiners so that evaluation of answer books should be as objective as possible.

The Review

Meaning and Significance of Item Analysis: Item analysis is a technique of determining whether an item is too easy to too difficult and to what extent it is able to discriminate between high and low achievers. The reliability and validity of any test depends on the reliability and validity of its items.

The item analysis is done both qualitatively and quantitatively.

Facility Value and Discriminating Index of an Item of a Test: Facility value and discriminating index are the two aspects of item analysis. The facility value refers to the number of students who can respond to the item with facility or rightly. Discriminating index indicates test's ability to discriminate between the high and the low achievements.

The difficulty level of a test item is indicated by the percentage of students who respond to the item correctly. Following is the formula for determining the difficulty level of an item.

$$\text{Difficulty level} = \frac{R}{N} = 10$$

Where R = The number of pupils who give the right answer of the item.

N = the total number of students who have tried the items.

Example: An item was answered correctly by 20 out of 24 students in the upper group and 12 out of 24 student in the lower group. We have to find out the difficulty level of the item. Should the item be considered difficult, moderate or easy? What would be the discriminating index of the item?

$$\text{Difficult level} = \frac{20+12}{48} = \frac{32}{48} = \frac{2}{3} = .666 = .67$$

Result, The item is moderate

$$\text{Index of discrimination} = \frac{20-12}{24} = \frac{8}{24} = \frac{1}{3} = .33$$

Definition and Meaning of a Standardized Test: Following definitions throw light on the various aspects of a standardized test and bring out its meanings:

In the words of Newkirk and Greene, "A test is standardized (i) if it is composed of exercises that have been selected in the light of usual teaching practice and evaluated as to innate difficulty, and (ii) if it is accompanied by norms or standards permitting the interpretation of results in levels of accomplishment.

The Dictionary of C.V. Good explains a standardised test as "a test for which content has been selected and checked empirically, for which norms have been established, for which uniform methods of administering and scoring have been developed and which may be scored with a relatively high degree of objectivity."

According to Lee J. Cronbach "A standardized test is one in which the procedure, apparatus and scoring have been fixed so that precisely the same test can be given at different times and places. "

According to Thomas: "...a standardized test is one which has been given to so many people that the test makers have been able to determine fairly accurately how well as typical person of a particular age or grade-in school will succeed in it."

From above it is concluded that a standardized test is one for which norms have been established. A norm is an average or typical score which measures achievement in any trait. A standardized test is prepared after several trials of a test to a large number of students.

Important Characteristics of a Standardized Test: Ross has given the following characteristics of a standardized test.

(i) The content is standardized, i.e., item-selection has been done vigorously, after careful scrutiny and by competent judges.

(ii) Administration is standardized, i.e., directions, time-limit etc. are worked out carefully.

(iii) Scoring has been standardized, i.e., scoring keys are prepared, definite rules for scoring have been formulated etc.

(iv) Interpretation has been standardized, i.e., norms for various groups are provided.

Standardized tests have assumed such an important role in the guidance programme that the two terms 'Guidance' and 'Tests' have become synonymous terms.

They are very useful for the following reasons:

1. They give us objective and impartial information about an individual.

2. Since they give us information in an objective manner, it becomes easier to convince the guardians of the assets and limitations of their wards.

3. They provide information in much less time than provided by any other device.

4. Since there is a definite way of expressing the results of these tests in the form of percentiles or standard scores, it has the same significance for all the guidance workers and ail of them have the same interpretations.

5. These tests measures those aspects of the behaviour which otherwise could not be obtained.

6. In subjective observation we may overlook shy children but these tests discover such cases also.

The Categories

1. General intelligence or scholastic aptitude tests.

2. Special abilities or aptitude tests.

3. Achievement tests.

4. Interest tests or inventories.

5. Personality tests or personal adjustment tests.

Evolution and Growth

1. Before finalisation, a test is tried out and administered on a number of subjects for the expressed purpose of refining its items by subjecting the performances of the 'standardization' sample to pertient statistical analysis. The purpose is to ensure that items with adequate level of difficulty and which are capable of discriminating between the superior examinee and the inferior examinee have places in the test.

2. The validity and reliability of a standardized test are ensured right from the beginning of its construction.

3. A standardized test provides instructions and norms for the future users of the test. Such norms usually include pertinent details about the following:

   (i) The age, gender and academic background etc. of the sample used to lay down the norms.

   (ii) The mean score of the sample on the tests.

   (iii) The standard duration and variance of the sample on the test.

   (iv) The size of the sample.

   (v) Conversion tables for interpreting raw scores.

4. A standardized test is constructed by test specialists or experts.

5. A standardized test generally covers a broad or wide area of objectives and content common to the school system within a given geographical area.

6. Test items of a standardized test cover a large segment of knowledge and skills than the teacher-made test.

In short following steps are followed for the standardization of a test/tool:

1. Proper planning.
2. Adequate preparation.
3. Try-out of the test.
4. Preparation of proper norms
5. Preparation of a manual containing instruction for administering a tool/test, scoring and interpretation of data.

Role of Teacher

Teachers prepare achievement, diagnostic and prognostic tests for several occasions. Important features of a teacher-made tests are given below.

(i) They attempt to assess comprehensively the extent and degree of student's progress with reference to specific class-room activities.

(ii) They permit the teacher to ascertain an individual pupil's strengths, weaknesses and needs.

(iii) They provide immediate feedback for the teacher as to the effectiveness of his teaching methods and accordingly can make necessary adjustments and improvements.

(iv) They motivate the students.

(v) They are simple to use.

(vi) They provide information which is the basis for a report on the progress of students.

Functions of a Testing Programme

Class-room Functions	*Guidance Functions*	*Administrative Functions*
1. Grouping pupils for instruction within a class.	1. Preparing evidence to guide discussions with parents about their children.	1. Forming of and assigning to class room groups.
2. Guiding the planning of activities for specific individual pupils.	2. Building realistic self-pictures on the part of pupils.	2. Placing new students.
3. Identifying pupils who need special diagnostic study and remedial instruction.	3. Helping the pupil with immediate choices.	3. Helping in determining eligibility for special groups.
4. Determining reasonable achievement levels for each pupil and evaluating discrepancies between potentiality and achievement.	4. Helping the pupil to set educational and vocational goals.	4. Helping to determine which pupils are to be promoted.
5. Assigning course grades.	5. Improving counsellor, teachers, and parent understanding of problem cases.	5. Evaluating curricula, curricular emphasis and curricular experiments.
		6. Evaluating teachers.
		7. Evaluating the school as a unit.
		8. Improving public relations.
		9. Providing information for outside agencies.

Elements	*Comparative Study* *Standardized Test*	*Teacher-Made Test*
Purpose	Measurement of educational outcome of students of a number of schools.	It is intended to measure the outcome of a teacher's teaching or the outcomes of learning in his class. They are specific purposive.
Scope	Its scope is very wide. Several sections engaged in educational enterprise can use these tests.	Its scope is very limited. It is confined to the area of teaching of a particular teacher.
Accuracy	A standardized test is more accurate as experts are associated with it.	A teacher-made test is comparatively less accurate as the teacher may not be well versed with testing.
Refinement	Standardized tests are duly edited.	A teacher-made test is rather crude.
Coverage of curriculum	A standardized test covers the state or regional curriculum.	It covers a very small area of curriculum.
Sources	A standardized test uses several sources i.e. research workers, expects, teachers etc.	A teacher-made test is based on the experience of the teacher.
Norms	A standardized test provides norms.	A teacher-made test does not contain norms.
Publication	A standardized test is published	It is not published as it is made for local use only.

The Limitations

1. Tests are often ambiguous and unclear.
2. Tests are either too short or too lengthy.
3. Tests do not cover the entire content.
4. Tests are usually hurriedly conducted.
5. Tests serve a limited purpose.

Teachers use the tests made by them at introductory stage, development of the lesson stage, recapitulatory stage and for home assignments. They prepare tests for weekly, monthly, quarterly and annual assessments. They also prepare admission tests.

Thorndike and Hangen point out the following points distinction between the standardized test (i.e., commercially distributed test) and the teacher-made test for his own class.

1. The standardized test is based on the general content and objectives common to many schools across the country, whereas the teacher's own test can be adapted to content and objectives specific to his own class.
2. The standardized test deals with large segments of knowledge or skill, whereas a teacher-made test can be prepared in relation to any specific limited topic.
3. The standardized test is developed with the help of professional writers, reviewers, and editors of test items, whereas the teacher-made test must usually rely upon the skill of one or two teachers.
4. The standardized test provides norms for various groups that are broadly representative of performance throughout the country, whereas the teacher-made test has usually been given only to the pupils in a single class or school.

The Characteristics

The distinctive features of the standardized test represent important advantages for some purpose and disadvantages for others. Basing the test upon a careful analysis of the common objectives expressed in textbooks, courses of study, and reports of committees of professional societies should guarantee that the thinking of many specialists has entered into the test plan. However, a published test is fixed for a period of years in terms of broad, common objectives. It is not a flexible tool. It cannot be adapted to special current needs, to local emphasis, or to particular limited units of study.

The Importance

The value of standardized tests lies particularly in situations in which comparisons must be made-comparisons of a school with other schools, comparison of achievement in different areas by a pupil or a school group, or comparison of achievement with the potentiality for achievement indicated by an aptitude test. The norms provided with standardized tests make such comparisons readily possible. For a school, achievement may be compared with national norms. The standing of a single pupil, or of several pupils coming from different schools, may be determined by reference to the norms for the test. The age or grade equivalents, percentiles or standard scores of a pupil on tests in different subjects may be compared to establish his relative level of achievement, or these converted scores may be compared with a similar score from an aptitude test to see whether achievement is consistent with what we would expect from the pupils' aptitude.

The chief characteristics of standardized tests that differentiate them from teacher-made tests are:

1. A standardized test is more objective.

2. A standardized test is more reliable.

3. A standardized test is more valid.

4. A standardized test is easy to administer.

5. A standardized test makes scoring easier.

6. It is economical.

7. It is comprehensive.

On the other hand a teacher-made test is more useful for specific issues that concern the daily teaching-learning situation faced by the teacher and the students. A teacher-made test is very helpful to the class-room teacher to modify the learning of experiences according to the specific situations. Thus elements of individuality and 'specificity' are more predominant in teacher-made tests.

In the light of these differences, we propose that chief reliance should be placed on teacher-made tests when we want to test in order to:

1. See how well students have mastered a limited unit of instruction.

2. Determine the extent to which distinctive local objectives have been achieved.

3. provide a basis for assigning course marks.

Standardized tests should be used when we wish to test in order to:

1. Compare achievement with potentiality for an individual or a group.

2. Compare achievement of different skills or in different subject areas.

3. Evaluate the status of pupils from different schools or classes on a common basis.

4. Make comparisons between different classes and schools.

5. Study pupil growth over a period of time to see whether progress is more or less rapid than might be expected.

QUESTIONS

1. Define a standardized achievement test. How is it measured? State its merits and limitations.

2. Explain the meaning of a teacher-made test. State its merits and limitations.

3. Differentiate between a standardized test and a teacher-made test. State when you would use a standardized test and when teacher-made test.

4. Explain the procedure for the construction of an achievement test.

5. What do you understand by the blue-print of an achievement test. State the elements of a blue-print with special reference to types of items and weightage to them.

6. Write a short note on item analysis in the construction of an achievement test.d

13

The Teenage

The term adolescence is derived from a Latin word 'adole-scence' meaning 'to grow', 'to mature'. Now this term primarily implies to emerge or to 'achieve identity'. It is very difficult to define exactly the period of life which constitutes adolescence. No sharp chronological boundaries may be fixed to this period. Generally speaking, it covers a period of seven or eight years, normally from 12 to 18 or 20 with large variations in many cases. Some children may manifest traits of its advent as early as the 10th year while others may manifest it till the fifteenth or sixteenth year. Twelve or thirteen may be considered as the normal period for boys in India and even for girls when adolescence begins.

Concept and Meaning

Adolescence is best defined in relation to puberty. This is the period which begins with puberty and ends with the general cessation of physical growth; it emerges from the later childhood stage and merges into adulthood.

According to G. R. Medinnus and R.C. Johnson, "Adolescence begins when signs of sexual maturity begin to occur in both physical and social development and ends when the individual has assumed adult roles and is concerned in most ways as an adult by his reference group."

A. T. Jersild observes, "Adolescence is that span of years during which boys and girls move from childhood to adulthood mentally, emotionally, socially and physically."

According to Dorthy Rogers, adolescence is "a process rather than a period, a process of achieving the attitudes and beliefs needed for effective participation in society."

The Hadow Report in England has described this stage as, "There is a tide which begins to rise in the veins of youth at the age of eleven or twelve. It is called by the name of adolescence. If the tide can be taken as flood, and a new voyage began in the stream and along the flow of its current, we think it will move on to fortune."

WHO defines adolescence both in terms of age (spanning the ages between 10 and 19 years) and in terms of a phase of life marked by special attributes. These attributes include:

- Rapid physical growth and development
- Physical, social and psychological maturity, but not all at the same time
- Sexual maturity and the onset of sexual activity
- Experimentation
- Development of adult mental processes and adult identity

- Transition from total socio-economic dependence to relative independence

To distinguish adolescents from other similar (and sometimes overlapping) age groupings, which however differ in these special characteristics, WHO has also defined youth and young people.

- Youth—persons between 15 and 24 years
- Young people—persons between 10 and 24 years.

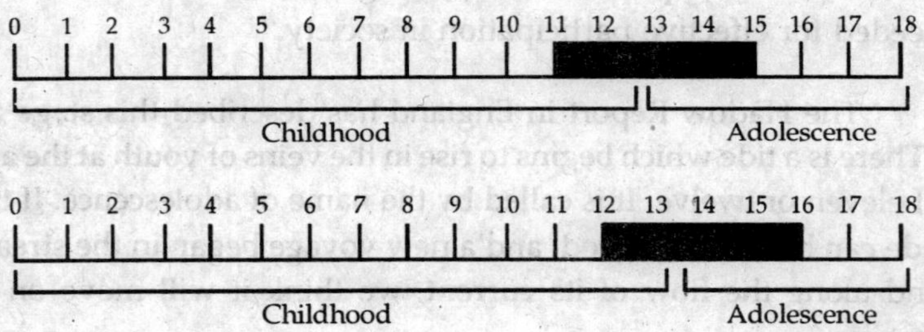

Fig. Puberty overlaps the end of childhood and the beginning of adolescence

Significant Features

1. The adolescent is a combination of opposites. Sometime he is an altruist and sometimes a miser. On the one hand, he behaves like a child in many ways and on the other hand he likes to be treated as an adult. He wants to have the privileges of adulthood but does not want to undertake its obligations and responsibilities.

2. The adolescent of lacks experience though he may exhibit a 'know-it-all' attitude.

3. He regards himself as more suited than the adults and grown- ups to frame rules, laws, codes and morals which will be just and true.

4. He is intensely emotional. He fluctuates between two extremes. He may be active and happy at one time and moody and dull at another.

5. He is seeking his own place in the life around him.

6. There is a strong tendency of self-assertion which is prominent owing to the new orientation which sets in life.

7. The adolescent wants to free himself from bondage. There is a tendency to revolt against authority.

8. The growth of intelligence reaches its maximum during this period.

9. The adolescent is extremely passionate for expressing his own opinions and appreciation.

10. A group of adolescents sets to practical work with Great zeal and works patiently.

11. He responds more readily to the influence of the teacher than of the parents.

12. There is unlimited admiration for some adult whom he considers to be outstanding. An adolescent is essentially a hero-worshipper.

13. There is interest in and emphasis on physical attractiveness and good grooming.

14. Girls are more interested in boys than boys are in girls; of course both are interested in the opposite sex.

15. In extreme cases, homosexuality (association with the same sex) is established.

16. An adolescent exhibits exuberant imagination. This period is characterized as a period of day-dreams.

17. He wants to form small groups or gangs.

Particular Requirements

Although in many respects, several needs of adolescence stage are similar to the needs of the other stages but they are quite different in the matter of intensity and forcefulness. The following chart illustrates the specific needs of the adolescence.

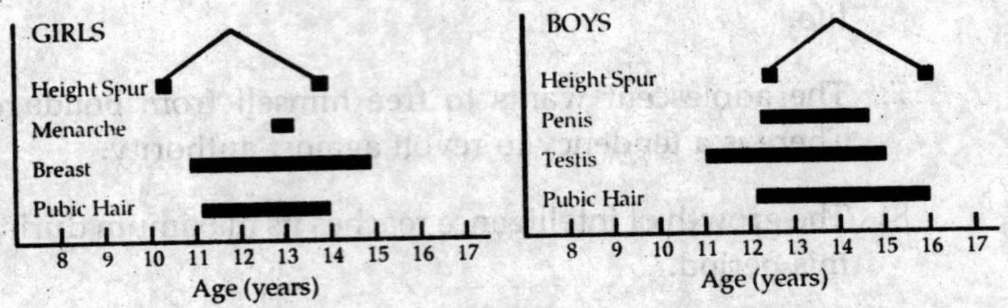

Fig. Pattern of Development of Secondary Sex Characteristics in Boys and Girls

Significant Specific Needs of the Adolescence

Physical Needs	*Social Needs*	*Emotional Needs*	*Intellectual Needs*	*Moral Needs*
1. Enough nutrition for physical develop-ment.	1. Acceptance in the society. 2. Suitable peers.	1. Heightened emotions. 2. Recogni-tion of self identification.	1. Heightened curiosity. 2. Indepen-dent	1. Search for values. 2. Equality thinking.
2. Channels for the uti-lisation of abundant energy.	3. Adjustment in the group and society. Equal 4. treatment	3. Arousal of sexual emotions. 4. Development of confidence.		
3. Acquaintance with body development aspects.				
4. Sex				
5. Security				

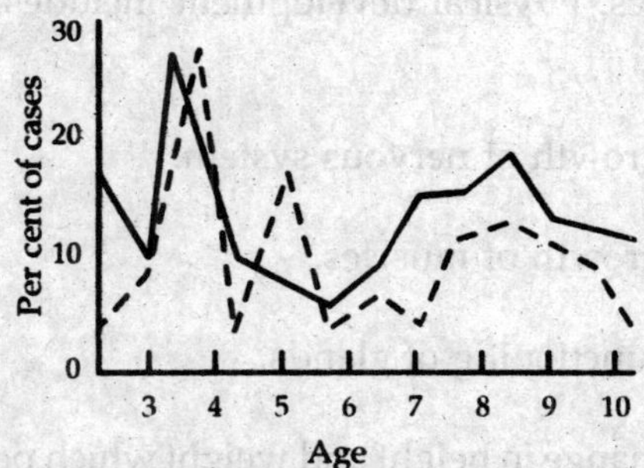

Fig. Irritability tends to increase early in puberty and then to decline

General Requirements

Hall has very emphatically observed, "A ton of knowledge, bought at the expense of an ounce of health which is the most ancient and precious form of wealth and worth costs more than its value." Similar views have been expressed by Carlyle when he writes, "We manufacture clever devils by the thousand because health is not the object of party politics." Great seer Swami Vivekananda has also stressed the importance of well-built bodies when he remarks, "What India needs today is not the Bhagwad Gita but the football field." Our schools must give due importance to this aspect of education. W.M. Ryburn remarked "We need in Indian Education-a general philosophy of physical education-we need a conception of education in which physical education takes its rightful place and in which its vital importance is recognised."

A properly directed physical development programme should result in health, happiness, efficiency and character.

Education on Health

Physical education relating to physical development is that field of education which deals with muscle activities and their related responses. Physical development includes the following aspects:

(i) It is growth of nervous system.

(ii) It is growth of muscles.

(iii) It is functioning of glands.

(iv) It is change in height and weight which people normally observe.

(v) It is development of sex.

Physical development and growth include the physical as well as psycho-motor changes in an individual. Physical development also includes qualities like courage, endurance and self-control.

Growth and Development

At the adolescent stage, marked changes take place in the following domains:

(i) Height and weight.

(ii) Bodily proportions.

(iii) Change in voice.

(iv) Increase in motor performance.

(v) Sexual changes.

Sexual Changes: Sexual changes are very prominent during the period of adolescence.

(a) *Primary Sex Features*

1. Boys develop their sex organs.

2. Sex glands-the gonads-start producing sperms. Boys may suffer from night dreams.

3. The growth of sex glands among girls is not visible. The first menstrual flow is indicative of their sexual growth.

(b) *Secondary Sex Features*: These features are not related to sex organs but are indicative of sexual maturation which is a part of adolescence. These are different in the case of males and females. Among the males the features are:

(a) Growth of public hair around the sex organ,

(b) Hair in the arm pit, legs, arms and the chest,

(c) The growth of beard, and

(d) The tone of the voice deepens.

Among the girls the growth of sex organs is not visible. Other changes are:

(a) The development of breasts,

(b) Increase in the width of lips,

(c) A rounded appearance of body and limbs,

(d) Growth of pubic hair, and

(e) A shrill voice.

Sexual identity includes the expression of sexual needs and feelings and the acceptance or rejection of sex.

Adolescence period is the onset of puberty. Puberty implies a series of physical changes that make the organism capable of reproduction.

Puberty leads to sexual activity, erotic fantasy, experimentation and masturbation.

The period of puberty is a difficult one for most of the adults.

Physical Growth and Development: A programme of physical growth and development is not confined to the playground but should pervade the class-room and in fact the entire school programme. Physical development in the class-room may take the following forms:

1. Direct instruction emphasising the necessity of having a good physique may be given.
2. Suggestions regarding the maintenance of good health are very helpful:
3. Emphasis on right postures should be laid.
4. Provision of good seating and lighting arrangements in the class-room, thereby impressing upon them the importance of studying under healthy surroundings should be made.
5. Providing ample opportunities to the children for physical activity should be given its due importance.
6. Medical examination of school children by the school doctor should be made at suitable intervals.
7. Physical exercise for every child should be compulsory in the school.

8. Various activities promoting physical development should be well planned and children should be encouraged to take part in these activities.

9. Activities like woodwork, spinning and weaving, book binding, gardening etc. may be introduced in the school as a group project. Such activities will lead to motor development as well as promote co-operation, and emotional adjustment among students.

10. At this stage students also have sexual development. It is necessary for us to impart them sex education.

11. Teachers should be conversant with norms of motor development of the child.

12. A variety of co-curricular activities should be introduced to provide outlets for the development of emotions and instincts which have a close link with physical growth and development.

Summary: Montaigne has very aptly remarked, "Physical education does neither train up the soul nor body, but the whole man." Froebel rightly stated, "Early education must deal directly with the physical development and influence the spiritual development through the exercise of senses."

Development of Mind and Sentiments

Emotional development is one of the major aspects of adolescence growth and development. Not only adolescent's physical growth and development is linked with his emotional make-up but his aesthetic, intellectual, moral and social development is also controlled by his emotional development. To keep one's emotions under control and be able to conceal them is considered a mark of strong and balanced personality. Therefore, adolescents must be trained to control their emotions and achieve a mental balance and stability which will lead to individual happiness and social efficiency.

The term emotion is derived from the Latin term, 'emovere' which means 'to stir,' 'to agitate,' 'to move' or 'to excite.'

Woodworth, by making use of this explanation defined emotion in the following way: "Emotiòn is a 'moved' or 'stirred up' state of an organism. It is a stirred up state of feeling-that is the way it appears to the individual himself. It is a disturbed muscular and glandular activity-that is the way it appears to an external observer."

Crow and Crow have defined emotion in the following way: An emotion 'is an affective experience that accompanies generalized inner adjustment and mental and psychological stirred up states in the individual, and that shows itself in his overt behaviour.'

According to Kimball Young, "Emotion is the aroused psychological state of the organism marked by increased bodily activity and strong feelings directed to some subject.

How Emotions Work? All of us observe a large number of persons and objects in the world. We have some feelings for them in our mental make-up. Sometimes our feelings become strong either in favour or against the object or individual or an occasion. This disturbs our mental balance. This disturbance is known as Emotion. It not only disturbs our mind, but the entire organism. It is expressed in various movements and expressions of body and it tries to adjust to face the situation.

Major Elements

1. We have emotions due to our intensity of feeling. The depth of intensity differs from individual to individual.

2. The expression of emotions is universal in nature, i.e., it is found in all living beings.

3. Every individual has his own outlet of emotions in his own way.

4. Our expressions of emotions are related to a person, object, idea or work.

5. Sometimes the expression of emotion leads to the loss of thinking power.

6. Our emotional expression is related to our instinct.

7. Our emotions persist for sometime and then they disappear.

8. Expression of emotions leads to changes in our behaviour.

9. Emotions rise abruptly but die slowly.

A suitable educational programme needs to be developed to enable the adolescents to control their emotions and obtain a mental balance and stability which will mark for individual happiness and social efficiency.

Emotions can be suitably modified by the following mechanisms:

(i) Redirection

(ii) Sublimation

(iii) Catharsis

(iv) Inhibition

Forcès at Work

Some of the important factors which disturb the emotions of adolescents in school are:

1. Lack of security.
2. Economic disparities.
3. Faulty methods of teaching.
4. Fearful atmosphere in school.
5. Emotionally unbalanced teacher.
6. Traditional concept of discipline.
7. Poor physical conditions in schools.
8. Disregard of individual differences.
9. Lack of co-curricular activities.
10. Lack of sex education.
11. Faulty examination system.
12. Faulty curriculum.

Role of the School and the Teacher in satisfying the Needs of the Emotional Development of the Adolescent. Following are the ways for meeting the needs of the adolescents:

1. Providing equal treatment irrespective of considerations of wealth, status or gender of the adolescents.
2. Using dynamic and progressive methods of teaching-learning.

3. Love and affection on the part of the teacher to be made the basis of work.

4. Balanced emotional behaviour of the teacher himself.

5. Creative and democratic classroom and school discipline.

6. Healthy physical conditions in the school.

7. Due regard to individual differences of the adolescents.

8. Due regard to the individuality of the adolescents.

9. Adequate provision for a variety of co-curricular activities.

10. Provision of sex education.

11. Rich and varied curriculum.

Societal Factors

Meaning of Social Development. Educators have defined social development in a number of ways.

Freeman and Showel observe, "Social development is the process of learning and conforming to group standards, mores and traditions and becoming imbued with a sense of oneness, inter-communication and co-operation."

H. E. Garret states, "Socialization or social development is the process whereby the biological individual is converted into a human person."

E.B. Hurlock thinks, "Social development means the attaining of maturity in social relationships."

Herbert Sorenson writes, "By social growth and development we mean increasing ability to get along well with oneself and others."

Thus social development refers to the process of development by which a child acquires the necessary attitudes, skills and values that make him an acceptable member of the group to which he belongs.

Characteristics of Social Development: Following are the important characteristics of social development during adolescence:

1. Adolescence is marked with too much sex consciousness resulting in sexual social relationships.
2. During adolescence loyalty becomes very much pronounced and adolescents are in a mood to sacrifice their selfish interests for the greater cause of the group, society and nation.
3. Adolescence stage is often marked with increased friendly relationships.
4. Emotional behaviour of the adolescent dominates his social characteristics and qualities.
5. There is too much diversity in the adolescents regarding their social interests.

To sum up, we may say that the adolescence is a period of maximum social awareness, increasing and intimate social relationships.

Factors Affecting Social Development: Important factors are given below:

Personal Factors: These include: (i) Physical strength and health, (ii) Level of intelligence, (iii) Emotional set up.

Environmental Factors: These comprise : (1) Family environment, (2) Social and physical environment of the school, (3) Peer group relationships and gang influence, (4) Community environment, (5) Social clubs, (6) Mass media.

According to T.P. Joseph, an adolescent wants a friend 'someone to be trusted', 'someone to talk', 'someone who is dependable.'

Harrocks and Benimoff observe regarding the peer influence on the adolescence as, "The peer group is the adolescent's real world, providing him a stage upon to try himself and others.'

School's Atmosphere

The function of the school has considerably changed in the rapidly changing civilizations. The traditional function of imparting the basic skills of the three R's is now no longer considered to be adequate to meet the present challenge. The present day school has also to perform some of the functions of the family. It must develop certain desirable social habits. It is through co-curricular and extra-curricular activities that the task of social development can be achieved more successfully. It is only the sympathetic understanding and sincere desire of the teacher to act positively in an un-prejudicial manner that can help.

Class in the Process of Socialization: Class provides innumerable opportunities to the adolescents to move and mix with other groups. This is the beginning of the social development of the child. Here children get many chances to mix without any distinction of caste, colour or creed. The teachers are expected to be vigilant to ensure that the students do not think in terms of untouchability, caste distinction and other prejudices.

Role of the Teacher in Social Development: A teacher can play a vital role in the social development of adolescent under his change. He exerts a great influence upon the development of the personality of the adolescent.

Following are the important suggestions for the social development of the adolescent:

1. Adolescents may be taken from time to time to public places like museums, courts and places of historical importance etc to observe social interaction.

2. People engaged in different economic activities or vocations may be invited to school for giving a description of what they do and how useful their work is to the nation. This will enable the adolescents to be acquainted with those around them in the society.

3. Work experience will enable the adolescents to have first hand experiences of the activities pursued in farms and factories.

4. Adolescents should be acquainted with the social events like the celebration of the birthdays of leaders.

5. The school programme should be full of numerous co-curricular and curricular activities in which adolescents meet, co-operate and learn from each other's personality.

6. The introduction of common school dress, common lunch, etc., in the schools will prevent adolescents of poor and lower middle classes from facing inferiority complex due to the ego of the children of the well-to-do families.

7. Teachers and parents may encourage the adolescent to mix in inter-caste and regional groups.

8. The teachers and the parents should respect the personality of adolescents.

9. The mechanism of praise and blame, reward and punishment should be carefully used for the social development of the adolescents.

10. Appropriate social education may be provided to the parents so that they understand the significance of the social development of the adolescents.

11. The teachers should demonstrate democratic outlook.

12. Community activities like camps, common meals, social services etc., should be frequently organised.

13. There should be a close co-operation between the teachers and parents on matters relating to the proper social development of the adolescents.

14. Adequate stress may be laid on group activities.

15. Stories depicting self-sacrifices made by great men for the cause of general good may be told to adolescents so that they are motivated to rise above petty gains and work for the betterment of the humanity.

16. The teachers should not show any discrimination. They must ensure a safe and healthy social development in which the adolescents may imbibe desirable values of freedom, equality, integrity, honesty, patriotism etc.

Concluding Remarks: The task of social development of the adolescent is not an easy one. The educational thinkers point out very emphatically that certain conditions in the learning-teaching situation must be created and made available in the school so that it may become an effective instrument of social development. These conditions are: (i) A democratic social climate in the school; (ii) Effective interpersonal relationships; (iii) Motivated learning situations; (iv) Group methods of teaching; (v) Social discipline; (vi) School-community inter-relationships; (vii) Student participation and involvement in the school management; (viii) A rich programme of co-curricular activities.

Mental Demands

Meaning of Intellectual Development: Mental or intellectual development implies the growth and development of those abilities and capacities of the adolescents that enable them to accomplish a task that needs complex cognitive abilities and enable them to adjust their behaviour to the ever changing environmental conditions. Cognitive abilities include abilities like sensation, perception, imagination, memory, reasoning, understanding, generalisation, interpretation, problem-solving and decision-making etc. In fact the most part of the school programmes relates to mental developments.

Characteristics of the Mental Development of the Adolescents: The adolescents learn to reason and seek answer to 'how' and 'why' of every thing rationally and scientifically. Power of critical thinking and observation is much developed. They are more creative and inquisitive. They are almost critical of everything. They develop a lot of imagination. This becomes the beginning of the artist, inventor, philosopher, poet and writer etc. in the adolescent. An adolescent tends to become day-dreamer.

Factors Affecting Intellectual Development: Intellectual development of the adolescent in the school is affected by curricular and co-curricular programme, teaching-learning environment, and the role of the teachers.

Measures for the Satisfaction of Intellectual Needs or Intellectual Development of the Adolescents: Among the important factors are:

(i) Provision of rich curriculum.

(ii) Provision of streaming.

(iii) Provision of varied activities like debates and discussions.

(iv) Provision of socialised teaching.

(v) Project work related to subjects.

(vi) Subject related educational tours.

(vii) Library and reading room facilities.

(viii) Problem solving teaching-learning.

(ix) Challenging questions.

(x) Exploratory activities.

Evolution of Morality

***Meaning of Moral Development*:** By morality we mean conformity to the moral code of the social group. The term comes from the Latin word 'mores', meaning manners., customs or folkways. To act in a moral way means to act in conformity to group standards of conduct. Morality also includes a sense of right or wrong-a behaviour which has to do with the conscience of the individual. Moral behaviour is learnt. Moral standards vary from group to group depending upon what has been accepted by the group as the socially approved behaviour. True morality comes from within the individual. It is internal in nature and not imposed by external authority. Immoral behaviour is that behaviour which is unfavourable to the group.

Bowley and others are of the view that a person of moral character has the following qualities: (i) Self-control, (ii) Reliability, (iii) Persistence in action, (iv) Industry, (v) Feeling of responsibility, (vi) Consciousness.

Several thinkers equate morality with character.

B. N. Jha has stated that character is "a mental factor of the individual, which determines his social behaviour. It is a mental organisation which lies at the back of all his connotations."

A person of character has the following characteristics in his behaviour:

(a) He is firm and not impulsive in his behaviour.

(b) He is not dominated by others in his actions.

(c) He has a strong sense of self-respect and is governed by his self-regarding sentiment.

(d) He is intelligent and cheerful in his behaviour.

(e) He is hard working and faces difficulties with courage and optimism.

(f) He is idealistic in his approach. His inner and outer self is dominated by some ideals.

Role of the School Environment: Behaviours and norms adopted in the immediate environment influence the adolescent in shaping his moral behaviour. It is very unfortunate that generally elders observe double standards of morality. We hardly practice what we preach. These double standards are observed by adolescents. It is, therefore, very essential that elders set high standards of morality.

Role of the Teacher: It has been stressed again and again that nothing can be more helpful in moulding the adolescent's moral behaviour than the teacher's own conduct. A teacher has to set a high standard of moral behaviour before the adolescent.

The school plays a very important role in the moral development of the adolescent. Through the organisation of various curricular and co-curricular activities, teachers can foster among children various moral qualities. In the teaching of different subjects like languages and social studies etc., teacher may stress moral qualities like love, sacrifice, self-control, truthfulness and uprightness, etc. Social service programmes should be undertaken on a large scale. Self government may be organised.

A comprehensive programme of guidance and counselling needs to be organised.

QUESTIONS

1. Explain the meaning of adolescence. State its main characteristics.

2. "A teacher should not only know his subject but the student as well" Discuss with reference to Indian adolescent students.

3. "Adolescence is the period of storm and stress". Comment on this statement.

4. "There is a tide which begins to rise at the age of eleven or twelve. It is called by the name of adolescence." Elucidate this statement.

5. Describe the significant specific needs of the adolescence. State how these needs can be met?

6. "The adolescence period is period of heightened emotion." Explain this statement and suggest measures for the development of emotions.

7. State the mechanisms of satisfying the emotional needs of the adolescents. What is the role of the school in this?

8. "The adolescent is faced with the identity crisis." Explain in this regard the need for social development as well as individual development of the adolescent.

9. Mention the intellectual and moral needs of the adolescents. State measures for the satisfaction of these needs.

14

Abnormal Kids

Meaning of a Slow Learning Child: In the words of Prof. T. N. Birkett, "A slow learning child is one whose capacity for learning the kind of material which is taught in the ordinary school is limited by some deficit in intellectual capacity. Limited intelligence, however, is the chief characteristic of the slow learning child.

Categories of Slow Learners: Following are the main categories of slow learners:

Children, whose capacity for education or training is limited by low intelligence, cover a fairly wide I.Q. range from approximately 40 to 80 or 90. However students whose I.Q. ranges between 50/55 and 85/90 are capable of benefiting from the kind of education which is offered within the normal school system. These may be subdivided into two groups:

(a) The Educable Mentally Retarded (I.Q. range 50 to 70).

(b) The Dull Normal (I.Q. range 70 to 85).

Students whose I.Q. range is between 35/40 and 50 are usually termed as Trainable Mentally Retarded. Provision for education of such children may be made outside the normal school system.

Significant Features

'Sullivan summarises the characteristics of these children as follows:

1. Short attention and concentration span.
2. Slow reaction time.
3. Limited ability to evaluate materials for relevancy.
4. Limited powers of self-direction.
5. Limited ability to work with abstractions and to generalize.
6. Slowness to form association between words and phrases.
7. Failure to recognise familiar elements in new information.
8. Habits of learning very slowly and forgetting very quickly.
9. Very local point of view.
10. Inability to set up and realize standard of workmanship.
11. Lack of originality and creativeness.
12. Lack of ability to analyse, to do problems solving or think critically.
13. Lack of ability to use higher mental processes.

Identification of Slow Learners: Following methods are usually employed to identify the slow learners.

1. Achievement Tests.
2. Intelligence Tests (Individual)
3. Intelligence Tests (Group)
4. Observation by teachers and others including the school counsellor.
5. Diagnostic Tests.

Facilities Available

Diagnostic Tests: Diagnostic tests should be employed in working with slow-learning children.

Curricula According to Interests: Courses and curricula should be selected by the students with the help of their counsellors on the basis of aptitude, interest and need.

Vocational Programmes: Vocational programmes should not be forced upon slow-learners. Such children do not always have the necessary aptitude to acquire vocational skill.

Special Classes: Special classes for slow-learning children should be organized. However, partial segregation is preferable to total segregation.

Partial Segregation: It has been stated, "These children should be included in the total school set-up, regularly participating in assembly programmes, organised play, and other activities enjoyed by all children."

Short Assignments: Assignments given to the students should be broken up into short and simple units. The problems should be clearly explained.

Drill Work: Sufficient drill work should be done.

Summaries: Frequent summaries of the important points of discussion should be used.

Praise: Slow-learners should be praised occasionally when they have done their assignments properly.

Proper Evaluation: Good set of tools should be used.

Close Supervision: Supervision should be very close.

Use of Audio-visual Aids: Auditory and visual aids facilitate their learning.

Opportunities for Creative Expression: Opportunities for expression of creativeness with their hands for slow-learning children should be provided.

Equality of Opportunity in Recreational Programmes: The whole programme of recreational activities, athletics, music, art, dramatics, etc., should be opened to all on an equal basis. Mones summarizes the advantages which the slow-learners will get as, "When these pupils are accepted in secondary schools, the school clubs, the bands, the patrols, the clean-up squads, the down and ground squads, the cafeteria patrols, athletics teams-are all possible instrumentalities of their education. If they can find educational outcome as a means of developing traits, attitudes, purposes, and satisfactions, that will give them a sense of integrated personality.

Remedial Teaching: Remedial teachers who meet such students twice a week may be appointed.

Co-operation of All Agencies: All agencies engaged in the children's welfare work should co-operate.

Exceptional Children

Meaning of Socially Disadvantaged Children: According to the National Policy on Education, the socially disadvantaged children are those children who belong to the following categories:

1. Scheduled Castes Children.
2. Scheduled Tribes Children.
3. Other Backward Classes (OBC's) Children.
4. Tribal Areas Children.

Statutory Safeguards

Article 15: Prohibition of Discrimination on grounds of religion, race, caste, sex or place of births sub-section (4) states, "Nothing in this Article or in clause (2) of Article 29 shall prevent the State from making any special provision for the advancement of any socially and educationally backward classes or for the Scheduled Castes and the Scheduled Tribes.

Article 46: It reads, "the State shall promote with special care the educational and economic interests of the weaker sections of the people, and in particular, of the Scheduled Castes and Scheduled Tribes and shall protect them from social injustice and all forms of exploitation.

Article 338: It makes provision for the appointment of a Special Officer for SCs and STs.

Article 390: It envisages the appointment of a Commission to investigate the conditions of the Backward classes.

Development of Learning

The Education Commission 1964-66, in chapter VI entitled 'Equalisation of Educational Opportunity and Social Change' very aptly observed, "One of the important social objectives of education is to equalise opportunity, enabling the backward or under-privileged classes and individuals to use education as a lever for the improvement of their conditions. Every society that values social justice and is anxious to improve the lot of the common man and cultivate all available talent must ensure progressive equality of opportunity to all sections of the population. This is the only guarantee for the building up of an egalitarian and humane society in which the exploitation of the weak is minimised." The Commission further stated, "The education of the backward classes in general and the tribal people in particular is a major programme of equalisation and of social and national integration. No expenditure is too great for this purpose." Alas! We have not paid heed to these words of wisdom. Non-implementation of this vital recommendation has led to disintegrative tendencies, hatred and strife.

Policies on education-the National Policy on Education, 1968, 1986 and modified Policy Formulation 1992-all stress upon speedy action for the promotion of education of the deprived sections.

The Identification: Children belonging to the four categories of sections of population as mentioned above automatically come under the category of socially disadvantaged children. Such children cannot be treated inferior on the basis of I.Q. They may not show the desired results on account of lack of facilities. They may have the potential to show good results provided ancillary facilities are made available to them.

Methods of Teaching

Preparatory Classes and Compensatory Instruction: Many children belonging to the Scheduled Castes and Scheduled Tribes come from a comparatively poor environment. They may not be neat or smart. Their usage of standard language may be poor. Their vocabulary is underdeveloped as compared to their peers. They may not have formed the initial mathematical concepts. On the other hand they may be more enthusiastic to learn. Because of the lack of a congenial home environment, these children may not be in a position to complete their home assignments. Their parents are usually employed as landless labour or in other manual or agrarian activities. Therefore, such children are not able to conceptualise their future as educated persons.

There is the need to conduct some preparatory classes for children coming from the Scheduled Castes and Scheduled Tribes. The primary objective of conducting such classes is to raise the school entry ability level of such children. This is also helpful in having a somewhat homogeneous grouping in the class. The classes may be conducted two to three weeks in advance of the general admissions. Classes may be conducted on healthy habits, personal and environmental cleanliness, eating habits etc. The children may also be helped in improving the pronunciation of the words and picking up standard language. For this, they may be motivated to participate in discussions, recitation and story-telling etc. Initial concepts of mathematics may also be introduced.

Remedial Instruction: Students coming from Scheduled Castes and Scheduled Tribes are also likely to be deficient in the scholastic areas. The school may provide some remedial education programmes. Adoption of instructional strategies, such as peer group learning, monitorial assistance, diagnostic testing and tutoring would help to improve the educational levels of these learners.

Provision of outdoor games and activities, co-curricular and work experience activities will also help in the retention of such children in the schools and create an interest in them for continuing schooling.

Monitoring of Programmes: A Standing Committee of the Central Advisory Board of Education (CABE) under the Chairmanship of Minister of Human Resource Development may be constituted to monitor and review implementation of all educational programmes for the deprived sections.

Incentive Schemes: Incentive schemes in operation for the promotion of the education of the deprived sections may be evaluated and appropriate strategies evolved in the light of such studies.

Role of the Teacher: Following are the important points which a teacher should take into account while teaching the students.

1. The teacher should take interest in meeting the needs of every type of child.

2. The teacher should ensure that his own behaviour and behaviour of students is free from bias.

3. The teacher must ensure that the interaction amongst the students is normal.

4. The teacher should understand the learning process in the context of characteristics of learners.

5. The teacher should appreciate that the special educational needs of the students reflect the special requirement of a learner calling for specific adjustment in regular educational programmes.

6. The teacher should keep in view that special needs can arise from physiological, intellectual, social and economical reasons.

7. The learner should be given importance as an individual rather than as a disabled or as a scheduled caste or scheduled tribe or a girl.

8. Educational adjustment has several dimensions like curriculum decision, class-room organisation, special teaching techniques and aids etc.

9. A teacher should be sensitive to the needs of socially disadvantaged learners.

10. The teacher should have a close link with parents to ensure regular attendance.

11. The teacher should make the parents aware of the special educational and otter facilities in the school and the neighbourhood and impress upon them to make use of them.

12. The teacher should find out specific areas of deficiency in learning.

13. The teacher should take all possible steps to develop self-concept and positive image among such learners.

14. Special incentives be provided to such students.

15. The teacher's own example in his behaviour towards students belonging to these castes is the most effective and powerful way to build up a congenial climate.

16. The school staff should ensure non-discrimination between the children of Scheduled Castes, Scheduled Tribes and other communities.

17. The school staff should avoid the use of the caste names or derogatory words while calling roll calls or naming children.

18. Teachers should provide equal opportunities to all the children to participate in the curricular and co-curricular activities of the school, including games.

19. Frequent meetings between the staff, school teachers and parents of Scheduled Castes and Scheduled Tribes children should be arranged. The details of the schemes for promoting education amongst Scheduled Castes and Scheduled Tribes should be explained to the parents at these meetings. It should be impressed upon them that they must continue the education of their children.

20. Special attention should be paid to motivating parents to educate girls.

21. Teachers should suggest to illiterate parents the advantages gained by attending functional literacy classes in the adult education centre.

Sentimental Aspects

There are learners with socio-emotional problems of varying intensity. Most of such learners can be identified and tackled with ordinary means and with a little more special attention.

It is observed that at some point in their school career, between 2 to 5 per cent of children become so disturbed socially and emotionally that they experience great difficulty to make desirable progress in studies and to adjust to the demands of the society in acceptable ways, unless they are given special guidance, either through psychological services or by placement in special units.

1. They are emotionally immature.
2. They do not possess a balanced self-regarding sentiment.
3. They are not able to face failures bravely.
4. They do not have a rational attitude towards sex.
5. They are over anxious.
6. They have inferiority complex.
7. They are withdrawn.
8. They find it difficult to adjust to and within the self.
9. They find it difficult to everyday social requirements and relationships.

Diagnosis of Problems

Projective Techniques: Following types of projective techniques may be used to find out the problems if they are very acute.

Causes Leading to Socio-emotional Problems

Family Circumstances	Personal	School	Teachers	Peers
	Some physical defect	1. Unattractive School Environment 2. Unsuitable curriculum or wrong choice of subjects 3. Lack of curricular activities 4. Lack of discipline	1. Unsympathetic teachers 2. Uninspiring methods of teaching.	1. Undesirable interests and activities of peers 2. Non-acceptance in the group

Economic	Psychological	Social
(i) Problem of unemployment or semi-employment (ii) Low economic status	(i) Over possessive parents (ii) Unrealic expectations from childrens (iii) Faulty home discipline (iv) Use of abusive language (v) Lack of role model:parents (vi) Unequal parental treatment to siblings (vii) Fear of insecurity	(i) Loss social status of the family (ii) Broken homes (iii) Fear of insecurity (iv) Some anti-social stigma to the family

(i) Play situations.

(ii) Story telling and story completion.

(iii) Incomplete sentence technique.

(iv) Original drawings and paintings.

(v) Free association and dream analysis.

(vi) Thematic Apperception Test (TAT)

2. Sociometric Tests.

3. Situational Tests.

4. Personal Documents

5. Parent's information.

6. Case conference.

The Syllabus

Following measures may be adopted to meet the socio-emotional needs of the learners:

1. Provision of normal curriculum.

2. Provision of normal co-curricular activities.

3. Sympathetic attitude of the teachers to understand the needs of such children.

4. Provision of an environment of security.

5. Protecting them for 'bully' students.

6. Career guidance.

7. Vocational guidance.

8. Counselling.

9. Cooperation of all agencies in the welfare of children.

It may be observed that usually the learners with socio-economic problems are at par with normal children in intelligence and capacity to learn. It is only their socio-emotional state of affairs that hinders their growth. They are not to be segregated from normal children.

Disabled Children

A physically handicapped child is one who is affected with a physical impairment that in any way limits or inhibits his participation in normal activities. Impairment implies abnormalities of body structure and appearance. It represents disturbance at the organ level. The impairment may be of a serious type or it may be slight in degree. For instance, a person hit by polio may be having only 15 per cent impairment on a certain part of the body or may have a total loss of mobility. Similarly, the visual defect may be total and it may not be restored. Other visual impairments may not pose serious problems and may be overcome with some aids.

Generally speaking, the physically handicapped may be classified as

1. The cripple.

2. The blind or near blind or partially blind.

3. The deaf or hard of hearing.

4. The language handicapped.

5. Cerebral palsied.

6. Orthopaedically handicapped.

In addition, the chronically ill children who may have health problems like heart defects or cardiac problems, epilepsy, allergies, diabetes, rheumatism, muscular and tuberculosis etc. also fall in the category of physically handicapped children.

Objectives of Education: Following are the chief objectives of the education of the physically handicapped children:

1. To reach the maximum level of effectiveness in school subjects.
2. To pursue those curricular matters that strategically determine effective living for specific type of handicapped school children.
3. To consider the mental as well as the physical hygiene of handicapped school children and to take suitable measures.
4. To develop rational patterns in the handicapped that will produce achievement in school and out of school.
5. To produce in the handicapped a desire to participate in the activities of non-handicapped persons.
6. To develop a realistic self-concept in handicapped children.

Case for Educating Them

The education of handicapped children has to be organized not merely on humanitarian grounds, but also on grounds of utility. Proper education generally enables a handicapped child to overcome largely his (or her) handicap, and makes him a useful citizen. Social justice also demands it. It has to be remembered that the Constitutional Directive on compulsory education includes handicapped children as well. Very little has been done in this field so far on account of several difficulties. There is much in the field that we could learn from the educationally advanced countries which in recent years has developed new methods and techniques, based on advances in science and medicine.

The primary task of education for a handicapped child is to prepare him for adjustment to a socio-cultural environment designed to meet the needs of the normal. It is essential, therefore, that the education of handicapped children should be an inseparable part of the general educational system. The differences lie in the methods employed to teach the child and the means the child uses to acquire information. These differences in methodology do not influence the goals of education. This form of education is, therefore referred to as 'special'.

Pattern of Education of the Physically Handicapped Children: Following are the usual patterns of education of the handicapped:

Integration: Integration implies that the education of the handicapped should be so organised that they freely mix up with normal children. This can be achieved in various ways:

(a) Having regular classes for all children.

(b) Deliberate architectural planning to allot space for regular classes and special classes separately but in the same building.

Partial Integration: The brightest and the handicapped children join with regular groups for carefully selected experiences, games and play.

Total Segregation: Under this system, the handicapped children are completely separated from other children. They are taught in special schools.

Fundamental Principles for the Education of the Physically Handicapped Children are :

1. Recognition of the handicap of the child by the teacher as early as possible.
2. Taking all available correctional measures.
3. Development of favourable attitude towards the child.
4. Diagnostic and remedial work by the guidance counsellor.

Effects of Physical Handicaps on Children: A physical handicap may directly or indirectly create the following types of problems for the children and their parents:

Academic Performance: (i) Physically handicapped children generally work below their capacity in several areas. (ii) Some of the physically handicapped children find it difficult to deal with abstract concepts.

Emotional Reactions or Social Relationships: (i) Quite a large number of physically handicapped children suffer from feelings of inferiority. (ii) They also suffer from feelings of failures. (iii) Normal children are at times not only indifferent to the handicapped but also make fun of them. Thus the handicapped children are withdrawn. (iv) Aggressive feelings and tensions get accumulated in the handicapped as they have fewer opportunities for expressing their feelings. (v) Sometimes parents', teachers' and students' attitudes may make a physically handicapped child feet 'unwanted' or 'rejected'. (vi) Handicapped children are more prone to accident and injury. Thus, they are not in a position to participate in several co-curricular activities. This also creates a feeling of disgust in them.

Difficulties Ahead

The handicapped child is unable to participate in desirable normal activities of the daily life. He, therefore, needs satisfying substitute interests.

The physically handicapped child also faces emotional problems as he feels that others have a low opinion about him and develops a feeling of hatred for others or of self-pity.

The physically handicapped child is not necessarily mentally deficient. In the majority of cases, he possesses normal intelligence. it is, therefore, very necessary that the mental powers of the handicapped are exploited fully and suitable opportunities provided to generate hope in life and compensate for his physical disability.

The major problem of the physically handicapped is to identify at the earliest the impairment and make arrangement for adequate adjustment. The handicap that is obvious at birth is easily identified. Other impairments take time to be identified.

Following points may be considered while providing educational facilities for the handicapped children:

1. *Normal Curriculum:* The majority of the physically handicapped children are just normal except for their physical handicap. Such children should be provided all those educational activities which are meant for the normal children, keeping in mind, of course, their physical disability.

2. *Special Classes:* For the partially sighted students, special classes may be organised.

3. *Special Equipment and Methods of Teaching:* Blind children need special equipment and medium for their education. They also need special teaching, methods like the following.

   (i) For the teaching of mathematics, stress is laid on mental work.

   (ii) Embossed diagrams are used in geometry.

(iii) Relief maps and globes may be used for the study of geography.

4. *Special Subjects:* (i) Modelling may be substituted for drawing and painting. Blind children derive pleasure from working with clay and plasticine.

   (ii) Dramatic art may be cultivated.

   (iii) Music may be given adequate encouragement.

5. *Physical Education:* Corrective posture work, gymnastics, running, wrestling and sports etc. should form part of the physical education programme.

6. *Vocational Education and Handicrafts:* A variety of handicrafts may be taught to the physically handicapped.

7. *Therapeutic Assistance:* Special programmes in the form of speech-therapy, physio-therapy, play therapy should be undertaken to help physically handicapped children make the correct and maximum use of whatever abilities and capacities they possess.

8. *Education for Living in Society with Handicap:* Handicapped children have to live in a world of normal people. They, therefore, should be provided all types of education, training and guidance which enable them to face their disability realistically and make suitable adjustments accordingly and live without bitterness and meet unpleasant situations boldly.

Provisions for Learning

Prof. K. C. Panda (2000) mentions the following types of education services to be provided to the exceptional children, depending upon the nature and intensity of the handicap.

1. Regular class-room with minor in-class support.
2. Regular class-room with weekly 'itinerant' teacher.
3. Regular class-room with daily resource room supplemental programming.
4. Resource room with several hours of daily regular class-room instruction and non-instructional activities.
5. Regular room with limited hours of weekly non-instructional activities with regular classmates.
6. Self-contained special class-room.
7. Special day school.
8. Homebound or hospitalization.
9. Residential.

Various Methods

Integration implies the existence of following elements:

1. Sharing the same class-room, resources and opportunities by the handicapped as well as the regular students.
2. Providing special services needed for the exceptional (handicapped) students in the regular schools.
3. Having handicapped (disabled) students follow the same schedule as normal (non-disabled) students.
4. Involving disabled students in several academic courses and co-curricular activities including art, field trips, music and exercises etc.

5. Enabling disabled students to use library, playground and other facilities at the same time as normal students use.

6. Encouraging friendly relation between disabled and normal students.

7. Arranging for disabled students to receive their education in the regular environment of the community when feasible.

8. Advising all students to understand the limitations of the disabled students and accept human differences.

9. Enrolling children with disabilities in the same schools they would have attended if they were not disabled.

10. Attending to parents concern about their disabled children seriously.

11. Providing an appropriate individualised programme.

To sum up; integration approach is a particular orientation towards providing education to the majority of the handicapped children.

It is estimated that nearly 10 per cent of handicapped students receive most of their education in regular schools. An additional 20 to 25 per cent students are enrolled in special classes located in the same building.

1. He should learn about the students handicapping conditions.

2. He should understand the common characteristics of the handicapped children.

3. He should appreciate the common difficulties that the handicapped children experience.

4. He should learn about the special materials the handicapped children use, e.g., pushing a wheel chair up or down stairs etc.

5. He should meet the special education teacher to chalk out appropriate strategies to meet the special needs of the handicapped children.

6. He should accept appropriate behaviour in order to stimulate continuous effort.

7. He should seek the co-operation of normal students to improve the psychological climate of the class so that the disabled students are encouraged to put in their best.

Role of the Teacher

1. He should identify the academic or physical adaptations needed in the class-room for the disabled students.

2. He should develop programmes to prepare disabled students for entry into regular classes.

3. He should involve parents in setting appropriate goals for their students.

4. He should prepare a variety of activities that will involve the entire class in grouping patterns that are flexible.

5. He should design a variety of alternative teaching strategies.

6. He should prepare a flexible time schedule for learning as well as physical and social needs of each student.

7. He should fully co-operate with the regular teacher.

Essential Tools

1. Braille writer for the teacher.
2. Braille books.
3. Braille slates and stylus for students.
4. Abacus for the teaching of mathematics.
5. Braille sheets of paper.
6. Low vision aids.
7. Large print books.
8. Braille bulletin boards.
9. Equipment for teaching industrial and other arts.
10. Tape-recorders and cassettes.
11. Braille type duplicating machines.
12. Teaching aids.
13. Class-room furniture.

In the special programmes the handicapped children are isolated from the normal ones and placed in special institutions. In the educationally advanced countries, however, a great deal of stress is now being laid on the integration of handicapped children into the regular school programmes. This has two important advantages: reduction of costs and promoting mutual understanding between handicapped and the non-handicapped children. This has also its disadvantages. For instance, many handicapped children find it psychologically disturbing to be placed in an ordinary school.

To develop integrated programmes adequately, attention will have to be paid to the following matters:

1. The preparation of teacher will need emphasis and attention. This will necessitate a considerable increase in the capacity of existing training institutions and the establishment of new ones.

2. It is necessary to co-ordinate the efforts of different agencies working in the field.

3. It is also necessary to develop adequate research in the problems of integrated programme.

Statutory Provisions: With the coming into force of the 'Persons with Disabilities Act, 1955, there is now a statutory responsibility of the Central, State and Local Governments in India, to provide free education in an appropriate environment to all disabled children upto the age of 18 years.

Centrally sponsored Scheme for the Disabled Students: The Department of Education, Ministry of Human Resource Development, Government of India has been implementing the Scheme for Integrated Education of Disabled Children (IEDC) since 1974.

Significant Elements

Following are the important features of the scheme:

1. The scheme includes pre-school training for disabled children and counselling for their parents.

2. Cent per cent financial assistance is provided as per prescribed norms for facilities for disabled children. This covers cost of books and stationery, uniforms, transport and escort allowance for severely handicapped children, reader allowance for blind children and equip-

ment which includes educational aids and assistive services.

3. The scheme also provides assistance to non-governmental Organisations (NGOs), engaged in the field of integrated education.

4. *Polytechnics:* Two polytechnics for disabled students have been set up at Mysore and Kanpur.

5. *Curriculum for Teacher Training:* The NOTE (National Council for Teacher Education) has developed curriculum for teacher training and orientation so that both general teachers as well as resource teachers are trained to handle disabled children.

6. *NCERT Programmes:* The NCERT has also taken up several programmes in this area.

7. *India-Australia Training and Capacity Building Project (IACBP):* The programme includes:

   (i) Intensive training of 10 teacher educators in Australia to turn them into Master Trainers.

   (ii) Further training by the Master Trainers along with three Australian experts in various places in India.

   (iii) A study tour of 6-10 Officers of the Government of India and State Governments as well as educational institution to have first hand experience in Australia in the field of IEDC.

   (iv) Technological exchange programme in this field.

Coverage: The IEDC scheme is being operated in 26 States/UTs through nearly 15,000 schools and over 55,000 children are being benefited under this scheme.

Teaching the Blind

Children whose vision is so impaired that they can see objects at a distance of 20 ft. which a normal eye can see at a distance of 200 ft. are legally blind. The totally blind children read Braille. Blindness affects the life of the individual in the physical, mental, social, educational and vocational aspects.

Usually for blind children, going to school implies admission to a residential school for the blind (Braille classes). Of late some attempts have been made to integrate them with the normal children by admitting to them to normal schools but the coverage of blind population of the students in this respect is not significant. A blind school aims at assisting the blind child, through the use of special methods and aids, in his adjustment to the world in which he has to live as an adult.

Schools for the blind usually provide for activities such as dancing, scouting, and dramatics.

Special equipment and methods of teaching are employed for the education of the blind.

Particular attention is given to practice on type writer because it permits written communication with the seeing.

(i) As many as concrete experiences as possible, either by letting them observe the object as such or by providing replicas, may be provided to the blind students.

(ii) Blind children at least during the primary classes, should be taught by a unit plan of instruction.

(iii) Topics of the units may consist of everyday experiences such as provision shops, post offices etc.

(iv) Self-activity should be made an integral part of the education of the blind.

The Handicap

Several children do not have sufficient vision. They find it difficult to read the writing on the blackboard clearly. There are partially sighted children also. Some can read only large print. Visual impairment results in several learning problems. Children with visual impairments may have enormous capacity to work. However, this depends upon the nature of the impairment.

Identification of Children with Visual Impairments: It is very necessary to identify each category of children with visual impairments. Medical treatment may become necessary in some cases. Parents also need to be informed.

Children with visual impairment may be identified from the following:

1. Having watery eyes.
2. Rubbing eyes frequently.
3. Reddening of eyes frequently.
4. Covering one eye and titling the head forward.
5. Holding objects and books close to the eyes.
6. Asking help from others when taking notes from the blackboard.
7. Blinking frequently-squinting eyelids together.
8. Complaining about headache following close eye work.
9. Bumpening into people or objects.
10. Skipping words or lines while reading.
11. Having poor eye-hand coordination.

12. Moving head forward and backward while looking at distant objects.

Visual handicap is defined in terms of visual acuity, field of vision and visual efficiency. Snellen chart, developed by Herbart Snellen, a Dutch doctor, is used to assess the visual ability. The chart starts with a big 'E' which a normal eye can at a distance of 200 ft.

Visual acuity is not the only criteria for measuring acquision of basic skills. Following tests are used for measuring intellectual abilities.

1. The Blind Learning Aptitude Test.
2. The Haptic Intelligence Scale for the Adult Blind.

Role of Teacher

1. Children with visual impairment may be seated in the front rows so that they can read the writing on the blackboard without any difficulty or pressure.

2. Such children may be given training in listening with comprehension.

3. Books with bold letters may be provided to such children.

4. Radio and T.V. broadcasts may be arranged for to such children.

5. Efforts may be made to procure cassettes in different curricular areas. State Institutes of Education or State Councils of Educational Research and Training or District Institutes of Education and Training or Centres or Institutes of Educational Technology may be approached for this purpose.

6. Blind children need Braille script books.

7. School doctor may be consulted from time to time.

8. Co-operation of the parents be sought in the follow-up work.

Procedure for Distinction

Listening plays an important role in academic learning. Hearing problems interfere with the achievement of the students. It is, therefore, desirable to identify such children and take steps to meet their educational needs. Such children may be identified as under:

- Some observable deformity of the ear or ears.
- Frequent complaints of pain in ears.
- Frequent scratching of ears.
- Frequent discharge from ears.
- Turning head on one side to hear better.
- Frequent requests to teachers to repeat questions and directions etc.
- Making errors in taking dictation or notes.
- Displaying speech difficulty.

Guidelines

1. Children with hearing problems may be given front seats.

2. While speaking, the teacher may use a reasonable level of pitch.

3. The teacher should avoid mumbling.

4. The teacher should avoid speaking too fast.

5. Students should be encouraged to speak gradually and steadily.

6. Other students of the class may be asked to give due consideration to such students.

7. A lot of visual aids may be used in the class-room.

8. Some of the hearing problems can be corrected through drill and practice.

9. Medical help may be needed if speech disorder is due to an organic defect in speech mechanism.

Identification: Such children can be easily identified as their impairment is usually observable.

1. Deformity may be observable in fingers, hands, legs, neck or waist etc.

2. Showing difficulty in sitting, standing and walking.

3. Showing difficulty in picking up and holding objects and putting them on the ground.

4. Frequently complaining of pains in the joints.

5. Experiencing difficulty in holding the pen to write.

6. Walking with jerks.

7. Experiencing difficulty in the movement of limbs.

8. Amputated limbs.

Locomotor Impairment

1. The teacher should accept such children as he accepts other children.

2. The teacher should avoid sarcasm for the disability of the child.

3. Other children should be advised to appreciate the disability and show due regard to such children. They should be made to understand the disability.

4. Seating arrangement in the class may be adjusted to the specific needs of such students.

5. Reasonable opportunities for participation in recreational activities, sports and games should be provided to these children.

6. Remedial teaching may also be arranged for them.

QUESTIONS

1. Explain the term exceptional children. Classify such children. Why should their needs be attended to?

2. Identify the gifted children. What types of educational provisions in terms of curriculum, methods of teaching and evaluation should be made?

3. How will you arrange for the education of the gifted children? What will be the special features of this programme?

4. Who is an under-achiever child? Suggest a suitable educational problem for under-achiever children.

5. Who is a slow-learner child? How would you identify him? What type of educational programmes should be prepared?

6. Explain the concept socially disadvantaged child. Or why is it necessary to meet his demands? Suggest suitable educational programmes to meet his demands.

7. Who are slow learners with socio-emotional problems? What are the causes leading to these problems? What curriculum provisions, methods of teaching would you make for meeting their needs?

8. Distinguish between an under-achiever and a slow learner child. Suggest educational programmes.

9. "Under-achievement is a major problem in schools today." Discuss the causes responsible for this. What in your opinion are the special provisions a school should make for the under-achievers?

10. What do you mean by exceptional children? What are the educational needs of exceptional children?

11. "Under-achievement is a manifestation of a hidden psychological problem." Accepting the position stated above, how can you as a teacher help an under-achiever realize his/her potential?

12. Explain the meaning of physically handicapped children. Why should their education receive attention?

13. State the problems related to the education of the physically handicapped children. Suggest suitable educational problems for them.

14. Explain various approaches *i.e.,* Integration/mainstreaming and special approach to the education of the physically handicapped children. State their merits and demerits.

15. What do you understand by integration/mainstreaming approach to the education of the physically handicapped children? State the role of the teacher when integrated system of education comes into operation.

16. Write brief notes on (i) Centrally sponsored scheme for the disabled children, (ii) Education of the Blind.

17. State the main types of physical impairments and the educational programmes for them.

18. Write notes on: (i) Education of children with physical impairment. (ii) Education of children with hearing and speech impairment, (iii) Education of children with locomotor impairments.

15

Disabled Taughts

Exceptional children refer to those children whose needs are very different from the majority of the children in the society and who differ from the majority in their emotional, mental, physical and social characteristics. Such children cannot develop themselves under normal classroom conditions and special environment has to be created for them.

In the words of W. M. Crunchshank, "An exceptional child is he who deviates, physically, intellectually, emotionally and socially so marked from normal growth and development that he cannot be benefited from a regular class-room programme and needs special treatment in school."

According to Kirk, "An exceptional child is one who deviates from normal or average child in mental, physical and social characteristics to such an extent that he requires a modification of school practices or special educational services or supplementary instruction in order to develop to his maximum capacity."

Crow and Crow have observed, "The term a typical or exceptional is applied to a trait or to a person possessing the trait if the extent of deviation from normal possession of that trait is so great that because of it the individual warrants and receives special attention from his fellows and his behaviour responses and activities are thereby affected."

Significant Features

1. He is markedly different from the normal child.
2. The difference may be emotional, mental, physical or social.
3. An exceptional child needs a special environment.
4. The special environment may be provided in the normal system of schooling or in a special school. In case of some categories of exceptional children, only special schools can meet their needs.

Broad Classification of Exceptional Children

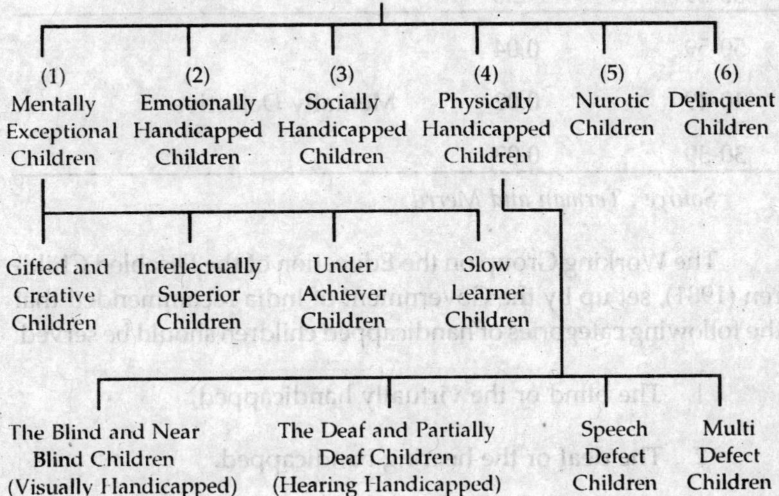

Categorisation of Children on Intelligence Quotient (IQ) on Stanford Revision (USA)

IQ	Percent	Classification
160-169	0.3	
150-159	0.2	Very Superior/Gifted/Creative
140-149	1.1	
130-139	3.1	
120-129	8.2	Superior/High Average
110-119	18.1	
100-109	23.5	Average
90-99	23.0	
80-89	14.0	Low Average
70-79	5.6	Borderline Defective
60-69	2.0	
50-59	0.04	
40-49	0.02	Mentally Defective
30-39	0.03	

Source : Terman and Merril

The Working Group on the Education of the Disabled Children (1981), set up by the Government of India recommended that the following categories of handicapped children should be served:

1. The blind or the virtually handicapped.
2. The deaf or the hearing handicapped.
3. The orthopaedically handicapped.

4. The educable and trainable mentally retarded.

5. The cerebral palsied.

6. The neurologically handicapped, including epileptic.

7. Children with speech and language disorders.

Dr. V. V. Karnath's Classification of Indian Children

I. Q.	*Category*
140 and above	Near genius or Genius
130-139.9	Extraordinary
120-129.9	Very superior
110-119.9	Superior
99-109.9	Average or Normal
80-98.9	Backward
70-79.9	Very Backward
60-69.9	Borderline
40-59.9	Moron
20-39.9	Imbecile
Below 20	Idiot

Case for Educating Them

Following are the important considerations for making provision for the education of the gifted children:

1. Regular classes for normal children do not meet the needs of exceptional children. Hence they need separate classes.

2. Under normal conditions, exceptional children may develop behaviour problems.

3. The principle of equalisation of educational opportunities highlights that exceptional children should have opportunities to develop themselves to the maximum.

4. Proper opportunities will make them economically self-sufficient.

5. Special categories of children like deaf, dumb, blind, etc. require special school's learning.

Creative Kids

Meaning of the Gifted and the Creative: In simple language a gifted child is one who can make outstanding contribution in any area of national life. Giftedness generally speaking includes actual or potential qualities of creativity, emotional stability and social adaptability. Following are the important definitions of gifted children:

James Drever is of the view that "children possessing high intellectual ability, generally or in a particular field are gifted children."

Terman and Oden state, "Gifted children are far above the average in physique, social adjustment, personality traits, school achievement, play, information and versality of interests."

In the words of Hillingworth, "By a gifted child we mean one who is far more educable than the generality of children are. The greater educability may lie along the lines of one of the arts, as in music or drawing, it may lie in the sphere of mechanical aptitude, or it may consist in surpassing power to achieve literacy and abstract knowledge."

Paul Witty states, "Those whose performance in a worthwhile human endeavour is constantly remarkable as well as those who are academically superior."

R. J. Havighurst observes, "Gifted children are those individuals from kindergarten to high school age who show unusual promise in some socially useful area and whose talent might be stimulated."

Broadly speaking 'gifted children' should include all those children who give promise of creativity of a high order in any worthwhile line of human endeavour. They have superior ability that can make them contribute to the quality of living in society. Therefore, we include not only the intellectually gifted but also those who show promise in music, the graphic arts, creative writing, dramatics, mechanical skills and social leadership. Nevertheless, here we are dealing with children having gifted intellectual ability.

While discussing education of the gifted, the creative and the intellectually superior, it may be observed, that in essence, all these three types of children may be placed in the same category. In practice, it is very difficult to formulate separate policies. These categories differ in degrees only and not in kind.

Wide Variety : In the words of Hollingworth, "By a gifted child we mean one who is far more educable than the generality of children are. The greater educability may lie along the lines of one of the arts, as in music or drawing, it may lie in the sphere of mechanical aptitude, or it may consist in surpassing power to achieve literacy and abstract knowledge." Paul Witty, Ruth Strang, Havighurst and many others think that the term gifted children should include all those children who give promise of creativity of a high order in any worthwhile line of human endeavour. They have superior ability that can make them contribute to the quality of living in society. Therefore, we include not only the intellectually gifted but also those who show promise in music, the graphic arts, creative writing, dramatics, mechanical skills and social leadership.

Special Qualities

1. Very high I.Q.
2. Ability to apply knowledge to unfamiliar situations.
3. Ability for abstract and symbolic thinking.
3. Annoyance with details.
4. Attention span long for age.
5. Curiosity indicated by asking serious questions.
6. Dislike of rigid time schedule.
7. Energy level (physical and intellectual) very high.
8. Exposure needed limited and fewer repetitions to learn.
9. Intense interest in one area.
10. Knowing a lot about things of which other students are unaware.
11. Learning commensurate with that expected of older students, often start of reading at an earlier than average age.
12. Memory very extraordinary.
13. Often thinking faster than they write (can result in sloppy work).
14. Spontaneous and diverse interests.
15. Standards and goals unusually high.
16. Vocabulary very high and mature expressive ability enormous.

Those students who show some or several of the characteristics mentioned above are referred to by many adjectives such as 'genius', 'gifted' and 'talented' etc.

Categories of Gifted Children: Usually following are considered as the categories of the gifted on the basis of Intelligence Quotient (I.Q). (Stanford Revision-USA).

I. Q.	*Percent of Population*
160-169	0.3%
150-159	0.2%
140-149	1.1%
130-139	3.1%
120-129	8.2%

On the basis of Dr. V.V. Kamat's classification, 120 I.Q. may be considered as the lower limit of giftedness.

Usually it is said that nearly 2 to 3 per cent of the population may be placed under the category of the gifted children.

Special Attention on the Education: It is of great importance to bring out the hidden 'gem-like' potentialities in pupils not only for the interest of such students but for the interest of the humanity as a whole. The following lines fully illustrate this:

"For many a gem of purest ray serene. The dark unfathomed caves of the ocean bear. Full many a flower is born to flouriest unseen. And waste its sweetness on the desert air."

We are interested in the gifted on account of the following considerations:

1. There is a limited pool of ability and special talent in every country. This must be identified and developed to save it from loss.

2. The gifted individuals have played an important role in the preservation and advancement of civilization.

3. Values of democracy will be realized in the fullest sense when we recognize the full range of ability within our total population.

4. Many gifted children languish in educational institutions simply because they are not aware of their 'gifts' and the school programmes do not provide them enough motivation and challenge.

5. We need leaders for our business, education, research and government etc. These leaders are provided by this class of gifted children.

***Adjustment Problems*:** A gifted child may become a problem for the parents and the teacher if he is not handled properly. Following problems may arise:

1. When he is not properly guided, he utilises his superior intelligence in mischief, indiscipline, gang-formation and revolts against his elders. He becomes a nuisance.

2. Because of lack of opportunities and lack of recognition, he sometimes develops inferiority complex.

3. Too much of recognition or applauses by the parent or teacher also develop in him boastful conceit.

4. There is lack of stimulation for him in the subjects of his interests when he does not get opportunities of progressing according to his own pace.

5. He revolts against the parents and teachers when they do not recognise him, and sometimes creates mischief in order to catch their attention or to show his superiority.

***Identification*:** For identifying the gifted children, following techniques are employed:

1. Intelligence Tests (Individual)

2. Intelligence Tests (Group)

3. Achievements Tests and Batteries.

4. Observations by Teachers and others.

It may be observed that reliance should not be made only on one technique.

Enrichment Programmes: Enrichment consists in giving the gifted child the opportunity to go deeper or to range more widely than the average child in his intellectual, social and artistic experience. Such a programme may be characterized by (1) emphasis upon the creative or the experimental; (2) emphasis on the skill of investigation and learning; (3) independent work, stressing initiative and originality; (4) high standard of accomplishment; (5) co-operative planning and activity that provides opportunity for leadership training and experiences in social adjustment; (6) individual attention given by teacher to student; (7) first-hand experiences; (8) flexibility of organization and procedure; (9) extensive reading; and (10) concern with community responsibility.

The Triple Track Plan: In this type of learning plan, there are three tracks:

(a) The first is for the dull child who may cover it in a longer duration of time.

(b) The second one is for the average child who covers it in an average period of time.

(c) The third is for the child of superior intelligence. He covers the entire work in a shorter period of time due to his intelligence, efforts and initiative.

Such a system has been adopted in most of the schools in the United States.

Rapid Promotion: Gifted children should be promoted to the next higher grade as soon as they achieve the target of a particular grade.

Special Schools: In some countries special schools are organised for gifted children. Some educationists have pointed out some limitations in organising such schools.

Acceleration: Acceleration offers opportunity for a gifted pupil to move at a pace appropriate to his ability and maturity and to complete an educational programme in less than the ordinary amount of time. It involves advancing the gifted child rapidly from grade to grade in school so that he enters college earlier than others.

Segregation or Ability Grouping: The gifted pupils may be placed in special groups for all or part of the school day. The purpose of ability grouping is usually to provide for enrichment of children's experiences in both depth and breadth, and to permit the children to stimulate one another.

Summer Programmes: Special cultural and educational programmes may be organised for gifted children during the summer season. This approach is being tried in U.S.A. and in a limited measure in our country as well.

Scholarships: Gifted children should be given special scholarships for pursuing their studies. This will lead the gifted child in the right direction.

Special Visits: Groups of gifted children may formally visit places of historical, industrial, geographical and economic interest. This would enable them to understand and appreciate important places of social value also.

Contact with Eminent Persons: Gifted children may show interest in any special field of activities. Their meetings may be fixed up with persons of eminence of that particular field.

Vocational and Personal Guidance and Counselling: The gifted children should receive proper guidance in all areas of life so that their total development is of an optimum level.

The role of the counsellor in the promotion of talent can be very important. The counsellor with his detailed knowledge of each talented student is in a unique position to formulate a programme of enrichment for him and to suggest the necessary modifications in the curricular and extra-curricular requirements. Where special counsellors are not available, this task will fall on the teachers. It will, therefore, be necessary to train teachers for this responsibility through in-service seminars and special courses. It should be impressed on them that the class-room atmosphere and the attitudes of teachers is of considerable importance. In a social and educational set-up like ours where the relationship between the teacher and the taught is still largely authoritarian, the general tendency is to suppress any urges and interests that deviate from the class norm. The first requirement for the promotion of talent, therefore, is for the teachers to create an atmosphere of free expression in the class-room and to provide opportunities for creative work.

Summary: We may remember these words of wisdom said by AX Whitehead, "Any race which does not value trained intelligence is doomed."

The Deprived Lot

We usually hear parents and teachers making such remarks as "Sohan is bright and intelligent. We do not understand why he gets so poor marks," or "Lata could do much better if she really tried and took an interest in her studies. She has the ability." Such remarks indicate that most of us are aware of the fact that many school children work far below of their expected level of intellectual development. If such situations are not corrected, students gradually lose interest in academic work and may generally drop-out from school. They become a liability not only to themselves and their parents but also to the society. It is, therefore, very necessary to identify under-achievers early. We must help them to progress in their work.

***Meaning and Characteristics of the Under-achiever Children*:** There is no set definition of the under-achiever children. Several writers and experts do not refer to under-achiever children as a special category of children. They club this category with the slow learning children. Some authors and experts use terms like mentally retarded children and backward children. Hence there is a lot of confusion regarding the use of terms. An underachiever child generally speaking is one whose achievement falls below the level of his natural abilities.

Some experts regard an under-achiever child one who compared with other children of the same chronological age shows marked educational deficiency. The generally accepted meaning of under-achievement implies that a student's academic achievement is below on certain norm or standard which is expected of him on the basis of his potential ability. This means that we consider a student an under-achiever when his achievement is not at par with his intelligence.

From a broader point of view, an under-achiever child is one who has high potential in fields other than intellectual also but he is not using his potential adequately.

According to John Holt, an under-achiever child fails to develop more than a tiny part of the tremendous capacity for learning, understanding and creating with which they was born.

(i) An under-achiever with superior intelligence but having average performance in school subjects.

(ii) An under-achiever with average intelligence but whose achievements are significantly below a reasonable level of age and who does not appear to be making much progress.

(iii) The dull and the slow learner who is not working up to his capacity and is capable of improvement.

(iv) One who is highly creative and talented in fields other than intellectual but has not been able to develop his creative powers and talents to the full.

(v) An under-achiever who has lived under deprived, restricted and un-stimulating conditions for prolonged periods during early childhood and therefore, shows low scores on an intelligence test. His achievement is usually unsatisfactory in the school situation.

Unhealthy School and Class-room Environment: This refers to the following:

1. Absence of social security.
2. Absence of emotional security.
3. Faulty curriculum.
4. Ineffective and uninspiring methods of teaching.
5. Authoritative and unsympathetic attitude of the teacher.
6. Faulty class-room organisation.
7. Lack of co-curricular activities.
8. Lack of equipment.
9. Overcrowded classes.
10. Lack of effective guidance and counselling.

Factors Responsible for Under-achievement

(1) *Physical Factors*	(2) *Intellectual Factors*	(3) *Emotional Factors*	(4) *Factors Relating to Home*	(5) *Factors Relating to the Community*	(6) *Factors in School*
1. Poor physique of the child. 2. General disability of the child. 3. Chronic illness 4. Lack of stamina etc. These present a child from doing his best in the academic field.	1. Weakness in some specific area of cognitive functioning. 2. Poor power of attention and concentration. 3. Lack of aptitude for a particular subject. 4. Lack of curiosity 5. Lack of eagerness to learn	1. Emotional insecurity Emotional 2. immaturity.	1. Unfavourable physical conditions. 2. Un favourable parental relations leading to tension and worries. 3. Inconsistent disciplinary methods. 4. Siblings relations and perental fondness for some children and indifference to others. 5. Lack of encouragement by parents to child's school work. 6. Frequent transfer of parents.	1. Neighbourhood social group norms. Peer influence	Discussed separately

The Distinction

1. Use of intelligence tests.
2. Achievement tests.
3. Observation.
4. Parents view.
5. Socio-metric techniques.
6. Participation in co-curricular activities.

The Assessment

Role of the Teacher: Curriculum would be the same for the under-achiever and the normal child. In the case of the under-achiever, the role of the teacher assumes special significance, He is expected to take the following measures to bring about achievement in the under-achiever:

1. All possible efforts should be made by the teacher not only in detecting of under-achievement but also in trying to understand the nature of the problem in each individual case. A child may be carefully observed in different situations. Relevant information about his development may be found out. Parents may also be contacted and consulted. The school counsellor, if any, may be approached to study the under-achiever. Thereafter a remedial programme suitable to child's needs may be prepared and implemented.

2. At the early stages, attempts should be made to lay the foundations of good work habits and attitudes in children.

3. Emotional support by teachers should be provided to children. This will help them in meeting the developmental tasks which are a part of their normal growth.

4. Tensions in child's environment should not be allowed to build up. Sympathy and patience should be the watch words.

5. Genuine interest in the welfare of the students should be taken.

6. A few periods per week should be set apart for a small group of under-achievers for solving their problems.

7. One or two periods per week may be devoted for individual counselling to such students.

8. The under-achiever should be encouraged at his performance and thus helped in building his self confidence.

9. Outlets for children's tensions through provision of play in the form of dramatics, games, sports and a varieties of other self expressive and creative activities should be provided.

10. Assignment should be adapted to the needs of students.

11. Special care should be taken to accept the under-achiever child as a unique individual. His particular needs should be immediately attended to.

12. Efforts may be made to re-establish child's confidence in himself.

13. Remedial work for the under-achievers should be undertaken.

14. Class teacher should seek the cooperation of other teachers and the parents of the under-achievers.

15. In case of deep-rooted emotional problems which lie at the root of under-achievement, referral may be made to a child guidance clinic after taking the parents into confidence.

16

State of Society

While discussing various needs and problems of development of the adolescents, it is important to keep in view the following important points.

Needs Give Birth to Problems: Problems create worries and anxieties which in turn result in fears. Satisfaction or dissatisfaction of the needs thus have a great bearing on the development of the personality of the adolescent.

Needs → a Problems → Worries → Anxieties → Fears

The interrelatedness of the various aspects of the development of the personality of the adolescent may be illustrated as under:

A proper balance has to be struck between traditional values and modern values.

Ethical, moral and spiritual values on the one hand and scientific and technological values on the other hand have to be taken note of while considering adolescence needs and problems.

New Trends

Far reaching changes have been taking place in recent years in all societies, Schools, as social institutions have to rethink the way they are structured. At present, by and large, they tend to be based on the 20th century. Other models for schools need to be considered if students' development, especially of adolescents is to be enhanced.

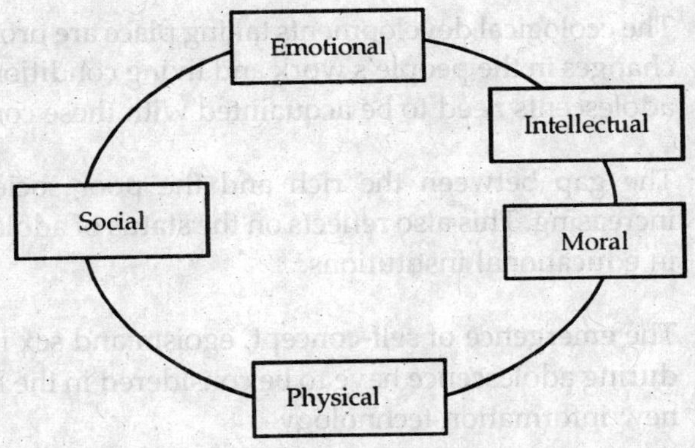

Various Aspects of the Development

Following are the developments which affects adolescence growth and development and create new problems:

1. New developments in information technology including computer aided learning, inter-active video and television offer important opportunities to improve the quality of many adolescents. At the same time they exercise an adverse influence also. Developments in this area, however, require a large investment of effort and finance. In many developing countries, the reality is that only a few elite schools would have such technology, thus aggravating the equity problem.

2. The current trends towards democratization in the societies will hopefully promote better understanding. In

order to support such a change, we will need an education for the adolescents which enables them to live harmoniously in the plural society of today.

3. The global problems we face with the environment will acquire a new responsibility on the adolescents.
4. Human rights and dignity still be an issue at the forefront of our concern.
5. The ecological developments taking place are producing changes in the people's work and living conditions. The adolescents need to be acquainted with these concerns.
6. The gap between the rich and the poor societies is increasing. This also reflects on the status of adolescents in educational institutions.
7. The emergence of self-concept, egoism and sex instinct during adolescence have to be considered in the light of new information technology.
8. Schools alone cannot influence the adolescents in the fast changing societies. In a world where mutual respect and co-operation is essential, it will be important to develop environment at school, at home and in wider society in which adolescent's self-esteem is enhanced.

Various Dimensions

1. Support by society for the career development of adolescents and counselling.
2. School's responsibility for career development as well as moral development of adolescents.
3. Constructive and co-operative educational environment.

4. Creation of a 'pedagogy of democratic fellowship' in which adolescents collaborate and support each other in their learning.

5. Classrooms to be mini-social realities in which adolescents assume different roles including those of leadership.

6. Teachers to play the role of facilitators, organisers and managers of learning.

7. Science courses to give students the opportunity to consider the social, economic and ecological impact of scientific and technological innovations.

8. Environmental Science to play an important role in helping the adolescents appreciate the interdependence of living things and the fragile balance in the biosphere.

9. Providing equality of opportunity.

10. Technology courses to be designed in such a way as they address students' needs in their own environment.

11. Along with mother tongue, foreign language to be given greater attention in the case of adolescents whenever needed.

12. Providing suitable television programmes to adolescents.

13. Encouraging the involvement of adolescents in the mass media programmes meant for them.

14. Introducing a variety of vocational courses for the adolescents.

15. Developing skills of thinking, planning, communicating, organising, problem solving, monitoring and assessing.

16. Developing educational systems to reinforce rural development programmes.

17. Introducing non-military national service for adolescents.

18. Greater-learning opportunities at work places.

19. Programmes for balanced personal opportunities.

20. Programmes for developing in the adolescents a sense of service and the advancement of public good.

21. Developing in the adolescents skills how to learn.

22. Laying emphasis on the development in the adolescents values of self-awareness and esteem and confidence in order to deal with a rapidly changing world.

23. Developing in the adolescents a positive outlook for the future.

24. Developing in the adolescents a commitment to promote interpersonal development.

25. Promoting in the adolescents values of tolerance and respect for different perspectives and views, cultures, religious and races and towards opposite sex and to disabled people.

The Difficulties

Adolescence is marked by specific attitudes and behaviour patterns. Among the most important of these according to E.B. Harlock are: (i) Feeling of vague status during transitional period (ii) A period for important changes: (a) Heightened emotionality (b) Rapid sexual maturing (c) Marked physical changes (d) Major changes in adolescents interests and behaviour patterns. (iii) A dreaded attitude (iv) Unrealism (v) Threshold of adulthood.

Adolescence has been called a period of 'Challenge and Potential'. The adolescent has enormous potential-physical, ideational and intellectual. At the same time he is faced with great challenges on account of his rapid physical growth, soaring as well as falling ideals, his search for identity as he is neither considered as a child nor an adult, his growing sexual desires, heightened emotions and lack of appropriate energies for channelising his enormous energy. All these issues and problems make the adolescence period as the period of 'Stress anal Storm'. An adolescent is faced with several alternatives on account of his 'conflicts and dilemmas'. 'To do or not to do' attitude creates several problems the solution of which needs guidance and counselling. Since an adolescent, in general, has the notion of 'knowing all things', several difficulties confront him.

Significant Features

Some of the important specific characteristics of adolescence problems and worries as given by various thinkers are briefly described here.

Becoming Independent: J. A. Hadfield (1962) is of the view, "When we speak of adolescent as growing up we mean that the youth is leaving behind the phase of protective childhood and is becoming independent."

Age of Ideals: Jean Piaget defines adolescence as, "the age of great ideals and the beginning of theories as well as the time of simple adaptation to life."

Rapid Physical Growth and Development: Rate of growth is so rapid in some cases as it seems almost 'as they go to bed one night as children and wake-up the next morning as adults.'

Health and Adolescence: It has been stated, "A growing youth has a wolf in his stomach." At this period appetite for food is often enormous. There is a widespread notion that "this is physically a critical period." Various ailments that often manifest themselves are anaemia, nosebleed, nervousness, growing pains, palpitation of the heart and especially among girls, headache, etc.

Programme of Adolescents : 14-18 years Age Group

Objectives	*Context*	*Approach*
1. To help adolescents develop into a responsible adult.	Knowledge of the phenomenon of ovulation, foetal development and birth of a baby. Marriage for reproduction, need of assistance at birth.	a) Talks with the aid of audio-visual aids. b) Emphasis on leading highly moral and ethical life in the interest of family happiness and community peace.
2. To make adolescents understand venereal diseases.	Different venereal diseases. This mode of infection and their damaging effect on the patients.	Causes of these diseases, their symptoms and the conditions of the patients should be illustrated by means of films, film strips and pictures.
3. To make adults aware of promiscuity and prostitution.	Danger's of promiscuous sex relations. Its adverse influence on the family life and its being a great social evil. Prostitutes as chief sources of the spread of vene real diseases.	Frank discussion. Students to be told emphatically that all extramarital sex relations must be avoided in the interest of personal health and family happiness.
4. To make student careful of homosexuality.	Homosexual an unethical and unnatural practice. An offence under law punishable by imprisonment. Can convey vene real diseases	Adolescents must not be permitted to go out with strangers. They should be motivated to utilise their surplus energy and spare time in sports, cultural programmes, community welfare service and nation building activities. Such programmes should be systematically organised.

Sex and Adolescence: One writer has remarked, "Sex powers permeate the whole body and the entire life of feeling and thought and will."

Emotions and Adolescence: In the words of Richmond, "Adolescence is the heyday of the emotional life, the blossom time of all those feelings and emotions which depend at bottom upon sex." Masterson has observed, "Emotional disorders frequently arise during adolescence. Such disorders range from simple depression to being over anxious about health to suicidal thoughts or attempts." Many adolescents who engages in delinquent, bizarre, or self-abusive behaviour do so as a cell for help during a difficult period. Some adolescents use drugs, alcohol, or sex as a response to emotional disorders. The emotions of the adolescents drive them from one extreme to the other. At one time a boy or a girl may be shiftless, lazy or at another full of enthusiasm and energy.

Steps to be Taken

1. A friendly, open-mindedness classroom climate, free of embarrassment to students should pervade.

2. Students should be free to ask questions which trouble them.

3. Answers given by the teachers should be honest and sensible.

4. Sex should be talked in an objective and a matter-of-fact way like any other subject.

5. A question box may be used in which adolescents may put questions anonymously if they do not feel free to ask questions in the class.

6. Films and other aids may be used to clarify concepts.

7. An adequate number of books on sex education should be kept in the open shelf school library.

QUESTIONS

1. Explain the interrelatedness of the various aspects of the development of the personality of the adolescent.

2. State the factors in the society which influence adolescents. Describe the directions which would be helpful to find suitable solutions to adolescents problems.

3. State the specific problems and worries of adolescents.

4. "The 'search for identity' and 'dealing with sexuality' are the most compelling concerns of adolescents." Discuss. As a teacher describe what would you specifically do to help adolescents in these areas.

5. Adolescence ought to be re-defined as a period of 'challenge and potential' and not one of 'storm and stress'. Discuss in the context of the developmental tasks of adolescence.

17

Educational Counselling

Webster's Dictionary defines counselling as "Consultation, mutual exchange of opinions, deliberating together."

Wrenn says, "Counselling is personal and dynamic relationship between the two individuals-one of whom is older or more experienced than the younger, who together approach a more or less well defined problem of the younger or less experienced or less wise, with mutual consideration for each to the end that the problem may be more clearly defined and that the one who has the problem may be helped to a self-determined solution of it."

Counselling is a process in which a pupil is approached by the counsellor on an individual basis and is helped in arriving at a decision or making choice finding a direction.

Types of Counselling: There are three types of counselling:

1. Directive Counselling
2. Non-Directive Counselling.
3. Eclectic Counselling

Directive Counselling: E.G. Williamson favours this type of counselling. It is counsellor directed counselling. Counsellor is the leader or it is he who dominates. It is the counsellor who discovers the problem, diagnoses it and provides a solution to it. Majority of the talking is done by the counsellor. In this type of counselling, the emphasis is upon the problem. What caused the problem? How can it best be solved?

According to Andrews and Willy, the basic assumptions of the directive counselling can be:

1. Counsellor has superior training, experience and information and is competent to give advice about how a problem is to be solved.

2. The maladjustment of an individual does not entirely impair the intellectual ability of the client, hence counselling is primarily an intellectual process.

3. Because of such factors as bias, the client is not always capable of solving his problems.

4. The objectives of counselling are achieved primarily through a problem solving situation.

Role of the Counsellor in Directive Counselling: The role can be portrayed by presenting the various steps the counsellor uses:

(a) *Analysis:* The collection of pertinent data by a variety of tools and techniques.

(b) *Synthesis:* The mechanical and graphical organisation of the data.

(c) *Diagnosis:* Drawing a conclusion about the causes of disturbance.

(d) *Prognosis:* A prediction of the future development of the student's problem.

(e) Counselling and Treatment

(f) Follow-up and Evaluation

Merits

1. It takes less time and is economical with respect to time.

2. The counsellor comes to the solution soon. This gives him happiness.

3. Directive counselling gives more significance to the intellectual rather than to the emotional aspect of individual's personality.

Demerits

1. It kills the initiative of the child and as such it makes him somewhat helpless.

2. It does not guide the counsellee to be efficient and he cannot express himself freely.

3. There is lot of regimentation in it because of the dominant role played by the counsellor. It is undemocratic.

4. Lastly, the counsellee is made dependent upon the counsellor.

Non-Directive Counselling: Non-Directive Counselling is also known by various other names such as permissive counselling or counsellee or client-oriented counselling. Carl Rogers is the leading exponent of this type of counselling.

This type of counselling is totally opposite to directive type of counselling. In non-directive counselling, the counsellor remains silent to the maximum and allows the counsellee to speak freely about the problem. The counsellor passes an occasional remark as to keep his client on the track. The counsellor asks a few questions. In this way the counsellor helps the pupil to think out the solution of the problem himself. Complete responsibility is placed on the individual and the counsellee plays the primary role.

Counsellor's Importance

Carl Rogers has outlined the role of the counsellor by listing down the following steps in the said type of counselling:

The individual or the counsellee comes for help.

The helping situation is usually defined.

The counsellor encourages the counsellee to express his feelings freely.

The counsellor accepts and clarifies negative feelings.

Negative feelings or impulses are followed by tentative expressions of the positive impulses.

Counsellor accepts and recognizes positive feelings of the counsellee.

This provides a basis on which the counsellee can go ahead to the new level of integration.

Counsellor clarifies possible course of action.

Counsellee develops further insight, a more complete and accurate understanding of the problem.

Merits

1. In the present day personnel work, the non-directive counselling movement may be linked to the progressive

movement in education. Both stress the freedom of the individual.

2. As therapy, it has indisputable values.

3. Non-directive counselling can be compared to confessions made in the church and as such when one is allowed to talk, one brings one's repressed thoughts to the surface and relieves one's tensions.

4. This facilitates integrated positive action.

5. This develops a feeling of increased independence on the part of the counsellee.

Demerits

1. It is a time consuming process. The counsellee may begin a never ending dialogue.

2. In view of above, it may deprive many other counsellor to seek necessary counselling.

3. The resources, judgement and wisdom of the client cannot be relied upon.

4. How most problems be solved by simply talking out things in the interview situation is a big limitation.

Eclectic Counselling

Eclectic counselling is a combination and synthesis of directive and non-directive types of the counselling or viewpoints. As stated earlier, the two extremes forms of (Directive and Non-Directive) are combined. Here both the counsellor and the counsellee are active and co-operative. Both do the talking turn by turn. The problem is solved jointly.

This also raises one problem-how much freedom should the counsellee be allowed? Answer is simple-fifty per cent. But the factors of the personality of the counsellee and the situation should also be taken into consideration.

To Conclude: In the absence of any clear-cut indication of the superiority of one counselling method over another, the eclectic approach seems justified provided it is coupled with the positive concept that counselling is essentially a learning process for both the counsellor and the counsellee.

The Procedure

So whatever be the type, it has been found out that counselling process has the following five characteristics:

1. Counselling is a professional service.
2. Counseling is centred upon the problems of the client.
3. Good counselling results in client-made decisions.
4. Counselling is one to one process.
5. Counselling must be on the accuracy of the counsellor's prediction.

Core Issues

It is sometimes said that guidance is the heart of education and counselling as the heart of counselling.

Guidance is relatively a broader term and counselling is one of the services under the guidance programme.

Need for guidance arises when an individual is confronted with some problems. Problem may be solved by providing information. This is the initial phase of guidance. The individual having the problem may be charged with emotion. It may be unable to adjust himself with the environment on account of emotional tension. In such a situation he needs counselling to overcome tension.

Various Approaches

There are two methods of guidance: (i) Individual guidance, (ii) Group guidance.

Group guidance includes the following techniques:

1. Talks by teachers, school counsellor and experts on educational matters.
2. Use of audio-visual aids, including electronic media to disseminate career information.
3. Career conferences and exhibitions.
4. Group discussions.
5. Orientation courses.
6. Parent-teacher meets.
7. Commercial and industrial visits.
8. T.V. talks and panel discussions.
9. Counselling.

Individual Guidance includes the following techniques:

1. To tell an individual about his potentialities.
2. Orientation to the individual to educational, vocational and avocational opportunities and requirements.
3. Assisting individuals to adjust themselves to various situations.

4. Assisting the individual to assess himself what he is.
5. Assisting the individual to appreciate where he is.
6. Assisting the individual to become aware of his assets and limitations.
7. Assisting the individual to find his own path in accordance with his assets and limitations.
8. Assisting the individual to follow his chosen path.
9. Assisting the individual to promote his career.

QUESTIONS

1. State the meaning, nature and purpose of guidance.
2. What is the meaning of educational guidance? Why is it needed? What is its scope?
3. "Individual differences are the basis of all guidance and counselling." Explain in this context the aims and purposes of guidance and counselling.
4. Explain how guidance and counselling is useful to the adolescent.
5. State the problems of the adolescents in India. Suggest a suitable programme of guidance for them.

18

Educational Guidance

Basic Requirement

The need for guidance is based on the fact that every individual needs help. Jones has very rightly observed that everyone needs assistance at some time in his life, some will need it constantly and throughout their entire lives, while others need it only at rare intervals at times of great crisis. There always have been and will continue to be people with an occasional need for the help of the more experienced persons in meeting problem situations.

The need for a comprehensive programme of guidance has become imperative in view of the following considerations:

1. Complex nature of society.
2. Individual differences.
3. Changed agricultural, commercial and industrial patterns of the country.
4. Changed occupational pattern of the country.

5. Changed occupational structures.
6. Changed educational pattern of the country.
7. Need for conservation of human energy.
8. Vocationalisation of education.
9. New researches in educational psychology.
10. More leisure and the need for its proper utilisation.
11. Impact of electronic mass media.
12. Impact of press media.
13. Juvenile delinquency.
14. Urbanisation and congested cities.
15. Growing tension on account of increased stress.
16. Changed family structure and lack of guidance and counselling at home.
17. Employment of women in large numbers.
18. Need for correct understanding of religious matters.
19. Political exploitation.
20. Population explosion.
21. Industrial psychology and its requirements.
22. Search for identity of the youth.
23. Need for wholesome relations

24. Need for making educational choices.

25. Need for effective learning.

26. Need for proper involvement in co-curricular work.

The Background

During the late 1920s and early 1930s, in the U.S.A. for example, education and guidance were considered almost synonymous. During the same period, psychologists like Binnet, Cattell, Terman and Tbomdike introduced psychological testing in the field of guidance. About the middle of 1930s, the emphasis shifted and more attention was given to economic problems, placement or employment and occupational trends. More and more of assistance was given to the employer in order to make him more effective in his work. This trend was described by some writers as 'personal movement.'

Modern meaning of guidance concept, however, does not restrict itself to any one discipline. It is being influenced by sociology, psychology, economy and education etc.

The Concept

Following are the important definitions of guidance.

1. Chisholm states "Guidance seeks to help the individual discover his own talents in comparison to the opportunities of the world and help him prepare himself so that he can find or develop a place in which he can live a well balanced life and contribute his part to the welfare of his fellow men."

2. In the words of Ruth Strang, "Guidance is a process of helping every individual, through his own efforts, to discover and develop his potentialities for his personal happiness and social usefulness."

3. Dr. J.A. Humphreys and Dr. A.E. Traxler, define guidance as: "At any level, guidance implies that the individual attains self-direction just as fast and as far as his mental, social and emotional abilities permit. Guidance of the younger or less mature individual, of course, calls for closer direction than does guidance of the older or more mature individual. The term guidance, moreover, aptly applies to working with an individual all along the lines from early childhood into adulthood."

4. According to Jones, "Guidance involves personal help given by someone; it is designed to assist a person in deciding where he wants to go, what he wants to do, or how he can best accomplish his purposes; it assists him in solving problems that arise in his life. It does not solve problems for the individual, but helps him to solve them. The focus of guidance is the individual, not the problem, its purpose is to promote the growth of the individual in self-direction."

5. According to the Secondary Education Commission, "Guidance involves the difficult art of helping boys and girls to plan their own future wisely in the full light of all the factors that can be mastered about themselves and about the world in which they are to live and work. Naturally, therefore, it is not the work of a few specialists, but rather a service in which the entire school staff must co-operate under the guidance of some person with special knowledge and skill in this particular field. Guidance in this sense is not confined to the vocational field only. It covers the whole gamut of youth problems and should be provided in an appropriate form at all stages of education through the co-operative endeavour of understanding parents, teachers, headmasters, principals and guidance officers."

Salient Features

From above mentioned definitions, we conclude:

1. Guidance is assisting the individual to find his own place.

2. Guidance is assisting the individual to know his assets and liabilities.

3. Guidance is assisting the individual to find his path through his own efforts.

4. Guidance is assisting the individual to help himself for promoting his self-direction.

5. Guidance is assisting the individual to adjust himself.

6. Guidance is a point of view that reflects a positive towards oneself and others.

7. Guidance is assisting an individual to develop his potentialities and talents to the optimum level.

8. Guidance is helping the individual to make appropriate educational, personal, recreational and vocational choices.

9. Guidance is assisting the individual to establish harmonious relations with his parents, neighbours, peers etc.

10. Guidance programme is organised.

11. Guidance programme has a structure, system and personal.

12. Guidance consists of specialised services-testing, counselling, educational and vocational information, placement and follow-up.

13. Guidance programme is an integral part of the school programme.

The Objectives

The aims of guidance are :

1. Optimum development of the potentialities of an individual.
2. Orientation to the individual to educational, vocational and avocational opportunities and requirements.
3. Assisting individuals to adjust themselves to various situations.

The Practicability

An effective guidance programme comprises the following functions:

1. Assisting the individual to assess himself what he is.
2. Assisting the individual to appreciate where he was.
3. Assisting the individual to become aware of his assets and limitations.
4. Assisting the individual to find his own path in accordance with his assets and limitations.
5. Assisting the individual to follow his chosen path.
6. Assisting the individual to promote his career.

Various Angles

1. Career Guidance.

2. Civic Guidance.
3. Community Guidance.
4. Cultural Guidance.
5. Educational Guidance.
6. Emotional Guidance.
7. Family Relations Guidance.
8. Health Guidance.
9. Human Relations Guidance.
10. Leisure Time Utilisation Guidance.
11. Moral Guidance.
12. Personal Guidance.
13. Physical Guidance.
14. Professional Guidance.
15. Psychiatric Guidance.
16. Recreational Guidance.
17. Religious Guidance.
18. Sex Guidance.
19. Social Guidance.
20. Spiritual Guidance.
21. Vocational Guidance.

In fact there is no aspect of life which does not need guidance.

Meaning of Educational Guidance: Following definitions of educational guidance bring out the meaning of educational guidance.

In the words of G. E. Myers, "Educational guidance is a process concerned with bringing about between an individual pupil with his distinctive characteristics on the one hand, and differing groups of opportunities and requirements on the other, a favourable setting for the individual's development or education. If there is a single group, of opportunities and requirements, as is the case with a fixed curriculum, the problem is simply one of the education by the best methods possible in a setting already determined and not one of educational guidance."

Jones defines educational guidance as the assistance given to the pupils in their choices and adjustments with relation to schools, curriculum's, courses and school life.

Ruth Strang observes that educational guidance.is positive. It is a developmental programme concerned with the questions. What is this boy or girl good for? What kind of education will reveal his capacities and help him to develop them? According to the same author, educational guidance is intended to aid the individual in choosing an appropriate programme and in making progress in it. This involves (1) knowledge of the abilities and interests of the individuals, (2) awareness of a wide range of educational opportunities, and (3) programmes and counselling which help the individual to choose wisely on the basis of these two kinds of knowledge.

Brewer defines it as "Educational guidance is a conscious effort to assist in the intellectual growth of an individual-anything that has to do with instruction or with learning may come under the term of guidance."

Dunsmoor and Miller observe, "Guidance as a form systematic assistance whereby students are aided in achieving satisfactory adjustment to school and life."

In the words of Dr. K. G. Rama Rao, "Guidance in the wider context of a total curriculum and embracing education of everyone of the basic activity pattern-intellectual as well as social, economic as well as artistic, moral as well as spiritual, domestic as well as physical-becomes all inclusive as well as competes with instructional and testing or examining functions of the school in preparing the school-leavers for work and life in general."

Shirely, Hamrin and Clifforde Erickson write, "Guidance in the secondary school refers to that aspect of the education programme which is concerned especially with helping the pupil to become adjusted to his present situation and to plan his future in line with his interests, abilities and social needs. Guidance or personal work represents an organized effort on the part of the school, equipped with both a knowledge of the pupil and information as to opportunities, of an educational, a social and a vocational character to help the individual pupil become adjusted to his present situation in such a way as to provide the greatest development for him and to aid him in planning for his future. It is rightly said that this programme helps John see through himself and then to assist him in seeing himself through."

The Need: Educational guidance is needed to make the best use of the potential of children.

Lack of educational guidance has created what is known as the problem of 'educated unemployment.'

Lack of educational and vocational guidance has led to a dearth of suitable hands for many occupations needing a specialised training.

It has been rightly said, "Nothing but a well-organised network of guidance services throughout the country will save us from the impending tragedy."

Almost every system of education is based on two assumptions. The first is that every student should strive for maximum self- development and the other is that every student should take his place in the society as its useful member. These two assumptions imply that the school and community activities of a child should be based on some definite pattern. Educational guidance services must assist the child to achieve this end.

For achieving above purposes of guidance, several kinds of services are organised in the school.

1. To assist the student secure information regarding the possibility and desirability of further schooling.

2. To assist the student to know the purpose and functions of the different categories of senior secondary schools and other institutions.

3. To assist the student to know in detail the offerings and facilities of the school he might attend.

4. To assist him to know the requirements for entrance into the school of his choice.

5. To assist him to adjust himself to the curriculum, the school and the social life connected with it. Under this we may include:

   (a) To help the student in the selection of the subjects at the senior secondary stage.

   (b) To help him in the selection of textbooks and other instructional material.

   (c) To help him in developing study habits.

   (d) To help him in making satisfactory progress in various subjects.

   (e) To help him in the selection of hobbies.

(f) To help him in the selection of co-curricular activities.

(g) To help him in knowing the availability of scholarships, loans etc.

(h) To help him to find out his aptitudes, interests etc.

6. To assist him in building healthy social relationship.

7. To help him in selecting subjects in accordance with his vocational choice.

8. To assist him in knowing the various openings available after.

Typical Approaches

There are two important reasons which give rise to the necessity of a specialised guidance service. The first is that there is a marked difference in the curriculum of an elementary and secondary school and that of a higher secondary school. Curriculum of a Higher Secondary school is a diversified one which involves the problem of selecting subjects in class XI.

The second reason is that much emphasis is placed upon the vocational point of view. Important decisions are to be made in class XI and class XII. In class XI the selection of subjects is largely influenced by vocational requirements. Important decisions are taken and help is needed when the students are about to leave the school, either to secure jobs or to go to college or to some other type of further training.

Professional Guidance

The distinguishing mark between the two is the character of the dominating purpose. In vocational guidance, the vocational considerations are dominating, whereas in educational guidance 'making a life' in school is more important than 'making a living' after the school stage. Educational and vocational guidance are parts of the total guidance process by which an individual's potentialities are discovered and developed through his own efforts for his personal happiness and social usefulness. The student's vocational plan and selection of courses are functionally related.

The Schemes

1. Appraisal of the student by means of	(a) Tests and rating scales	
	(b) Parents ratings	
	(c) Diagnostic records	
	(d) Individual inventories	
	(e) Sociometric analysis	
	(f) Observations	
	(g) Anecdotes	
	(h) Case studies	
	(i) Cumulative records	
2. Adjustment by means of	(a) Change in the environment through	1. Socialised curriculum.
		2. Co-curricular activities.
		3. Physical surroundings
		4. Community resources.
		5. Educational and vocational opportunities.
		6. Group contacts.
	(b) Changes in the individual through	1. Interviews
		2. Developmental exercises.
		3. Instruction.
		4. Guidance.
		5. Group process.

Facilities Available

Following five types of guidance services are needed in a school :

Individual Inventory Service: Compilation of individual inventory giving detailed information about each student concerning his abilities and achievements in different areas is the first essential of every guidance programme in the school. This information should be kept up-to-date and is to be used for the good of the student. It may be compiled in the form of a cumulative record.

Information Service: Students of higher secondary schools generally need three types of information which is very helpful to them in making decisions about various cour-ses, occupations and institutions such as : (a) Information about colleges and training opportunities, (b) Informa-tion about available occupations, and (c) Information about scholarships and other financial help available during the training period. Information may be collected from papers and magazines, government notifications and bulletin's and information centers of the Employ-ment Exchanges, etc. The usefulness of this information will be lost if the information is not kept up-to-date. This information may be supplemented by talks of people from different occupations.

Counselling Service: Counselling service is regarded as the 'heart' of the guidance programme. This service must assist an individual in identifying, understanding and solving problems that confront him. Counselling can be done by a well-trained counsellor. A detailed discussion on the role of the counsellor is available elsewhere in this book.

Placement Service: This service implies help to the indivi-dual in obtaining employment. There are three stages of this service:

(a) Assessing the abilities, aptitudes, and interests of the individual student.

(b) Analysing several occupations, particularly the ones in which the student expresses his interest.

(c) Relating occupations and abilities.

5. *Follow-up Service:* This implies continuation of the programme to check the effectiveness of the programme.

Guidance and Education: Following are the main differences between guidance and education.

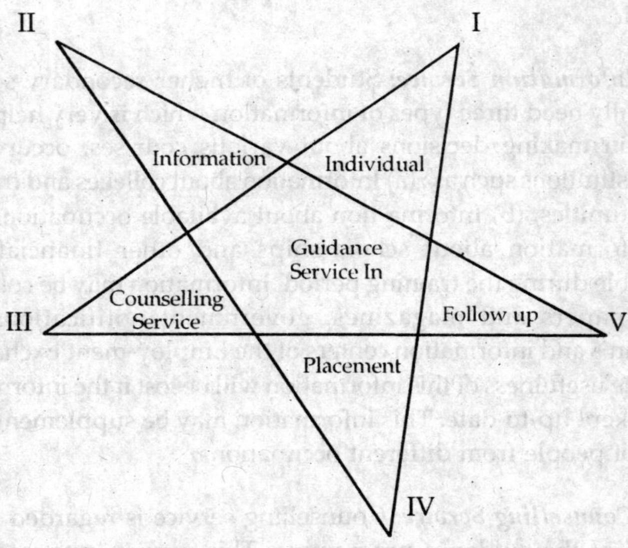

Diagram showing Guidance Services in the Schools

1. "All guidance is education but some aspects of education are not guidance, their objectives are the same-the development of the individual-but the methods used in education are by no means the same as those used in guidance," writes Jones.

2. Again the same author writes, "Education may take place, and often does, through the effort and initiation

of the individual alone. This is education, but not guidance."

3. There might be some element of compulsion in education but not in guidance.

4. Guidance is present when the co-operation of the individual is secured and when help is given to him. Guidance is the outgrowth of a philosophy of education that every child in a school system should have an opportunity for all round growth and development in order to achieve his greatest potential.

Meaning and Definition of Vocational Guidance: To quote Prof. G. E. Myers, "Vocational guidance is fundamentally an effort to conserve the priceless native capacities of youth and the costly training provided for youth in the schools. It seeks to conserve these richest of all human resources by aiding the individual to invest and use them where they will bring greatest satisfaction and success to himself and greatest benefit to society."

According to Super, "Vocational guidance is the process of helping a person to develop and accept an integrated and adequate picture of himself, and of his role in the world of work to test this concept against reality and to convert it into a reality with satisfaction to himself and benefit to society."

It may be stressed again that it is impossible to separate sharply the vocational aspects of guidance from other aspects of guidance such as educational, social, health, etc.

The Need: According to Myres, Vocational guidance is needed because of the following reasons:

Avoiding Wrong Profession and Economic Loss: If an individual stays in a wrong profession for a long time, he suffers economically and there is financial loss.

Checking Psychic Loss: If an individual stays in a wrong profession, he suffers from a psychic loss. The individual is not happy. He is frustrated. His family life is also affected.

Right Profession and Economic Advantages: Vocational guidance provides many economic advantages to the employers. Their problems are less because their workers enjoy job satisfaction.

Health Point of View: Proper profession is needed from the point of health of the individuals. If the profession is such where health breaks down, production suffers and morale of individuals goes down.

Personal and Social Values: There are a large number of personal and social values of vocational guidance. Leaving aside financial considerations, the worker's happiness, his personal development, his value as a social unit and his contribution to human welfare are all involved. Right vocational guidance helps us to achieve this objective.

Maximum Utilisation of Human Potentialities: Human potentialities are utilised to the maximum with the help of vocational guidance. The nation also derives benefit as the resources are utilised very profitably.